60 HIKES *within* 60 MILES
CHICAGO

INCLUDING AURORA, ELGIN, AND JOLIET

60 Hikes within 60 MILES

CHICAGO

INCLUDING AURORA, ELGIN, AND JOLIET

Ted Villaire

MENASHA RIDGE PRESS
Birmingham, Alabama

Library of Congress Cataloging-in-Publication Data

Villaire, Ted, 1969–
    60 Hikes within 60 miles, Chicago: including Aurora, Elgin, and Joliet /
Ted Villaire.—1st ed.
        p. cm.
Includes index.
ISBN 0-89732-566-4
    1. Hiking—Illinois—Chicago Region—Guidebooks. 2. Chicago Region (Ill.)—
Guidebooks. I. Title: Sixty hikes within sixty miles, Chicago. II. Title.

GV199.42.I32C458 2005
796.51'09773'11—dc22   2005047965

Cover design by Grant M. Tatum
Text design by Karen Ocker
Cover photo © Sarah Hadley/Alamy
Author photo by Michael Roberts
All other photos by Ted Villaire
Maps by Steve Jones

Menasha Ridge Press
P.O. Box 43673
Birmingham, AL 35243
www.menasharidge.com

**For Phillip (1936–1993) and Kathleen:
I could not ask for more supportive and loving parents.**

TABLE OF CONTENTS

TABLE OF CONTENTS

ACKNOWLEDGMENTS

My gratitude goes to all the staff and volunteers who provide the essential service of maintaining the parks and trails in the Chicago region. Without these committed individuals, our local sanctuaries wouldn't exist. In particular, thanks to staff at the Thorn Creek Nature Center, Starved Rock State Park, Bristol Woods County Park, and Goose Lake Prairie State Park. Thanks to friends, coworkers, and family (particularly to my brother, Lou) for their support and encouragement during the book's research and writing.

—*Ted Villaire*

FOREWORD

Welcome to Menasha Ridge Press's *60 Hikes within 60 Miles*, a series designed to provide hikers with information needed to find and hike the very best trails surrounding cities usually underserved by good guidebooks.

Our strategy was simple: First, find a hiker who knows the area and loves to hike. Second, ask that person to spend a year researching the most popular and very best trails around. And third, have that person describe each trail in terms of difficulty, scenery, condition, elevation change, and all other categories of information that are important to hikers. "Pretend you've just completed a hike and met up with other hikers at the trailhead," we told each author. "Imagine their questions; be clear in your answers."

An experienced hiker and writer, author Ted Villaire has selected 60 of the best hikes in and around the Chicago metropolitan area. From the greenways and urban hikes that highlight the lakeshore to flora- and fauna-rich treks amid state parks in the hinterlands, Villaire provides hikers (and walkers) with a great variety of hikes—and all within roughly 60 miles of Chicago.

You'll get more out of this book if you take a moment to read the introduction explaining how to read the trail listings. The "Topographic Maps" section will help you understand how useful topos will be on a hike, and will also tell you where to get them. And though this is a "where-to," not a "how-to" guide, those of you who have hiked extensively will find the introduction of particular value.

As much for the opportunity to free the spirit as well as to free the body, let these hikes elevate you above the urban hurry.

All the best,
The Editors at Menasha Ridge Press

ABOUT THE AUTHOR

Ted Villaire has hiked, paddled, camped, and bicycled widely in the western Great Lakes region. Recently, while riding his bicycle around Lake Superior, he discovered he thrives on a diet of smoked fish and candy bars. Villaire has worked as a freelance news reporter covering local government, education, business, and the environment/outdoors for a variety of newspapers, including the *Chicago Tribune* and the *Des Moines Register*. He also served as editor of a weekly community newspaper in Chicago. A graduate of Aquinas College and DePaul University, Villaire currently works as a publications editor for a large nonprofit organization headquartered in Chicago.

PREFACE

There's no arguing with the benefits of wandering through the woods. Whatever we're looking for—fresh air, exercise, time with (or away from) the family, a bit of adventure, or a momentary escape from the concrete grid—traipsing through the local landscape helps us take stock of ourselves and the world around us.

The best thing about hiking in the Chicago region is the variety of scenic spots, each with a distinctive topographical flavor, its own combination of plants and wildlife, and its unique seasonal ambience. When it's time to dodge city living for a while, a short trip to Lake Michigan is the first idea in the minds of many. Mesmerizing us every chance it gets, the Big Lake's endless blue horizon is no small part of the region's allure. Profoundly intertwined with the area's weather, economic and social history, and, of course, its visual charm, Chicagoans are fortunate to have this exquisite diversion in their front yard. Heading inland away from the lake, there is no shortage of patches of parkland that can provide us with a respite from our daily routines. These are places that invite us to trace the routes of meandering rivers, wander through expansive prairies, and scramble up steep, wooded hills. These are places we go to enjoy a picnic in a dappled oak savanna, or where we can sit on the edge of a quiet lake while admiring a field of water lilies beyond the weeping willows.

Spring and fall provide some of the best times to explore local trails: temperatures are moderate, bugs are dormant, the number of visitors is minimal, and lovely surprises often present themselves to those who look. Spring, of course, brings a sensory banquet as buds pop, wildflowers bloom, and the landscape becomes braided with intermittent streams. The only thing more pleasurable than the awakening of spring is getting hit with a Technicolor blast in fall. Places such as Deer Grove Forest Preserve, Morton Arboretum, and the Bailly/Chellberg Hike at the Indiana Dunes are a few spots where one can witness brilliant displays of autumn's leaves. Fall also offers opportunities to swim through a sea of prairie grass as the mauve stalks of big bluestem reach heights of eight to ten feet at places like Goose Lake Prairie State Park and Chain O' Lakes State Park.

Destinations swarming with visitors in the warmer months usually supply a pleasing solitude during winter. While the dead grasses, naked trees, and frozen streams of winter can seem stark and barren, the snowy landscape is alive with opportunities to follow the comings and goings of elusive creatures such raccoons, opossums, and coyotes. Winter serves up other delights, too. Opportunities for sledding and outdoor ice skating can be found at places such as Lakewood and Goodenow forest preserves and Oak Ridge Prairie County Park.

BORDERS.

BORDERS
BOOKS AND MUSIC
830 N. MICHIGAN AVENUE
CHICAGO IL 60611
(312) 573-0564

Educators Savings Week!
All current and retired educators
will receive 25% off most items
at Borders stores nationwide!
September 26 - October 2

BORDERS.

Returns to Borders Stores

Merchandise presented for return, including sale or marked-down items, must be accompanied by the original Borders store receipt or a Borders Gift Receipt. Returns must be completed within 30 days of purchase. For returns accompanied by a Borders Store Receipt, the purchase price will be refunded in the medium of purchase (cash, credit card or gift card). Items purchased by check may be returned for cash after 10 business days. For returns within 30 days of purchase accompanied by a Borders Gift Receipt, the purchase price (after applicable discounts) will be refunded via a gift card.

Merchandise unaccompanied by the original Borders store receipt, Borders Gift Receipt, or presented for return beyond 30 days from date of purchase, must be carried by Borders at the time of the return. The lowest price offered for the item, during the 6 month period prior to the return will be refunded via a gift card.

Opened videos, music discs, cassettes, electronics, and audio books may only be exchanged for a replacement of the original item.

Periodicals, newspapers, out-of-print, collectible, pre-owned items, and gift cards may not be returned.

Returned merchandise must be in saleable condition.

BORDERS.

Returns to Borders Stores

Merchandise presented for return, including sale or marked-down items, must be accompanied by the original Borders store receipt or a Borders Gift Receipt. Returns must be completed within 30 days of purchase. For returns accompanied by a Borders Store Receipt, the purchase price will be refunded in the medium of purchase (cash, credit card or gift card). Items purchased by check may be returned for cash after 10 business days. For returns within 30 days of purchase accompanied by a Borders Gift Receipt, the purchase price (after applicable discounts) will be refunded via a gift card.

Merchandise unaccompanied by the original Borders store receipt, Borders Gift Receipt, or presented for

PREFACE

Winter's fleeting daylight hours need not prevent you from seeking treatment for your cabin fever—many of the destinations listed in this book stay open after dark. Just bring a headlamp or a flashlight, or better yet, take a hike under the glow of a full moon. When hiking in fall and winter, be mindful that some parks may be closed for hunting, while others may provide restricted access, and still others will allow hikers and hunters to coexist. During hunting season, it's never a bad idea to call the park administration to ask about access and safety precautions.

Many people prefer hiking in summer, when the sun is warm, the greenery is lush, and kids are searching for something to do. Lake Michigan excursions such as the Cowles Bog and Dead River hikes are particularly fun for the family on hot summer days when you can kick off your shoes and float in the lake at the hikes' halfway points. It's true, summer is the most conducive season for combining your hike with a myriad of other outdoor pursuits like picnicking, playing Frisbee, casting a fishing line, or practicing your tai chi. It's also the time of year to combine hiking with a night or two sleeping under the stars at places like Chain 'O Lakes, Illinois Beach, and Shabonna Lake state parks.

Whatever the season, I can't stress enough the advantages of getting out on the trail as early as possible. Early mornings—the time of day when wildlife sightings outnumber sightings of people—deliver the most captivating moments: a line of deer leaping over a fence, steam rising off a pond on a cool spring morning, or a great blue heron fishing for frogs.

▶ CITY ON THE PRAIRIE

At the time of European settlement, the landscape of the Chicago region was mostly tallgrass prairie, an especially fertile type of grassland due to thousands of years of tall grasses decomposing. While this eastern edge of the nation's grassland is known for being productive farmland, farmers were initially in for an unpleasant surprise when they struggled to plow soil that seemed to have more roots than dirt. But once the sod was turned over and seeds were planted, their efforts were rewarded. To this day, Illinois continues to be a top producer of national staples such as corn and soybeans. While nearly all the tallgrass prairie has been cultivated, the remnants described in this book provide a taste of what it was like to trek through prairie grass growing as high as a horse's head.

Even though much of the native landscape was gently rolling prairie, numerous hilly wooded exceptions could always be found. Among those places spared from the

PREFACE

steamrolling effect of the last glacier were the steep hills scattered throughout McHenry and Lake counties, the wooded bluffs within the Palos/Sag Valley Forest Preserve, and the sandstone cliffs and canyons along the Illinois and Kankakee rivers. And later, after the last glacier began to recede some 14,000 years ago, the colossal sand dunes formed at the south edge of Lake Michigan.

▶ THE TRAILS

While the destinations in this book are scattered across three states and more than a dozen counties, there are a few places where trails are concentrated. The most accessible of these areas are the trails in the vicinity of the Palos/Sag Valley Forest Preserve (southwest of downtown) and the Indiana Dunes (southeast of downtown). In the far northeastern corner of Illinois is an assortment of good destinations in McHenry and Lake counties. Southwest of the city, beyond Joliet, a great collection of trails lies within the vicinity of the Illinois River and the Illinois & Michigan (I&M) Canal.

THE I&M CANAL TRAIL

Perhaps the most important development that led to Chicago becoming the economic and cultural capital of the Midwest was the digging of the I&M Canal in 1848. Running parallel to the Illinois and Des Plaines rivers, the canal provided a link between the Great Lakes and the Mississippi River. After the canal was completed, the task of getting grain from the Midwest's breadbasket to markets in Chicago and beyond suddenly became easier, and in the larger picture, shipping traffic could travel from the Atlantic Ocean to the Gulf of Mexico. For much of canal's life span the boats were pulled by mules along an accompanying towpath.

Today, 60 miles of the old towpath between Joliet and LaSalle has been preserved as a multiuse trail. This trail and its surrounding environs now offer some of the best hiking in the Chicago region. Sprinkled in the vicinity of the trail and the Illinois River are the high bluffs of McKinley Woods; sandstone cliffs and canyons of Starved Rock, Buffalo Rock, and Matthiessen state parks; and the largest tract of tallgrass prairie in the state, at Goose Lake Prairie State Park. There are also a dozen locks that were once used for raising and lowering boats along the canal, as well as a handful of charming little towns that grew up alongside the waterway.

INDIANA DUNES

Located on the southern tip of Lake Michigan, the Indiana Dunes offer great stretches of sandy beach, dense bottomland forests, and soaring mountains of sand overlooking the lake. Even though the dunes are bounded by steel mills, residential developments, and a power plant, the 17,200 acres that make up the national and state parks can feel surprisingly remote. At the state park and at the national lakeshore's West Beach and Cowles Bog trails, you'll encounter curious dune formations know as "blowouts," where forceful lake winds have scooped out huge bowls in the sand. Other hikes in the area, such as the Li-co-ki-we Trail and the Bailly/Chellberg hike, feature rolling oak savannas, gentle dune ridges, winding streams, and marshland active with birds. With quick access via the South Shore Rail Line, the dunes are an especially attractive destination for individuals using public transit.

PALOS AREA

The Palos/Sag Valley Forest Preserve hosts about 35 miles of trails that branch out and converge within 14,000 acres of woodland, lakes, ponds, sloughs, and rugged glacial terrain. Families visiting Palos will enjoy the Little Red Schoolhouse Nature Center, where they can take a short hike along the banks of Long John Slough and through groves of stately oaks, and then visit a small nature center featuring a menagerie of birds, snakes, and frogs, as well as a beehive under Plexiglas. Across the Des Plaines River, at Waterfall Glen Forest Preserve, a 10-mile loop trail through rugged wooded terrain winds around

A stairway leading up one of the monstrous sand dunes at Indiana Dunes State Park.

the Argonne National Laboratory. To the east, Lake Katherine Nature Preserve provides an unrivaled spot for a casual urban stroll. The most scenic and remote hiking destination in the Palos area is Cap Sauers Holdings, which is the largest roadless area in Cook County and one of the largest state-designated nature preserves in Illinois.

LAKE AND MCHENRY COUNTIES

Thanks to a glacier that dumped enormous heaps of dirt and gravel as it retreated from the area some 14,000 years ago, Lake and McHenry counties possess hills galore. Situated side by side in Illinois' far northeast corner, these counties are where you'll find destinations with names like Glacial Park, Moraine Hills State Park, and Marengo Ridge Conservation Area that hint at the area's geological legacy. The glacial heritage is also evident in the many types of wetlands dotting the landscape. When glaciers retreated, chunks of ice often would get left behind, leaving depressions in the ground that eventually became lakes, ponds, marshes, or bogs. This process created extensive wetlands at places such Volo Bog, Chain 'O Lakes State Park, and Moraine Hills State Park.

▶ **PICK A TRAIL, ANY TRAIL**

Even though the focus of this book is hiking, much of the information will be useful to cyclists, trail runners, cross-country skiers, snowshoers, parents with strollers, and wheelchair users. With a growing number of trails classified as "multiuse" (trails offering a wide, smooth, crushed-gravel surface), more people are seeing that there's more than one way to follow a

PREFACE

A boardwalk protects the fragile landscape at Cowles Bog.

trail. One mother I know, for example, runs along multiuse trails while her ten-year-old son rides his bicycle beside her. Hitting the trails is a great way for them to stay fit while spending time together outdoors.

Local hikers will want to keep an eye on the changes at Midewin National Tallgrass Prairie, the first national tallgrass prairie (pages 164–167). Several years down the road, the U.S. Forest Service will start opening some 40 miles of trails throughout the 19,000 acres that once hosted the largest ammunition-production plant in the world. While prairie restoration is planned for much of Midewin, large sections will be woodland.

As I mulled over the trails to include in this book, I sometimes found it difficult to eliminate one hike in favor of another. As much as possible, I leaned toward variety in terms of length, location, and scenic attractions. While I hope you enjoy the hikes I have laid out, keep in mind there are many more excellent hikes that are not among these 60. Some are included in the "Nearby Activities" sections of the various profiles, but many are not. In any case, good wishes to you and your companions as you ramble through the natural wonders of the Chicago region.

HIKING RECOMMENDATIONS

▶ 1 TO 3 MILES

Braidwood Dunes and Savanna Loop
Bristol Woods Hike
Buffalo Rock State Park Hike
Busse Woods Loop
Chicago Botanic Garden Hike
Crabtree Nature Center Hike
Deep River Hike
Goodenow Grove Hike
Goose Lake Prairie State Natural Area:
   Prairie View Trail
Goose Lake Prairie State Natural Area:
   Tallgrass Trail
Illinois Beach State Park: Dead River Loop

Iroquois County State Wildlife Area Hike
Jackson Park Loop
Joliet Iron Works Hike
Lakewood Forest Preserve Loop
Matthiessen State Park Dells Area Hike
McKinley Woods Loop
Palos/Sag Valley Forest Preserve:
   Little Red Schoolhouse Hike
Silver Springs State Park Loop
Starved Rock State Park: West Hike
Tekakwitha–Fox River Hike
Thorn Creek Hike

▶ 3 TO 6 MILES

Bong State Recreation Area Loop
Chain O' Lakes State Park: West Hike
Chicago Lakeshore Path: North Hike
Chicago Lakeshore Path: South Hike
Danada Forest Preserve Hike
Deer Grove Loop
Fullersburg Woods Loop
Geneva Lake: Bigfoot Beach Hike
Glacial Park Loop
Greene Valley Forest Preserve Loop
Indiana Dunes National Lakeshore:
   Bailly/Chellberg Hike
Indiana Dunes National Lakeshore:
   Cowles Bog Trail
Indiana Dunes National Lakeshore:
   West Beach Loop

Indiana Dunes State Park: Dune Ridge Loop
Kankakee River State Park Hike
Lake Katherine Trail
LaSalle Fish and Wildlife Area Loop
Marengo Ridge Hike
Midewin National Tallgrass Prairie Hike
Morton Arboretum East Hike
Oak Ridge Prairie Loop
Palos/Sag Valley Forest Preserve: Cap Sauers
   and Swallow Cliff Loop
Pilcher Park Loop
Ryerson Woods Hike
Shabbona Lake State Park Loop
Skokie Lagoons and River Hike
Veteran Acres–Sterne's Woods Hike
Volo Bog State Natural Area Hike

▶ OVER 6 MILES

Chain O' Lakes State Park: East Hike
Geneva Lake: North Shore Hike
Grand Kankakee Marsh Hike
Channahon State Park: I&M Canal Trail
Indiana Dunes National Lakeshore:
   Ly-co-ki-we Hike

Indiana Dunes State Park: Shoreline Loop
Moraine Hills State Park Hike
Pratt's Wayne Loop
Starved Rock State Park: East Hike
Waterfall Glen Forest Preserve Loop

HIKING RECOMMENDATIONS

▶ GOOD FOR YOUNG CHILDREN

Bristol Woods Hike
Buffalo Rock State Park Hike
Chain O' Lakes State Park: East Hike
Chicago Botanic Garden Hike
Crabtree Nature Center Hike
Deep River Hike
Fullersburg Woods Loop
Goodenow Grove Hike
Goose Lake Prairie State Natural Area: Prairie
  View Trail
Illinois Beach State Park: Dead River Loop
Indiana Dunes National Lakeshore:
  Bailly/Chellberg Hike
Indiana Dunes National Lakeshore: Cowles
  Bog Trail

Indiana Dunes National Lakeshore: West
  Beach Loop
Indiana Dunes State Park: Dune Ridge Loop
Indiana Dunes State Park: Shoreline Loop
Lake Katherine Trail
Matthiessen State Park Dells Area Hike
Morton Arboretum East Hike
Oak Ridge Prairie Loop
Palos/Sag Vally Forest Preserve: Little Red
  Schoolhouse Hike
Pilcher Park Loop
Silver Springs State Park Loop
Tekakwitha–Fox River Hike
Veteran Acres–Sterne's Woods Hike
Volo Bog State Natural Area Hike

▶ ACCESSIBLE BY PUBLIC TRANSPORTATION
(NO CABS REQUIRED)

Chicago Lakeshore Path: North Hike
Chicago Lakeshore Path: South Hike
Fullersburg Woods Loop
Indiana Dunes National Lakeshore:
  Cowles Bog Trail
Indiana Dunes National Lakeshore:
  Ly-co-ki-we Trail

Indiana Dunes State Park: Dune Ridge Loop
Indiana Dunes State Park: Shoreline Loop
Jackson Park Loop
Joliet Iron Works Hike
Lake Katherine Trail
Skokie Lagoons and River Hike

▶ URBAN HIKES

Chicago Botanic Garden Hike
Chicago Lakeshore Path: North Hike
Chicago Lakeshore Path: South Hike
Geneva Lake: Bigfoot Beach Hike
Geneva Lake: North Shore Hike
Jackson Park Loop

Joliet Iron Works Hike
Lake Katherine Trail
Skokie Lagoons and River Hike
Tekakwitha–Fox River Hike
Veteran Acres–Sterne's Woods Hike

▶ NO DOGS ALLOWED

Chicago Botanic Garden Hike
Crabtree Nature Center Hike
Morton Arboretum East Hike

Ryerson Woods Hike
Thorn Creek Hike

HIKING RECOMMENDATIONS

▶ SOLITUDINOUS HIKES

Braidwood Dunes and Savanna Loop
Bristol Woods Hike
Chain O' Lakes State Park: West Hike
Crabtree Nature Center Hike
Deep River Hike
Goodenow Grove Hike
Grand Kankakee Marsh Hike
Indiana Dunes National Lakeshore:
  Bailly/Chellberg Hike

Indiana Dunes National Lakeshore:
  Cowles Bog Trail
Iroquois County State Wildlife Area Hike
Lakewood Forest Preserve Loop
LaSalle Fish and Wildlife Area Loop
Marengo Ridge Hike
Midewin National Tallgrass Prairie Hike
Palos/Sag Valley Forest Preserve: Cap Sauers
  and Swallow Cliff Loop
Thorn Creek Hike

▶ HIKES FOR WILDLIFE VIEWING

Chain O' Lakes State Park: East Hike
Crabtree Nature Center Hike
Danada Forest Preserve Hike
Glacial Park Loop
Goodenow Grove Hike
Goose Lake Prairie State Natural Area: Prairie
  View Trail
Goose Lake Prairie State Natural Area: Tall-
  grass Trail
Grand Kankakee Marsh Hike
Greene Valley Forest Preserve Loop
Illinois Beach State Park: Dead River Loop

Indiana Dunes State Park: Dune Ridge Loop
Iroquois County State Wildlife Area Hike
Lakewood Forest Preserve Loop
LaSalle Fish and Wildlife Area Loop
McKinley Woods Loop
Midewin National Tallgrass Prairie Hike
Morton Arboretum East Hike
Palos/Sag Valley Forest Preserve: Cap Sauers
  and Swallow Cliff Loop
Pilcher Park Loop
Ryerson Woods Hike
Volo Bog State Natural Area Hike

▶ HIKES WITH WHEELCHAIR-ACCESSIBLE SECTIONS

Buffalo Rock State Park Hike
Chain O' Lakes State Park: East Hike
Channahon State Park: I&M Canal Trail
Chicago Botanic Garden Hike
Chicago Lakeshore Path: North Hike
Chicago Lakeshore Path: South Hike
Danada Forest Preserve Hike
Fullersburg Woods Loop

Greene Valley Forest Preserve Loop
Joliet Iron Works Hike
Kankakee River State Park Hike
Moraine Hills State Park Hike
Palos/Sag Vally Forest Preserve: Little Red
  Schoolhouse Hike
Waterfall Glen Forest Preserve Loop

▶ HIKES FOR SEASONAL WILDFLOWER VIEWING

Braidwood Dunes and Savanna Loop
Buffalo Rock State Park Hike
Chicago Botanic Garden Hike

Crabtree Nature Center Hike
Danada Forest Preserve Hike
Deep River Hike

HIKING RECOMMENDATIONS

▶ HIKES FOR SEASONAL WILDFLOWER VIEWING (cont'd)

Goose Lake Prairie State Natural Area:
  Prairie View Trail
Goose Lake Prairie State Natural Area:
  Tallgrass Trail
Illinois Beach State Park: Dead River Hike
Indiana Dunes National Lakeshore:
  Bailly/Chellberg Hike
Indiana Dunes National Lakeshore:
  Cowles Bog Trail
Indiana Dunes National Lakeshore:
  Ly-co-ki-we Trail
Indiana Dunes National Lakeshore:
  West Beach Loop
Iroquois County State Wildlife Area Hike

LaSalle Fish and Wildlife Area Loop
Marengo Ridge Hike
Matthiessen State Park Dells Area Hike
Midewin National Tallgrass Prairie Hike
Moraine Hills State Park Hike
Oak Ridge Prairie Loop
Palos/Sag Valley Forest Preserve: Cap Sauers
  and Swallow Cliff Loop
Pilcher Park Loop
Silver Springs State Park Loop
Starved Rock State Park: East Hike
Tekakwitha–Fox River Hike
Veteran Acres–Sterne's Woods Hike

▶ BUSY HIKES

Chain O' Lakes State Park: East Hike
Channahon State Park: I&M Canal Trail
Chicago Botanic Garden Hike
Chicago Lakeshore Path: North Hike
Chicago Lakeshore Path: South Hike
Fullersburg Woods Loop
Geneva Lake: North Shore Hike
Kankakee River State Park Hike
Lake Katherine Trail

Moraine Hills State Park Hike
Palos/Sag Vally Forest Preserve: Little Red
  Schoolhouse Hike
Skokie Lagoons and River Hike
Starved Rock State Park: West Hike
Tekakwitha–Fox River Hike
Veteran Acres–Sterne's Woods Hike
Waterfall Glen Forest Preserve Loop

▶ HILLY HIKES

Bristol Woods Hike
Chain O' Lakes State Park: West Hike
Deer Grove Loop
Geneva Lake: North Shore Hike
Indiana Dunes National Lakeshore:
  Cowles Bog Trail
Indiana Dunes National Lakeshore:
  West Beach Loop
Indiana Dunes State Park: Dune Ridge Loop
Indiana Dunes State Park: Shoreline Loop

Lake Katherine Trail
Marengo Ridge Hike
Matthiessen State Park Dells Area Hike
McKinley Woods Loop
Moraine Hills State Park Hike
Silver Springs State Park Loop
Starved Rock State Park: East Hike
Starved Rock State Park: West Hike
Tekakwitha–Fox River Hike
Veteran Acres–Sterne's Woods Hike

HIKING RECOMMENDATIONS

▶ RIVER HIKES

Buffalo Rock State Park Hike
Chain O' Lakes State Park: East Hike
Channahon State Park: I&M Canal Trail
Chicago Botanic Garden Hike
Deep River Hike
Fullersburg Woods Loop
Glacial Park Loop
Goodenow Grove Hike
Grand Kankakee Marsh Hike
Illinois Beach State Park: Dead River Loop
Indiana Dunes National Lakeshore:
  Bailly/Chellberg Hike
Kankakee River State Park Hike

Lake Katherine Trail
LaSalle Fish and Wildlife Area Loop
Matthiessen State Park Dells Area Hike
McKinley Woods Loop
Pilcher Park Loop
Ryerson Woods Hike
Silver Springs State Park Loop
Skokie Lagoons and River Hike
Starved Rock State Park: East Hike
Starved Rock State Park: West Hike
Tekakwitha–Fox River Hike
Thorn Creek Hike

▶ LAKE HIKES

Bong State Recreation Area Loop
Chicago Botanic Garden Hike
Chicago Lakeshore Path: North Hike
Chicago Lakeshore Path: South Hike
Crabtree Nature Center Hike
Geneva Lake: Bigfoot Beach Hike
Geneva Lake: North Shore Hike
Illinois Beach State Park: Dead River Loop
Indiana Dunes National Lakeshore:
  Cowles Bog Trail
Indiana Dunes National Lakeshore:
  West Beach Loop

Indiana Dunes State Park: Dune Ridge Loop
Indiana Dunes State Park: Shoreline Loop
Jackson Park Loop
Lake Katherine Trail
Lakewood Forest Preserve Loop
Moraine Hills State Park Hike
Oak Ridge Prairie Loop
Palos/Sag Vally Forest Preserve: Little Red
  Schoolhouse Hike
Pratt's Wayne Loop
Shabbona Lake State Park Loop
Silver Springs State Park Loop

▶ BEACH HIKES

Chicago Lakeshore Path: North Hike
Chicago Lakeshore Path: South Hike
Geneva Lake: Bigfoot Beach Hike
Geneva Lake: North Shore Hike
Illinois Beach State Park: Dead River Loop
Indiana Dunes National Lakeshore: Cowles
  Bog Trail

Indiana Dunes National Lakeshore: West
  Beach Loop
Indiana Dunes State Park: Dune Ridge Loop
Indiana Dunes State Park: Shoreline Loop

HIKING RECOMMENDATIONS

▶ GOOD HIKES FOR CYCLISTS/MOUNTAIN BIKERS

Chain O' Lakes State Park: East Hike
Channahon State Park: I&M Canal Trail
Chicago Lakeshore Path: North Hike
Chicago Lakeshore Path: South Hike
Danada Forest Preserve Hike
Deer Grove Loop
Fullersburg Woods Loop
Grand Kankakee Marsh Hike

Greene Valley Forest Preserve Loop
Kankakee River State Park Hike
LaSalle Fish and Wildlife Area Loop
Midewin National Tallgrass Prairie Hike
Moraine Hills State Park Hike
Pratt's Wayne Loop
Skokie Lagoons and River Hike
Waterfall Glen Forest Preserve Loop

▶ GOOD HIKES FOR RUNNERS

Bong State Recreation Area Loop
Bristol Woods Hike
Buffalo Rock State Park Hike
Chain O' Lakes State Park: East Hike
Chain O' Lakes State Park: West Hike
Channahon State Park: I&M Canal Trail
Chicago Lakeshore Path: North Hike
Chicago Lakeshore Path: South Hike
Danada Forest Preserve Hike
Deer Grove Loop
Fullersburg Woods Loop
Glacial Park Loop
Goodenow Grove Hike
Grand Kankakee Marsh Hike
Greene Valley Forest Preserve Loop
Indiana Dunes National Lakeshore:
  Cowles Bog Trail

Iroquois County State Wildlife Area Hike
Kankakee River State Park Hike
Lakewood Forest Preserve Loop
Marengo Ridge Hike
McKinley Woods Loop
Midewin National Tallgrass Prairie Hike
Moraine Hills State Park Hike
Moraine Hills State Park Hike
Palos/Sag Valley Forest Preserve:
  Cap Sauers and Swallow Cliff Loop
Pilcher Park Loop
Ryerson Woods Hike
Silver Springs State Park Loop
Skokie Lagoons and River Hike
Veteran Acres–Sterne's Woods Hike
Waterfall Glen Forest Preserve Loop

▶ GOOD HIKES FOR CROSS-COUNTRY SKIERS

Bong State Recreation Area Loop
Bristol Woods Hike
Buffalo Rock State Park Hike
Chain O' Lakes State Park: East Hike
Chain O' Lakes State Park: West Hike
Crabtree Nature Center Hike
Danada Forest Preserve Hike
Deer Grove Loop
Fullersburg Woods Loop
Glacial Park Loop
Goodenow Grove Hike

Goose Lake Prairie State Natural Area:
  Tallgrass Trail
Grand Kankakee Marsh Hike
Greene Valley Forest Preserve Loop
Illinois Beach State Park: Dead River Loop
Indiana Dunes National Lakeshore:
  Ly-co-ki-we Hike
Iroquois County State Wildlife Area Hike
Kankakee River State Park Hike
LaSalle Fish and Wildlife Area Loop
Marengo Ridge Hike

HIKING RECOMMENDATIONS

INTRODUCTION

Welcome to *60 Hikes within 60 Miles: Chicago*. If you're new to hiking or even if you're a seasoned trail-smith, take a few minutes to read the following introduction. We explain how this book is organized and how to use it.

▶ HIKE DESCRIPTIONS

Each hike contains eight key items: a locator map, an "In Brief" description of the trail, a key at-a-glance information box, directions to the trail, a trail map, an elevation profile, a trail description, and a description of nearby activities. Combined, the maps and information provide a clear method to assess each trail from the comfort of your favorite reading chair.

LOCATOR MAP

After narrowing down the general area of the hikes on the overview map (see inside back cover), the locator maps, along with directions given in the narratives, enable you to find the trailheads. (Once at the trailhead, park only in designated areas.)

IN BRIEF

A "taste of the trail." Think of this section as a snapshot focused on the historical landmarks, beautiful vistas, and other sights you may encounter on the trail.

KEY AT-A-GLANCE INFORMATION

The information in the key at-a-glance boxes gives you a quick idea of the specifics of each hike. There are 13 basic elements covered.

LENGTH The length of the trail from start to finish. There may be options to shorten or extend the hikes, but the mileage corresponds to the described hike. Consult the hike description to help decide how to customize the hike for your ability or time constraints.

CONFIGURATION A description of what the trail might look like from overhead. Trails can be loops, out-and-backs (trails on which one enters and leaves along the same path), figure eights, or balloons.

DIFFICULTY The degree of effort an "average" hiker should expect on a given hike. For simplicity, difficulty is described as "easy," "moderate," or "difficult."

SCENERY A rating of the overall environs of the hike and what to expect in terms of plant life, wildlife, streams, and historic buildings.

EXPOSURE A quick check of how much sun you can expect on your shoulders during the hike. Descriptors used include terms such as "shady," "exposed," and "sunny."

TRAFFIC Indicators of how busy the trail might be on an average day, and if you might be able to find solitude out there. Trail traffic, of course, varies from day to day and season to season.

INTRODUCTION

SURFACE   A description of the trail surface, be it paved, rocky, dirt, or a mixture of elements.

HIKING TIME   The length of time it takes to hike the trail. A slow but steady hiker will average 2 to 3 miles an hour, depending on the terrain. Most of the estimates in this book reflect a speed of about 2 miles per hour.

ACCESS   A notation of any fees or permits needed to access the trail (if any) and whether pets and other forms of trail use are permitted.

FACILITIES   What to expect in terms of restrooms, phones, water, and other amenities available at the trailhead or nearby.

MAPS   Which maps are the best, or easiest, for this hike and where to get them.

SPECIAL COMMENTS   These comments cover little extra details that don't fit into any of the above categories. Here you'll find information on trail-hiking options and facts, or tips on how to get the most out of your hike.

DIRECTIONS TO THE TRAIL
Used with the locator map, the directions will help you locate each trailhead.

TRAIL DESCRIPTIONS
The trail description is the heart of each hike. Here, the author provides a summary of the trail's essence and highlights any special traits the hike offers. Ultimately, the hike description will help you choose which hikes are best for you.

NEARBY ACTIVITIES
Look here for information on nearby activities or points of interest.

▶ WEATHER

During an average year in Chicago, the mercury slides up and down full length of the thermometer, spending two weeks above the 90-degree mark and nearly the same amount of time below zero. While few will want to linger outdoors during the extremes of local weather, the rest of the year is great for outdoor activities. Extremes aside, summer and winter are full of mild days that provide excellent opportunities for hiking. And for those who like to watch leaves change, flowers bloom, and birds migrate, spring and fall are a favorite time for a ramble.

While the seasons provide a bounty of possible weather conditions, there are sometimes major weather variations within the region. The most important factor contributing to local variations is the freshwater sea outside our front door: Lake Michigan absorbs heats more quickly and releases it more slowly than the land. As a result, the phrase "cooler by the lake" habitually rolls off the tongues of our weather forecasters. This phenomenon is most noticeable on summer days when a cool breeze is sweeping the lakeshore, but several blocks away the city feels like a sauna because of the heat-absorbing properties of asphalt. "Lake effect"—another way in which Lake Michigan influences local weather patterns—occurs when an air mass absorbs moisture as it passes eastward over the lake and then releases precipitation upon reaching land. Lake effect explains why snow often falls heaviest on the eastern and southern shores of Lake Michigan compared to the western shore.

With all these variations in Chicagoland weather, the word to remember is adaptability. If you want to continue hiking all year, it helps to have apparel for a range of conditions. Especially in spring, winter, and fall, consider bringing one or two more layers than you think you'll need. Even during a warm summer day, a trip to the lakeshore may require a sweater or a light windbreaker. Adaptability, however, is not just a question of wearing sandals or snowshoes, hiking shorts or insulated pants— it's also an attitude. Being adaptable means thinking less about how the weather ought to be and thinking more about ways to find pleasure in a variety of conditions.

AVERAGE DAILY TEMPERATURES BY MONTH

	JAN	FEB	MAR	APR	MAY	JUN
HIGH	30	35	46	58	70	79
LOW	14	19	28	38	59	68
MEAN	22	27	73	48	59	68

	JUL	AUG	SEP	OCT	NOV	DEC
HIGH	84	81	74	62	47	34
LOW	63	62	54	42	32	20
MEAN	73	72	64	52	39	27

▶ ALLOCATING TIME

On flat or lightly undulating terrain, the author averaged 3 miles per hour when hiking. That speed drops in direct proportion to the steepness of a path, and it does not reflect the many pauses and forays off trail in pursuit of yet another bird sighting, wildflower, or photograph. Give yourself plenty of time. Few people enjoy rushing through a hike, and fewer still take pleasure in bumping into trees after dark. Remember, too, that your pace naturally slackens over the back half of a long trek.

▶ MAPS

The maps in this book have been produced with great care and, used with the hiking directions, will direct you to the trail and help you stay on course. However, you will find superior detail and valuable information in the United States Geological Survey's 7.5-minute series topographic maps. Topo maps are available online in many locations. The easiest single Web resource is located at terraserver.microsoft.com. You can

INTRODUCTION

view and print topos of the entire United States there, and view aerial photographs of the same area. The downside to topos is that most of them are outdated, having been created 20 to 30 years ago. But they still provide excellent topographic detail.

If you're new to hiking, you might be wondering, "What's a topographic map?" In short, a topo indicates not only linear distance but elevation as well, using contour lines. Contour lines spread across the map like dozens of intricate spider webs. Each line represents a particular elevation, and at the base of each topo, a contour's interval designation is given. If the contour interval is 200 feet, then the distance between each contour line is 200 feet. Follow five contour lines up on the same map, and the elevation has increased by 1,000 feet.

Let's assume that the 7.5-minute series topo reads "Contour Interval 40 feet," that the short trail we'll be hiking is two inches in length on the map, and that it crosses five contour lines from beginning to end. What do we know? Well, because the linear scale of this series is 2,000 feet to the inch (roughly two and three-quarters inches representing one mile), we know our trail is approximately four-fifths of a mile long (2 inches are 2,000 feet). But we also know we'll be climbing or descending 200 vertical feet (5 contour lines are 40 feet each) over that distance. And the elevation designations written on occasional contour lines will tell us if we're heading up or down.

In addition to outdoor shops and bike shops, you'll find topos at major universities and some public libraries, where you might try photocopying the ones you need to avoid the cost of buying them. But if you want your own and can't find them locally, visit the United States Geological Survey website at topomaps.usgs.gov. The author also recommends topozone.com as a resource for topographic maps and software.

GPS TRAILHEAD COORDINATES

To collect accurate map data, each trail was hiked with a handheld GPS unit (Magellan Meridian). Data collected was then downloaded and plotted onto a digital USGS topo map. In addition to rendering a highly specific trail outline, this book also includes the GPS coordinates for each trailhead. More accurately known as UTM coordinates, the numbers index a specific point using a grid method. The survey datum used to arrive at the coordinates is NAD27. For readers who own a GPS unit, whether handheld or onboard a vehicle, the UTM coordinates provided on the first page of each hike may be entered into the GPS unit. Just make sure your GPS unit is set to navigate using the UTM system in conjunction with NAD27 datum. Now you can navigate directly to the trailhead.

Most trailheads, which begin in parking areas, can be navigated to by car. However, some hikes still require a short walk to reach the trailhead from a parking area. In those cases, a handheld unit would be necessary to continue the GPS navigation process. That said, however, readers can easily access all trailheads in this book by using the directions given, the overview map, and the trail map, which shows at least

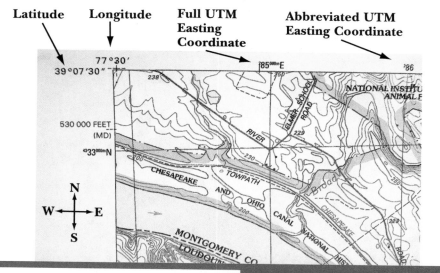

Latitude — Longitude — Full UTM Easting Coordinate — Abbreviated UTM Easting Coordinate

Easting coordinates and topo maps

one major road leading into the area. But for those who enjoy using the latest GPS technology to navigate, the necessary data has been provided. A brief explanation of the UTM coordinates follows.

UTM COORDINATES–ZONE, EASTING, AND NORTHING

Within the UTM coordinates box on the first page of each hike, there are three numbers labeled zone, easting, and northing. Here is an example from Skokie Lagoons and River Hike on page 207:

UTM Zone (NAD27) 16T

Easting 437475

Northing 4661092

The zone number (16) refers to one of the 60 longitudinal zones (vertical) of a map using the Universal Transverse Mercator (UTM) projection. Each zone is 6 degrees wide. The zone letter (T) refers to one of the 20 latitudinal zones (horizontal) that span from 80° South to 84° North.

The easting number (437475) references in meters how far east the point is from the zero value for eastings, which runs north-south through Greenwich, England. Increasing easting coordinates on a topo map or on your GPS screen indicate you are moving east. Decreasing easting coordinates indicate you are moving west. Since lines of longitude converge at the poles, they are not parallel as lines of latitude are. This means that the distance between Full Easting Coordinates is 1,000 meters near the equator but becomes smaller as you travel farther north or south. The difference is small enough to be ignored, but only until you reach the polar regions.

In the northern hemisphere, the northing number (4661092) references in meters how far you are from the Equator. Above the Equator, northing coordinates increase by 1,000

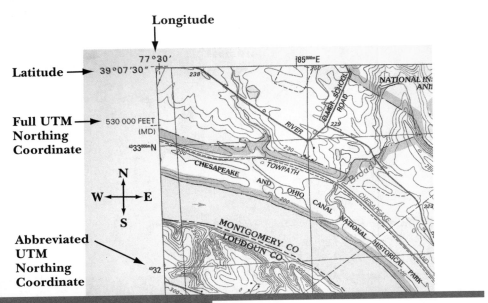

Longitude

Latitude

Full UTM Northing Coordinate

Abbreviated UTM Northing Coordinate

Northing coordinates and topo maps

meters between each parallel line of latitude (east-west lines). On a topo map or GPS receiver, increasing northing numbers indicate you are traveling north.

In the southern hemisphere, the northing number references how far you are from a latitude line that is 10 million meters south of the equator. Below the equator, northing coordinates decrease by 1,000 meters between each line of latitude. On a topo map, decreasing northing coordinates indicate you are traveling south.

▶ TRAIL ETIQUETTE

Whether you're on a city, county, state, or national-park trail, always remember that great care and resources (from Nature as well as from your tax dollars) have gone into creating these trails. Treat the trail, wildlife, and fellow hikers with respect.

1. Hike on open trails only. Respect trail and road closures (ask if not sure), avoid possible trespassing on private land, and obtain all permits and authorization as required. Also, leave gates as you found them or as marked.

2. Leave only footprints. Be sensitive to the ground beneath you. This also means staying on the existing trail and not blazing any new trails. Be sure to pack out what you pack in. No one likes to see the trash someone else has left behind.

3. Never spook animals. An unannounced approach, a sudden movement, or a loud noise startles most animals. A surprised snake or skunk can be dangerous for you, for others, and to themselves. Give animals extra room and time to adjust to your presence.

4. Plan ahead. Know your equipment, your ability, and the area in which you are hiking—and prepare accordingly. Be self-sufficient at all times; carry nec-

INTRODUCTION

essary supplies for changes in weather or other conditions. A well-executed trip is a satisfaction to you and to others.

5. Be courteous to other hikers, bikers, or equestrians you meet on the trails.

▶ WATER

"How much is enough? One bottle? Two? Three?! But think of all that extra weight!" Well, one simple physiological fact should convince you to err on the side of excess when it comes to deciding how much water to pack: A hiker working hard in 90-degree heat needs approximately ten quarts of fluid every day. That's two and a half gallons—12 large water bottles or 16 small ones. In other words, pack along one or two bottles even for short hikes.

Serious backpackers hit the trail prepared to purify water found along the route. This method, while less dangerous than drinking it untreated, comes with risks. Purifiers with ceramic filters are the safest, but are also the most expensive. Many hikers pack along the slightly distasteful tetraglycine-hydroperiodide tablets (sold under the names Potable Aqua, Coughlan's, and others).

Probably the most common waterborne "bug" that hikers face is *Giardia*, which may not hit until one to four weeks after ingestion. It will have you passing noxious rotten-egg gas, vomiting, shivering with chills, and living in the bathroom. But there are other parasites to worry about, including *E. coli* and *Cryptosporidium* (that are harder to kill than *Giardia*).

For most people, the pleasures of hiking make carrying water a relatively minor price to pay to remain healthy. If you're tempted to drink "found water," do so only if you understand the risks involved. Better yet, hydrate prior to your hike, carry (and drink) six ounces of water for every mile you plan to hike, and hydrate after the hike.

▶ FIRST-AID KIT

A kit may contain more items than you might think. These are just the basics:

Ace bandages or Spenco joint wraps

Antibiotic ointment (Neosporin or the generic equivalent)

Aspirin or acetaminophen

Band-Aids

Benadryl or the generic equivalent—diphenhydramine (an antihistamine, in case of allergic reactions)

Butterfly-closure bandages

Epinephrine in a prefilled syringe (for those known to have severe allergic reactions to such things as bee stings)

Gauze (one roll)

Gauze compress pads (a half dozen 4 x 4 in.)

Hydrogen peroxide or iodine

Insect repellent

Matches or pocket lighter

Moleskin/Spenco "Second Skin"

Snakebite kit

Sunscreen

Water-purification tablets or water filter (on longer hikes)

Whistle (more effective in signaling rescuers than your voice)

INTRODUCTION

▶ HIKING WITH CHILDREN

No one is too young for a hike in the woods or through a city park. Be mindful, though. Flat, short trails are best with an infant. Toddlers who have not quite mastered walking can still tag along, riding on an adult's back in a child carrier. Use common sense to judge a child's capacity to hike a particular trail, and always rely on the possibility that the child will tire quickly and need to be carried. To determine which trails are suitable for children, a list of good hikes for children is provided in the "Hiking Recommendations" section earlier in this book.

▶ SNAKES

Spend some time hiking in Chicagoland and you may be surprised by the variety of snakes in the area. Most snake encounters will be with garter snakes, water snakes, brown snakes, and perhaps an eastern hognose snake (while not venomous, the hognose can be intimidating, as it hisses and puts on a cobra-like display). The only venomous snake in the Chicago region is the massasauga rattlesnake. Sightings of this smaller-sized rattler are rare. You might spend a few minutes studying snakes before heading into the woods, but in any case, a good rule of thumb is to give whatever animal you encounter a wide berth and leave it alone.

▶ TICKS

Ticks are often found on brush and tall grass waiting to hitch a ride on a warm-blooded passerby. While they're most visible in the Chicago area in early and mid-summer, you should be on the lookout for them throughout spring, summer, and fall. Among the local varieties of ticks, deer ticks and dog ticks are the ones that can transmit diseases. Both of these ticks need several hours of attachment before they can transmit any diseases they may harbor. Deer ticks, the primary carrier of Lyme disease, are very small, sometimes the size of a poppy seed. While wearing shorts, I often find ticks hiding under the top edge of my socks (they need some type of backstop to start drilling into the skin). You can use several strategies to reduce your chances of ticks getting under your skin. Some people choose to wear light-colored clothing, so ticks can be spotted before they make it to the skin. Insect repellant containing DEET is known as an effective deterrent. Most importantly, though, be sure to visually check yourself at the end of the hike. And if it's prime tick season, you may want to perform a quick check every hour or so. During your post-hike shower, take a moment to do a more complete body check. For ticks that are already embedded, removal with tweezers is best.

INTRODUCTION

▶ POISON IVY

Recognizing and avoiding contact with poison ivy, oak, and sumac is the most effective way to prevent the painful, itchy rashes associated with these plants. In the Midwest, poison ivy occurs as a vine or groundcover, three leaflets to a leaf; poison oak occurs as either a vine or shrub, with three leaflets as well; and poison sumac flourishes in swampland, each leaf containing 7 to 13 leaflets. Urushiol, the oil in the sap of these plants, is responsible for the rash. Within 12 to 14 hours of exposure, raised lines and/or blisters will appear, accompanied by a terrible itch. Refrain from scratching because bacteria under fingernails can cause infection. Wash and dry the rash thoroughly, applying a calamine lotion to help dry out the rash. If itching or blistering is severe, seek medical attention. If you do come in contact with one of these plants, remember that oil-contaminated clothes, pets, or hiking gear can easily cause an irritating rash on you or someone else, so wash not only any exposed parts of your body but also clothes, gear, and pets if applicable.

▶ MOSQUITOES AND WEST NILE VIRUS

While not a common occurrence, individuals can become infected with the West Nile virus by being bitten by an infected mosquito. Culex mosquitoes, the primary varieties that can transmit West Nile virus to humans, thrive in urban rather than natural areas. They lay their eggs in stagnant water and can breed in any standing water that remains for more than five days. Most people infected with West Nile virus have no symptoms of illness, but some may become ill, usually 3 to 15 days after being bitten.

In the Chicago area, August and September are likely to be the highest-risk periods for West Nile virus. At this time of year—and anytime you expect mosquitoes to be buzzing around—you may want to wear protective clothing such as long sleeves, long pants, and socks. Loose-fitting, light-colored clothing is best. Spray clothing with insect repellent. Remember to follow the instructions on the repellent carefully and take extra care with children.

BONG STATE RECREATION AREA LOOP

IN BRIEF

Hiking around Wolf Lake, the centerpiece of Bong State Recreation Area, offers a pleasantly varied experience. The terrain on one side of the lake is flat or lightly rolling tree-speckled prairie, while the other side gives you dense woods, steep hills, and plunging ravines.

DESCRIPTION

In the early 1950s, the federal government determined that a jet-fighter base was needed to protect the Chicago and Milwaukee areas from enemy attack. Seventeen miles west of Kenosha, Wisconsin, a chunk of agricultural land spattered with woodlands, was chosen for the site. The federal government spent $29 million toward acquiring land from 59 farm families and beginning development for an air base designed to house 5,000 airmen. Three days prior to paving the 2.4-mile-long runway, the project was abandoned due to budget problems, possible air-space congestion, and concerns about the base being unnecessary.

In 1974, after much discussion and litigation, the state designated its first "recreation area" at the 4,515-acre base that was never to be. The aborted airbase and subsequent park were named after Richard Bong, a World War II ace fighter pilot from the far reaches of Northern Wisconsin. Bong, who died in 1945 while on a

KEY AT-A-GLANCE INFORMATION

LENGTH: 3.7 miles

CONFIGURATION: Loop

DIFFICULTY: Moderate

SCENERY: Lake, woods, prairie, ponds, marshes, and hills

EXPOSURE: Partly shaded

SURFACE: Mowed grass

HIKING TIME: 2.5 hours

ACCESS: 6 a.m.–11 p.m. A day pass is $10 per car for visitors with non-Wisconsin license plates, and $5 for those with Wisconsin plates. Hiking is not allowed on this trail when there is enough snow on the ground for cross-country skiing. When skiers take possession of this trail, hikers and snowshoers are invited to use a portion of the 12 miles of mountain biking trails in the northern section of the recreation area.

FACILITIES: Campground, picnic areas, beach, boat launch, visitor center

MAPS: Pick up a park map from the entrance station. USGS topos Paddock Lake, WI; Union Grove, WI

SPECIAL COMMENTS: Leashed dogs are welcome on this hike. Call the recreation area at (262) 878-5600 in the winter to see if this trail is open for hikers. Also, contact the park for camping information. The 217-site campground is open all year.

DIRECTIONS

From Chicago, take I-90/I-94 north, following I-94 as it branches off from I-90. Proceed along I-94 into Wisconsin, until reaching Exit 340. Head west (left) on IL 142 for 9.25 miles. After turning into the entrance of the park on the left, stop at the entrance station to pay admission and to receive a map. From the entrance station, take the first left, passing the Molinaro Visitor Station. The next left is the trailhead parking lot.

UTM Trailhead Coordinates for Bong State Recreation Area Loop

UTM Zone (NAD27)   16T

Easting   407710

Northing   4720375

entrance

142

visitor center

INTERPRETIVE TRL.

BLUE / GREEN TRL.

GREEN TRL.

HORSE TRL.

75

restrooms and fishing pier

beach and picnic area

BLUE TRL.

Wolf Lake

HORSE TRL.

N

BONG STATE RECREATION AREA LOOP

NO SCALE INDICATED

1

Michi City

421

23

65

IANA

38

NOIS

Kankake

I 94 33

16

355

44

13

FEET

| 1180 |
| 1120 |
| 1060 |
| 1000 |
| 940 |
| 880 |
| 820 |
| 760 |
| 700 |

0.82   1.65   2.47   3.7

MILES

30

60

22

21

55

test flight in California, still holds the fighter-pilot record for shooting down 40 enemy planes.

At the beginning or end of the hike, stop in at the visitor center to browse through an impressive collection of taxidermy specimens. Some of the more striking examples are the northern goshawk, snowy owl, and a dramatic portrayal of a coyote chasing a deer. For kids, there are bones, feathers, and pelts that can be picked up and examined.

Start the hike from the trailhead parking lot just east of the visitor center. Follow the blue and green arrows heading south to the boardwalk over the pond. After crossing the park road that leads to the Sunrise Campground, follow the Blue/Green Trail to the left. For the next mile or so, you'll encounter a handful of trail junctions; some of these are horse trails and some are connector trails to the campground. Fortunately, all the intersections are well marked with arrows and the respective color of the trail painted around the top of the post. For now, keep an eye on the posts marked with blue and green.

As the trail curves away from the road, it heads down into a wooded area next to a small pond. The hill on the right serves as a sledding hill in the winter; on the rise to the left is where campground sites are located. From the pond, the trail climbs a small hill, from which you'll see a grove of pine trees, a small prairie, and 150-acre Wolf Lake farther off. At the top of the next small hill, a junction of several trails comes together: follow the Blue/Green Trail on the left.

Hiking alongside the lake for 0.3 miles, you'll see stands of pussy willows on the lakeside and groves of pine on the land side. Soon, you'll pass a hunter's blind at the edge of the lake on the right, followed by a little knoll with a bench at the top. After squeezing between IL 75 and the lake, the trail rises into a densely wooded area, and then descends a steep hill under a canopy of gnarled oaks. At the bottom of the hill, the trail passes a pond connected to the lake. From here, head up another steep hill through a dense oak forest, and then enter a savanna area where a horse trail branches to the left.

Soon the trail descends into a picturesque ravine with a small stream snaking through it. The piles of rocks on the sides of this ravine were likely moved here from the adjoining prairies by early farmers. Coming out of the woods, the trail takes a quick turn to the right as it enters a prairie, crosses a small stream, and then drops down to the lake through thick stands of poplars and oaks. The trail runs to a bench at the water's edge, and then swings back out into the prairie. While walking through this section of the prairie, you'll see a couple of small marshes, an intersection with a horse trail, another trail leading to a hunter's blind, and farther ahead, several ponds in a range of sizes. Small patches of trees grow here and there at the edge of the ponds.

Soon, the path comes to a large picnic area that includes pavilions, a 300-foot beach, a concession stand, restrooms, and a small fishing pier. Continue ahead with the park road and wide-open prairie on the left of the trail. On the right, the landscape drops down to a long thin strip of cattail marsh between the trail and the parking lot. When you reach the ball diamond, a set of stairs leads down to the parking lot on the right. Soon, the trail descends a bit and then crosses the driveway for the

Gently rolling savanna on the edge of Wolf Lake.

boat launch. The landscape becomes more rolling and conifers become more abundant as you approach the crushed-gravel interpretive trail that runs to the lake and loops back. Near the first intersection with the interpretive trail, a picnic area and restrooms are situated through the trees on the left. Turn left at the trail junction after the second intersection with the interpretive trail, and continue straight ahead until you cross the park road and the boardwalk over the pond to arrive back at the trailhead parking lot.

Note: This trail passes near one duck-hunting blind on the shore of the lake, and in the vicinity of two others. The park remains open to all during hunting season, and assures visitors that this never has posed a problem. If you are uncomfortable hiking during hunting season, you may want to hike before or after hunting hours. Call the park for the hunting schedule.

▶ NEARBY ACTIVITIES

In Burlington, which is 8 miles northwest of the park on IL 142, you'll find a handful of locally owned and chain restaurants. For more eating options, head 17 miles east on IL 142 to Kenosha.

Bong Recreation Area offers 12 miles of mountain-biking trails north of IL 142. These trails are also open for hiking. On these trails, you'll encounter prairies, woodlands, wetlands, and an artificial ridge made from topsoil, cleared for the airfield's runway. With a few exceptions, the terrain is mostly flat or moderately rolling.

BRAIDWOOD DUNES AND SAVANNA LOOP

> ## IN BRIEF

While black-oak savanna dominates much of the setting for this short-but-sweet ramble, you'll also encounter wet swales, gentle ridges, and a rare sand prairie. This unusual landscape is home to an impressive array of wildflowers during much of the year.

> ## DESCRIPTION

In the late 1800s, Braidwood and its surrounding area in southwestern Will County was the cradle of an Illinois coal boom. It started in 1865 when a farmer struck a ribbon of coal while digging a water well. Over the next 50 years, mining companies bought large swaths of land while thousands of people flocked to Braidwood and quickly established nearby towns with names such as Coal City, Carbon Hill, and Diamond (named after "black diamonds").

Miners endured dangerous, dirty, and damp working conditions. Ceilings in the tunnels were low as they picked, shoveled, and pushed coal for ten hours a day to fuel the furnaces of Chicago. At least 74 miners died in an 1883 flood in the nearby Diamond Mine. A handful of labor and political leaders eventually emerged from Braidwood, including a former Chicago mayor, Anton Cermak, who worked in the mines until he was 17.

In the early twentieth century, the mines slowed, until 1928, when modern strip-mining methods took hold. The result was a boomerang-shaped strip-mined area starting roughly near the town of Morris, heading southeast toward the Kankakee River and angling south. Braidwood

> ## DIRECTIONS

Take I-55 south to Exit 238. Follow IL 129 south for 3.7 miles. Turn left (southeast) on IL 113 and proceed for 1 mile until reaching the preserve on the right.

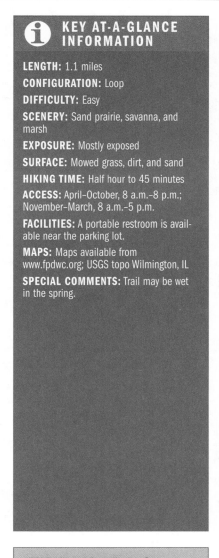

> ## KEY AT-A-GLANCE INFORMATION

LENGTH: 1.1 miles

CONFIGURATION: Loop

DIFFICULTY: Easy

SCENERY: Sand prairie, savanna, and marsh

EXPOSURE: Mostly exposed

SURFACE: Mowed grass, dirt, and sand

HIKING TIME: Half hour to 45 minutes

ACCESS: April–October, 8 a.m.–8 p.m.; November–March, 8 a.m.–5 p.m.

FACILITIES: A portable restroom is available near the parking lot.

MAPS: Maps available from www.fpdwc.org; USGS topo Wilmington, IL

SPECIAL COMMENTS: Trail may be wet in the spring.

UTM Trailhead Coordinates for Braidwood Dunes and Savanna Loop

UTM Zone (NAD27)   16T

Easting   399821

Northing   4568048

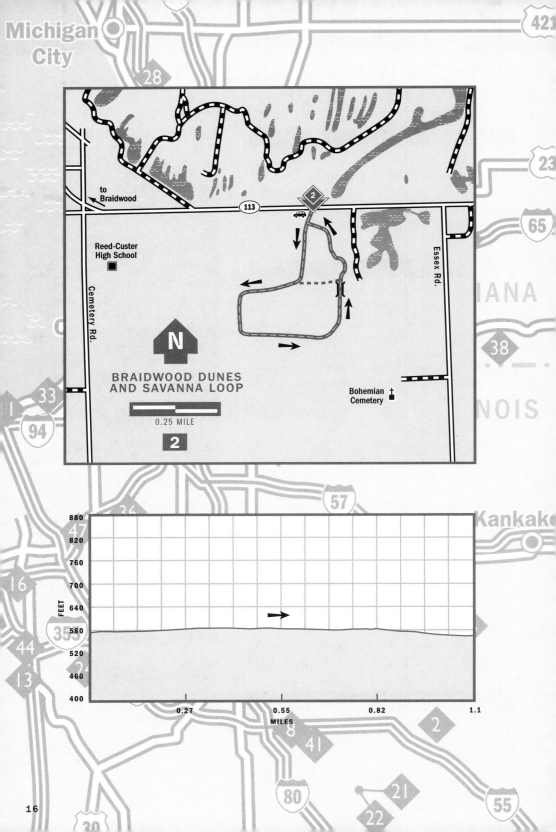

Michigan City

to Braidwood

113

Reed-Custer
High School

Cemetery Rd.

Essex Rd.

N

**BRAIDWOOD DUNES
AND SAVANNA LOOP**

0.25 MILE

2

Bohemian
Cemetery

FEET

880
820
760
700
640
580
520
460
400

0.27   0.55   0.82   1.1
MILES

Dunes and Savanna Nature Preserve, situated between two vast strip mines on property once owned by the Peabody Coal Company, is one of the few chunks of unscathed land within the path of the 20-mile-long boomerang. Braidwood Dunes not only survived the mining era, but also, due to its sandy and often wet ground, escaped the plow.

Dedicated in 1981 as a 259-acre state nature preserve, Braidwood Dunes is the legacy of a glacial lake that receded from the area some 11,000 years ago. While the dunes have blown away, the sandy ground and gently sloping ridges host plants and animals—such as the prickley pear cactus and the six-lined racerunner lizard—that one would expect to see in much sandier terrain such as the Indiana Dunes. Spring, summer, and fall bring an abundance of wildflowers and the attending butterflies and bumblebees.

Start the hike at the trail on the right that heads into the prairie. As you approach the grove of trees, stay right at the junction and follow the trail into a savanna. Look for scattered patches of thick moss on the ground as you hike along a line of shrubby trees on the left. In July, August, and into September, the savanna shimmers with bright yellow five-petaled flowers called the partridge pea. Soon, the trail surface gets sandy, and you'll see the sports fields near the back of Reed-Custer High School to the right. At the restricted-access sign, the trail turns left, cutting between a crowd of oak saplings on the right and a sandy savanna on the left. After passing stands of shrubs and a few towering oaks, you'll see dense clusters of ferns, sedge grasses, and raspberry and sand-cherry bushes. The trail may be overgrown in this section; the forest-preserve district does not mow the trail because the ground is wet along here (particularly in the spring).

At the next restricted-access sign, the trail turns left again. If the route becomes fuzzy due to high grass, just stay to the left next to the shrubs. Keep watch for the wet spots as you push through a labyrinth of bushes, ferns, and 6-foot stands of sedge grass. Suddenly, you're released from the thickets and walking along clearly defined trail through a savanna. After crossing the bridge spanning an intermittent stream, turn right at the junction and enter a dense woodland. As the trail runs toward the prairie, you may notice a profusion of small mounds of sand dug up by creatures making their homes. On the way back to the parking lot, the trail continues along the border of the woodland and prairie.

▶ NEARBY ACTIVITIES

Barely a mile from the Braidwood Dunes and Savanna, on former US Route 66, is a restaurant considered a local institution. In business for over 40 years, the 1950s-style Polk-a-Dot Drive-In is decorated with memorabilia and pictures of celebrities from the era. The menu is just what you'd expect: burgers, chicken, chili-cheese fries, shakes, and ice cream. Heading toward Braidwood on IL 113, turn right on IL 53. The Polk-a-Dot is on the left. Call (815) 458-3377 for hours.

BRISTOL WOODS HIKE

KEY AT-A-GLANCE INFORMATION

LENGTH: 2.6 miles

CONFIGURATION: Combo

DIFFICULTY: Easy

SCENERY: Oak and bottomland woods, marshes, pond, nature center, old town hall

EXPOSURE: Shaded

SURFACE: Dirt, grass

HIKING TIME: 1 hour

ACCESS: 7 a.m.–10 p.m.

FACILITIES: Picnic tables, shelter, toilets, playground

MAPS: Available in the nature center; USGS topo Paddock Lake, WI

SPECIAL COMMENTS: The nature center is open weekends 9 a.m.–4 p.m. In future years, expect to see expanded hours at the nature center and an interpretive brochure to accompany the numbered posts seen throughout the trail system.

UTM Trailhead Coordinates for Bristol Woods Hike

UTM Zone (NAD27) 16T

Easting 417414

Northing 4709201

▶ IN BRIEF

At Bristol Woods, hikers will enjoy the pleasantly rolling terrain covered in bottomland forest and oak woodland. Tree connoisseurs will enjoy the many oak specimens of considerable size, as well as a rare Native American trail-marker tree.

▶ DESCRIPTION

Once owned by a local parks commissioner, Bristol Woods offers visitors a pleasant stroll through nearly 200 acres of upland and lowland woods sprinkled with several small marshes. The park came into existence in the 1970s, when the county bought most of the property at a bargain price from Bob Pringle Sr., a one-time farmer who then served on the Kenosha County Parks Commission. Around the same time, the Pringle family also donated money toward the construction of a nature center. Now operated by volunteers from the Hoy chapter of the Audubon Society in Racine, the Pringle Nature Center has a nice collection of mounted birds and animals as well as habitat exhibits.

Starting the hike behind the nature center, you'll immediately come upon a tree with a strange crescent-shaped trunk. This 200-year-old oak is one of the last Native American trail-marker trees in Kenosha County. While this tree is slightly different, most trail-marker trees were created by stripping a sapling of all its branches and then bending it to the ground in the direction of

▶ DIRECTIONS

Follow I-90/I-94 northwest from Chicago. Stay on I-94 as it breaks off and follow it 45 miles north. Two miles into Wisconsin, take Exit 347, County Road Q. Turn left (west) and proceed for 2.5 miles until reaching County Road MB. Turn right (north) on CR MB and proceed 0.4 miles. The entrance to the park is on the left.

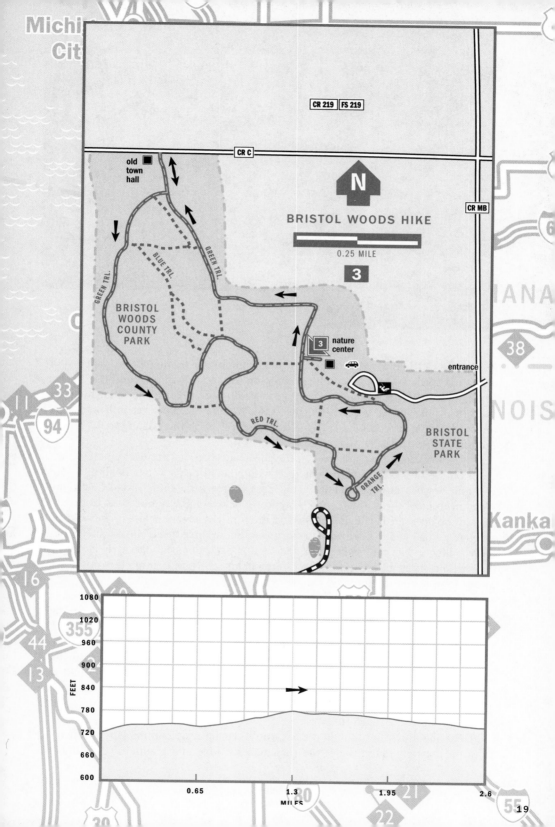

BRISTOL WOODS HIKE

0.25 MILE

3

A Native American trail-marker tree.

any number of important locations, such as camping or trading areas, sacred spots, or natural springs. Once a branch appeared on the top side in the middle of the bent trunk, this branch was allowed to grow skyward. The weight of the branch ensured that the trunk stayed bent. Later, the trunk beyond the lone vertical branch was removed. While this trail-marker tree lines up nicely with the existing trail, no one is certain what it originally pointed toward.

Just ahead, at the T-junction on the edge of a small marsh, turn right. Turn right again on the Red Trail (trails are marked with colored posts at nearly all junctions). Heading down a gradual incline, you'll pass by the little cattail pond in the open space in front of the nature center. Stay to the left as a grassy trail runs to the right toward the open area. The trail crosses an intermittent stream before it rises and runs through a small ravine filled with hickory, oak, and walnut trees. The terrain becomes more rolling as the trail swings left and then zigzags alongside the agricultural field on the right (keep an eye out for deer in the field). The trail eventually drops down a steep slope and heads through a small ravine strewn with deadfall.

After turning right at the Green Trail, the path guides you along a raised bed with a crushed gravel surface. An attractive bottomland forest appears on the right and a steep hill rises up on the left. Stay to the right and switch to the Blue Trail as it rises gradually toward the old town hall located on County Road C. A sign in front of the white wood-frame building explains that it was built in 1870 and actively used for the next 100 years. As you backtrack along the blue trail, skip the first trail that heads toward the back of the town hall. Instead, take the second right, the Green Trail, which leads through a small clearing with a picnic table and then climbs before taking a couple of banked turns.

Passing the White Trail on the left, you'll see more agricultural land through the trees on the right. From here, the trail makes a long and gradual decent under a canopy of large, eye-catching oaks. Watch for downy woodpeckers gliding between the specimens of burr, red, white, and black oak. Heading away from the agricultural field, the trail starts to drop. You may notice that the sides of this trail, as well as other trails at Bristol Woods, contain a good number of rocks and modest-sized boulders. Dropped off by the last glacier, these rocks were usually removed by farmers, so they wouldn't damage their plows. The abundance of rocks at Bristol Woods reveals that this area was never farmed; it was one of the few natural areas in the Chicago region to escape the plow. Just after the trail takes a sharp left turn at a large white oak, keep straight ahead on the Green Trail as you pass an unmarked trail on the right that connects with the Red Trail.

Arriving at a cluster of cottonwood and elm trees, turn right on the Red Trail as it leads past a bench. After a few turns and a series of intermittent streams, you'll see a marker at a grouping of cedars, followed by another intermittent stream that runs through a small gully. After the junction with the Yellow Trail, you'll pass a couple of huge white oaks, and then climb a bit before arriving at a bench situated under another cluster of cedars on a little hilltop. From the hill, walk down into a shallow ravine and then cross an intermittent stream that has carved out a rocky trough. A short climb brings you to a junction with the unmarked connector trail on the right; nearby you'll see a wall from a foundation of a former barn.

After a stretch of bottomland forest thick with bushes, you'll encounter another junction with a connector trail, as well as a marsh behind the trees on the left. Following a dense section of trail that is almost tunnel-like, turn right on the Orange Trail. Stay to the right and you'll see more marshland through the trees on the right. Complete the loop and then head back to the Red Trail.

Back on the Red Trail, look for the grove of apple trees, which were once part of a nearby farm. After passing a trail on the right that goes toward the park road, the trail leads you into a little ravine containing a grove of quaking aspen. This final section of the trail brings you beside several monster-sized oaks, some with knotty, arthritic limbs. Turn right on the Yellow Trail and then bear left back to the nature center.

▶ NEARBY ACTIVITIES

West of Bristol Woods is Silver Lake County Park, which offers several miles of hilly trails running above the lake through groves of oak and sumac, and pine plantations. Catch the beginning of the loop from the small parking area just inside the park entrance. Turning left on the park road at the entrance brings you to lakeside picnic area. Taking the road to the right brings you through a number of picnic areas sprinkled throughout the pleasantly hilly park. The park is open 7 a.m. to 10 p.m. From Bristol Woods, take County Road MB left (north) to IL 50. Follow IL 50 left (west) for 6 miles to County Road F. Turn left (south) on CR F, and the park entrance is nearly 2 miles ahead on the right.

BUFFALO ROCK STATE PARK HIKE

KEY AT-A-GLANCE INFORMATION

LENGTH: 2.5 miles

CONFIGURATION: Combo

DIFFICULTY: Easy

SCENERY: Cliffs and bluffs above the Illinois River, woodland, prairie, and giant mounds in the shape of a catfish, a turtle, a snake, a frog, and a water strider

EXPOSURE: Mostly exposed

SURFACE: Dirt, gravel

HIKING TIME: 1.5 hours (could be twice as long if you thoroughly explore the mounds)

ACCESS: 8 a.m.–sunset

FACILITIES: Playground, restrooms, water, ball diamond, soda machine

MAPS: Available at the park office; USGS topo Starved Rock, IL

SPECIAL COMMENTS: Wear long pants if you intend to explore the mounds. Few paths exist on the mounds, and the grass grows several feet high. For details about the conception and building of mounds, as well as dozens of great aerial photos taken at various stages of completion, take a look at the coffee-table book called *Michael Heizer Effigy Tumuli: The Reemergence of Ancient Mound Building*, by Douglass C. McGill.

UTM Trailhead Coordinates for
Buffalo Rock State Park Hike

UTM Zone (NAD27) 16T

Easting   340217

Northing   4576627

IN BRIEF

Located on a bluff overlooking the Illinois River, this small but charming park is home to an enormous outdoor sculpture. Mounds representing five different creatures invite visitors to walk around and explore this engaging homage to an old Native American practice.

DESCRIPTION

On a 90-foot-high mesa above the Illinois River, a 2,000-foot-long snake slithers along a rocky ledge, its head hovering on the riverbank. Nearby, an 18-foot-high frog looks ready to spring over the high sandstone cliff into the river. Made from earthen mounds, these and three other creatures at Buffalo Rock State Park are part of an outdoor sculpture called Effigy Tumuli. Paying homage to the 4,000-year-old practice of mound building among Native Americans, the artist Michael Heizer decided to represent creatures native to Illinois; the frog and the snake are accompanied by a catfish, a turtle, and a water strider. Commissioned in 1983 as part of an effort to reclaim 150 acres of strip-mined land polluted by toxic runoff, observers have said Effigy Tumuli is one of the largest sculptures since Mount Rushmore.

    The signs posted for each mound reveal that each creature's shape is fairly geometric, as if each

DIRECTIONS

From Chicago, take I-55 to I-80. After driving for 35.5 miles on I-80, take Exit 90. Turn left (south) on IL 23 and proceed for 1.3 miles. Turn right (west) on US 6 and drive for 1.2 miles to Boyce Memorial Drive, where you'll turn left (south). After 1 mile, veer left onto Ottawa Avenue. Buffalo Rock State park is 4.6 miles ahead on the left. As you get closer to the park, the name of Ottawa Avenue changes to North 27th Road or Dee Bennett Road.

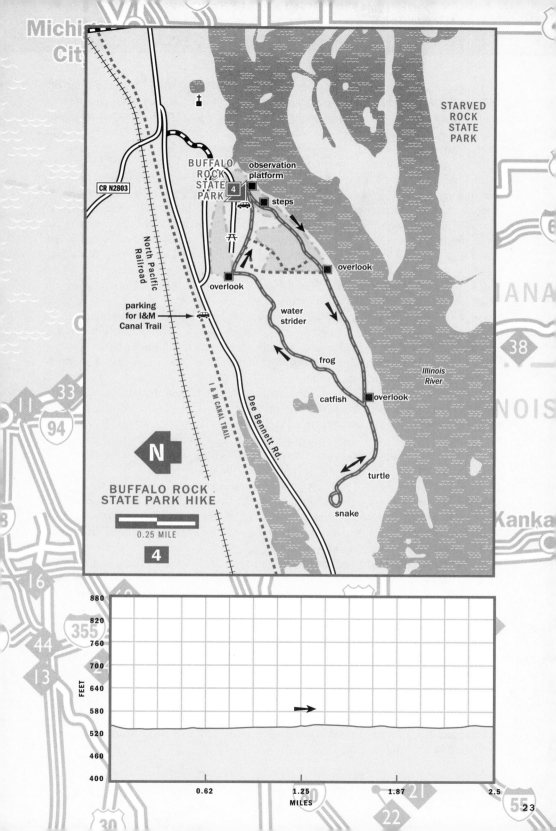

Michigan City

STARVED ROCK STATE PARK

CR N2803

BUFFALO ROCK STATE PARK

observation platform

4

steps

North Pacific Railroad

overlook

parking for I&M Canal Trail

overlook

water strider

frog

catfish

overlook

Illinois River

Dee Bennett Rd.

I & M CANAL TRAIL

N

BUFFALO ROCK STATE PARK HIKE

0.25 MILE

4

turtle

snake

Kanka

IANA

NOIS

FEET

880
820
760
700
640
580
520
460
400

0.62   1.25   1.87   2.5
MILES

was covered with flat plates. Visualizing the sculptures as a whole requires some off-trail exploration as you put the pieces together and notice a leg here and an antennae there. The view from above can only be imagined once you have a sense of what's on the ground. Best times to see the mounds are spring and early summer, when the grasses are short or matted, better revealing the shapes and lines.

As you enter the park on the steep park road, you'll pass a 40- to 50-foot sheer sandstone wall decorated with lichens, moss, ferns, and vines. Jewelweed and wild quinine grow near the base. At the top of the mesa, pull into the first parking lot on the left. The trail starts just beyond the restrooms at the bluff overlooking the river.

Before following the sign for the River Bluff Trail to the right, pay a visit to the observation platform and the short segment of trail at the top of the bluff off to the left. The rocky ledge 90 feet above the river provides a great view of the river to the east. While it's tough to tell from the overlook, the woodland on the opposite side of the river is actually a large island positioned at a wide point in the river. After following the bluff a bit farther to the left, turn around and begin the River Bluff Trail as it heads down a set of steps into an oak and hickory woodland. Shortly after passing a small ravine on the right, you'll notice a closed trail on the left and a short connecter trail to the parking lot on the right. Passing two more junctions on the right, you'll arrive at the edge of a prairie with a bench situated at another overlook. From here, a couple of islands are visible to the west in the river.

The trail continues between the heavily wooded bluff on the left and the prairie on the right. Along with big bluestem, Indian grass, and golden rod, the prairie is peppered with thick stands of tasseled sedge grasses in the wet spots. At 0.6 miles, the trees disappear on the left, providing a great view of the river and the farmland and woods on the opposite shore. Continuing on, cottonwoods, quaking aspen, and varieties of pine rise up again on the bluff and then disappear.

At 0.8 miles, stay to the left at the junction, and you'll see the sign for the catfish—the highest of the five earthworks in the park. Although not all of the mounds have trails going up on top of them, visitors are invited to walk on and around them. Hiking to the top of the earthwork helps to provide a better view of the entire sculpture and gets you a little closer to the ideal vantage point—about 100 feet straight up.

After the catfish, the trail brushes next to the turtle's back left leg and its tail as it slides down the slope and into the river (based on the size of its tail, this turtle is a snapper). The artist incorporated the existing bluff to serve as the turtle's shell and preexisting mounds by the river to serve as the turtle's front legs.

Like the turtle, the snake appears as though it's heading over the bluff and into the water. Climbing up on the zigzagging back of the snake provides a nice view of the nearby sandstone cliffs and the river beyond the thick stands of cottonwoods. The name of the park came from the Native American practice of running buffalos off these cliffs. With seven different parts, the snake is the most complex of the mounds. If bushwhacking sounds appealing, you can get the head of the snake by following the body of the snake to the right nearly to the tip of its tail. At the bottom of the bluff, head left toward the river and look for the 150-foot-wide head on the little promontory sticking into the river.

Heading back toward the parking lot, take a left at the catfish. As you get deeper into the prairie, the number of trees dwindles and the patches of sedge grasses grow larger and more frequent. Climbing up the gently rising back of the frog provides a nice view of the prairie and a view of the water strider just to the east. After passing through a grove of locust trees, you'll begin to see the patchwork of little ridges surrounding a low hump, which is easily accessible by following one of the water strider's two slender legs that come close to the trail.

After passing the water strider and returning to the woodland, turn left at the junction. This trail brings you to a platform with interpretive signs about the effigies. Continuing ahead, take the wood-chip trail to the left for a short walk to an overlook of the deep wooded ravine occupied by Dee Bennett Road and the Illinois and Michigan Canal. From the overlook, you'll see evidence of mining operations in the area. After the overlook, you can walk through the picnic areas to get back to the parking lot where you started the hike.

▶ **NEARBY ACTIVITIES**

Just a couple of miles west of the park on Dee Bennett Road is the Illinois Waterway Visitor Center at Starved Rock Lock and Dam. A platform on the second floor of the visitor center provides a great view of barges as they enter and leave the 600-foot-long lock. Several exhibits provide history on the Illinois Waterway, the first navigable connection between the Great Lakes and the Mississippi River. There are also books for sale and a replica of a pilothouse. Admission is free. Call (815) 667-4054.

Across from the entrance to Buffalo Rock State Park is one of the parking areas and access points for the 61-mile Illinois & Michigan Canal Trail, which runs from Joliet to LaSalle. Four miles west of the parking area is Utica; 2 miles east is Lock 12, and another 2 miles is Lock 11. Call (815) 942-0796 for a map and more information.

BUSSE WOODS LOOP

KEY AT-A-GLANCE INFORMATION

LENGTH: 1.4 miles

CONFIGURATION: Loop

DIFFICULTY: Easy

SCENERY: Woods, ponds, marshes, and a stream

EXPOSURE: Mostly shaded

SURFACE: Paved, gravel, hard-packed dirt

HIKING TIME: 45 minutes to 1 hour

ACCESS: 6:30 a.m.–sunset

FACILITIES: Picnic shelter, restrooms, water

TRAFFIC: Half of this hike uses the Busse Woods Bicycle Trail, which is popular with cyclists, in-line skaters, and runners. During summer, go early in the day to avoid the crowds on this stretch.

MAPS: For a map of the entire Busse Woods Bicycle Trail, contact the Forest Preserve District of Cook County at (708) 366-9429. USGS topo Palatine, IL.

SPECIAL COMMENTS: Consider bringing a bike along to ride the complete 11.2-mile paved trail. The south section of the preserve offers plenty of fishing spots, as well as boat rentals and a concession stand.

UTM Trailhead Coordinates for Busse Woods Loop

UTM Zone (NAD27)   16T

Easting   416626

Northing   4653578

IN BRIEF

This quick, pleasant, and easily accessible hike takes you through dense woods and near numerous small ponds at one of the largest forest preserves in Cook County. Although Busse Woods is busy at times, it's surprisingly quiet once you're off the paved trail.

DESCRIPTION

Busse Woods, also called the Ned Brown Forest Preserve, was one of the first forest preserves established in Cook County, and is now among the largest recreation and natural areas in this part of the Chicago region. The southern half of Busse Woods is dedicated mostly to the sprawling, 590-acre Busse Lake, which has arms extending in all directions forming a half dozen or so islands. The lake was created for recreation and to prevent the flooding problems that were occurring downstream on Salt Creek. To provide depth for boating and fishing, large sections of the lake have been dredged.

The northern half of the preserve is mostly occupied by Busse Woods, part of which is a national landmark registered with the U.S. Department of the Interior. Busse Woods is known for its variety of hardwoods and its spring flower displays, including the state flower, the purple-fringed orchid, which is endangered. Winding its way around the lake, through the

DIRECTIONS

From Chicago, take I-90/I-94 northwest. Stay on I-90 as you pass the I-94 turnoff and O'Hare Airport. Exit on Arlington Heights Road and turn left (south). Proceed for 0.8 miles. Turn right (west) on Higgins Road and continue for 1 mile. Take the second park-access driveway on the right. The paved trail crosses the driveway near the restrooms.

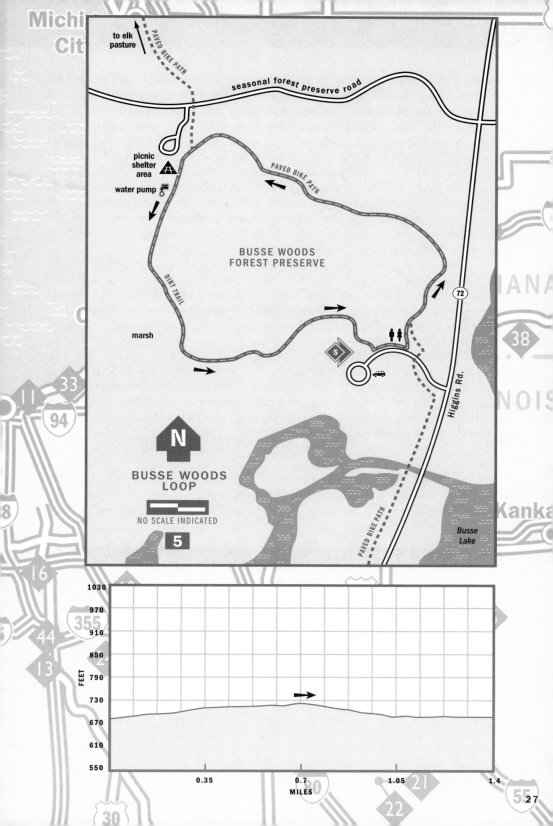

woods, and along Higgins Road, is an 11.2-mile paved trail much loved—especially on warm weekends—by bicyclists, in-line skaters, dog walkers, and hikers.

A little less than half of this hike is along the paved trail; the other part of the hike is surprisingly quiet, as it runs along a much less used gravel-and-dirt path. Catch the paved trail as it heads east near the restrooms. After following Higgins Road for 0.2 miles, the traffic noise drops off as the trail curves left. Like most of Busse Woods, this stretch of trail reveals a landscape that is densely wooded, faintly rolling, and often wet. Small, shallow ponds, often strewn with moss-covered dead-fall, occasionally interrupt the thick stands of trees. Growing near these little ponds are trees that can tolerate the wet conditions, such as ash and swamp-white oak. On this section of trail, look for several very small streams running through culverts under the trail, often ending or beginning in one of the shallow ponds.

At 0.6 miles, the trail enters an open picnic area with restrooms, a picnic shelter, and barbeque grills. In the far right corner of the meadow, beyond the water pump, is a trail marker where you'll begin the second half of this hike. If you have the time and the inclination, however, consider forging ahead on the paved trail for 1.25 miles to see a small herd of elk (read more about the elk pasture in the "Nearby Activities" section below).

Continuing ahead on the second half of the loop, cross the meadow as it gently slopes down toward the orange trail marker. As you follow this flat gravelly trail under a dense canopy of oak, sugar maple, and basswood, ignore the faint trails that occasionally branch off. Take a break and enjoy the sounds and smells of the woods at a large tree trunk lying trailside that works well as a bench. As the trail gradually curves to the left, you'll pass a large cattail marsh on the right.

Just before reaching a small meandering creek, you'll have to go around or climb over a big tree that has fallen on the trail. After stepping over the creek, you'll see the open space and the parking lot where you started the hike. Ahead, wetlands and more small ponds occupy both sides of the trail. After the trail curves to the right, you'll emerge from the woods at the back of the picnic shelter with Higgins Road on your left.

▶ NEARBY ACTIVITIES

Be sure to pay a visit to the 14-acre elk pasture just a mile east of the trailhead at the corner of Higgins Road and Arlington Heights Road, especially if you have kids along. The Potawatomi Indians called this area "Wapiti"—the Shawnee word for elk. Now, the surrounding community is named Elk Grove Village. This elk herd was established in 1925 when nine females and one male were brought by train from Jackson Hole, Wyoming.

Halfway through your hike, you can access about 2 more miles of dirt-and-gravel hiking trails at Busse Woods by turning left (north) at the forest-preserve road that runs from Higgins Road toward I-90. Follow this road for one-half mile until you reach the beginning of a trail near the Illinois Nature Preserve sign on the left side of the road. (This forest-preserve road is open to cars only during summer.)

CHAIN O' LAKES STATE PARK:
EAST HIKE

▶ IN BRIEF

Chain O' Lakes is full of natural treasures. The riches within the eastern section of the 6,023-acre park include expansive wetlands, gently rolling prairies, pleasant wooded areas, and a peaceful stretch of the Fox River—all accessed by a well-designed trail system.

▶ DESCRIPTION

As the largest state park in northern Illinois, Chain O' Lakes State Park seems to offer something for everyone. Along with prospects for camping, fishing, bicycling, and boating, there are picnic areas galore, playgrounds, boat and canoe rentals, and even horse rentals for the trails in the western section of the park (described on pages 33–35). With all this going on, it's no surprise that the park draws crowds—particularly boaters. Despite the busy atmosphere in the summer months, plenty of tranquil hiking is readily found once you get away from the boat launch and the picnic areas.

The trails in this eastern section of the park are laid out in four connected loops running north and south. The two south loops, hitting some of the busier sections of the park, brush up against Grass Lake and run through dense, hilly woods. The two north loops are notable for hilltop views, quiet prairies, and a brief rendezvous with the river.

▶ DIRECTIONS

Take I-90/I-94 northwest, following I-94 as it splits off northward. Exit I-94 at IL 173 (Rosecrans Road). Turn left (west) on IL 173 and proceed for 13 miles. At Wilmot Road, turn left (south). The Chain O' Lakes State Park sign appears on the left 1.7 miles ahead. Stop at the guardhouse for a park map, then continue on the park road for a mile before turning left at the sign for the park office. Park in the first lot on the right.

ℹ KEY AT-A-GLANCE INFORMATION

LENGTH: 7 miles

CONFIGURATION: 4 connected loops

DIFFICULTY: Easy

SCENERY: Hills, prairies, wetlands, and woods, with sections along Grass Lake and the Fox River

EXPOSURE: North 2 loops are mostly exposed; south 2 loops are mostly shaded.

SURFACE: 3 north loops are multiuse trails with a crushed-gravel surface; the south loop is mowed grass and dirt.

HIKING TIME: 3 hours

ACCESS: January–April, 8 a.m.–sunset; May–October, 6 a.m.–9 p.m.; park is closed for all activities except hunting during November and December.

FACILITIES: Water, restrooms, camping, picnic areas, concession stand, boat launch, and boat rental

MAPS: Park maps available at the guardhouse near entrance; USGS topo Fox Lake, IL

SPECIAL COMMENTS: Chain O' Lakes is one of only a handful of local trail systems that offer camping onsite. If you're interested in camping during the summer at one of the 137 sites in the park, consider visiting during the week for a quieter atmosphere. For weekend camping, reserve a site in advance by calling (847) 587-5512.

UTM Trailhead Coordinates for Chain O' Lakes State Park: East Hike

UTM Zone (NAD27) 16T

Easting 402187

Northing 4702067

CHAIN O'LAKES
STATE PARK:
EAST HIKE

NO SCALE INDICATED

6

While there are numerous places to start this hike, I recommend dropping in on the section near the park office. The office is easy to find, and provides sweeping views of the prairie, savanna, woods, wetland, and the Fox River in the distance. Once you find the trail on the east side of the parking lot, take it to the right for a counter-clockwise hike, saving the majority of the secluded areas and the river for the last leg.

As you head to the right from the parking lot on the Badger Trail, you'll see a rolling prairie on the left and a mixture of woods and savanna down the hill on the right. Soon, you'll have a nice view of the middle section of the park—open space dotted with marshes, ponds, and the occasional oak tree. After passing close to the park road a couple of times, you'll arrive at the junction of the Badger Trail and the Sunset Trail at 0.7 miles. Turn right and cross the park road before entering Deer Path Picnic Area, one of many picnicking spots clumped into this section of the park. South of the picnic area is where the Cattail Trail branches right, connecting hikers with 5.5 miles of less-used trails in the western section of the park (see profile 7 on page 33). Birders shouldn't miss the marsh halfway along the 0.8-mile Cattail Trail; for much of the year it's an excellent spot for seeing sandhill cranes (Chain O' Lakes Park is one of the few nesting sites in the region for these enormous gray birds with red foreheads).

Continuing on the Sunset Trail, cross the park road and stay to the right as you meet the other end of the Sunset loop at 1.3 miles. After passing by the North Pike Marsh Picnic Area, cross an arching steel-and-wood footbridge. At 1.7 miles into the hike, just beyond the Oak Grove Picnic Area, look for a marker on the right for Nature's Way Trail.

While Nature's Way Trail can be confusing because of a profusion of side trails leading to camping areas, the route is well marked and easily followed. Nature's Way Trail quickly brings you across the park road and into a thickly wooded area. Soon you'll be skirting a swampy pond on the right—look for great blue herons, sandhill cranes, and tree trunks chiseled by beavers.

After a sharp left turn at 1.9 miles, the trail brushes against a fenced-in irrigation field, then takes a sharp right turn before accompanying a park road through the Fox Den Camping Area. After 0.2 miles on the park road, follow the marker into the woods to the left. Immediately, there's a connector trail branching left that will trim 0.7 miles off this section of the hike. Ahead on the main trail, a grassy wetland known as a sedge meadow appears on the right. Soon, on the left, is another opportunity to shorten the hike via a brief connecter path marked as the Black Cherry Shortcut Trail. Continuing on the main trail, hikers will encounter the occasional patches of open space, as well as thick woods with large specimens of shagbark hickory and oak.

At 2.7 miles, the trail takes a hairpin left turn at the tip of a little wooded peninsula extending out into the sedge meadow. After the turn, you'll climb a hill and soon arrive at a bench with a fine view of Grass Lake, one of the largest of the nine lakes within the chain. The links in this chain were not always connected—in the early twentieth century, a series of channels were dug, linking together what is the largest concentration of lakes in the state.

Nearly a half mile after the little peninsula, hikers will pass a side trail that branches right to the boat launch and concession stand. After passing the boat-launch

Oak trees provide an attractive canopy.

parking lot and several side trails leading to camping areas, the trail crosses two park roads, and then returns to the Oak Grove Picnic Area.

Just beyond the North Pike Marsh Picnic Area, at 4 miles into the hike, take the Sunset Trail to the right. Intermittently, marshy spots appear through the trees to the right. Stay to the right at 4.5 miles when you reach the connection to the Badger Trail. Turn right again where there is a picnic table from which you can enjoy an expansive view of the grassy wetland. At 4.8 miles, the trail runs next to a swamp on the right, just before entering a tallgrass prairie fringed by oaks and conifers. Stay to the right at two successive trail junctions, which you'll encounter as you leave the Badger Trail and begin Gold Finch Trail.

Starting on the Gold Finch Trail, perfect rows of planted pine trees grow on the right. By the time you arrive at a picnic table next to a small pond at 5.6 miles, the terrain has flattened out considerably. After walking alongside a 0.2-mile-long cattail pond on the right, the trail arrives at an attractive slice of the Fox River. This is a good spot to scan the marshy shoreline for water birds, or sit on the bank and revive a pair of tired feet with a bath in the river. Following the riverbank for 0.2 miles, the trail heads back into the woods and passes under a canopy of oaks. Winding through woods, savanna, and stands of shrubbery, you'll soon pass another picnic table by a pond. At 6.9 miles, a trail branches right to the park office. Stay to the right at the next two trail junctions as you complete the Gold Finch Loop and return to the Badger Loop. At 7 miles, the trail arrives back at the parking lot.

▶ NEARBY ACTIVITIES

Gander Mountain Forest Preserve is located just 2.4 miles north of the Chain O' Lakes State Park entrance on Wilmot Road. The 290-acre preserve contains 2.5 miles of trails, access to the Fox River, and striking views from the 957-foot summit.

CHAIN O' LAKES STATE PARK:
WEST HIKE

▶ IN BRIEF

These trails offer an extremely pleasant jaunt through dense woods, pristine prairies, and over some of the biggest hills in Lake County.

▶ DESCRIPTION

When you compare the trails on the east and west sides of Chain O' Lakes State Park, notable differences emerge. While the east side of the park is fairly busy much of the year, especially near the picnic and camping areas, the west side seems more remote and wild. The east part of the park boasts the gleaming Fox River and shoreline of Grass Lake; the west side has woods that are often thick and dark and lush, possessing a fairytale-like appearance when they're draped in morning mist. Another difference is the terrain—the west side of the park reveals more glacial handiwork in the form of steep hills, tumbling ravines, and large bowl-shaped depressions.

Start this hike on the Blue Loop, which takes off from the northwest corner of the parking lot at the edge of the horse corral. The wide two-track gravelly path immediately brings you to a rolling landscape thick with oaks. Soon, a small savanna—peppered with goldenrod in summer and fall—appears on the right. After 0.2 miles, turn right at the four-way intersection. (With a couple of exceptions, you'll be staying to the right at every trail junction on this hike.) From the

▶ KEY AT-A-GLANCE INFORMATION

LENGTH: 5.25 miles

CONFIGURATION: 1 long loop and 2 small loops

DIFFICULTY: Easy to moderate

SCENERY: Woods, prairie, savannas, and wetlands

EXPOSURE: Mostly covered, except for the prairie sections

SURFACE: Loose gravel and dirt on 2 tracks

HIKING TIME: 2.5 hours

ACCESS: January–April, 8 a.m.–sunset; May–October, 6 a.m.–9 p.m.; November and December park is closed for all activities except hunting.

FACILITIES: Restrooms, water, horse rental (picnic tables and a concession stand are located in the eastern section of the park—see pages 29–32)

MAPS: Park map available at the guardhouse near entrance; USGS topo Fox Lake, IL

SPECIAL COMMENTS: Hikers share these trails with horses, and must provide them with the right-of-way. To learn about renting horses to ride on these trails May–October call (847) 587-5512.

▶ DIRECTIONS

Take I-90/I-94 northwest, proceeding along I-94 as it splits off northward. Exit I-94 at IL 173 (Rosecrans Road). Turn left (west) on IL 173 and proceed for 13 miles. At Wilmot Road, turn left (south). The Chain O' Lakes State Park sign appears on the left 1.7 miles ahead. Turn left 0.1 miles beyond the guardhouse, following signs for horse rental and horse-trailer parking.

UTM Trailhead Coordinates for Chain O' Lakes State Park: West Hike

UTM Zone (NAD27) 16T

Easting 401132

Northing 4701170

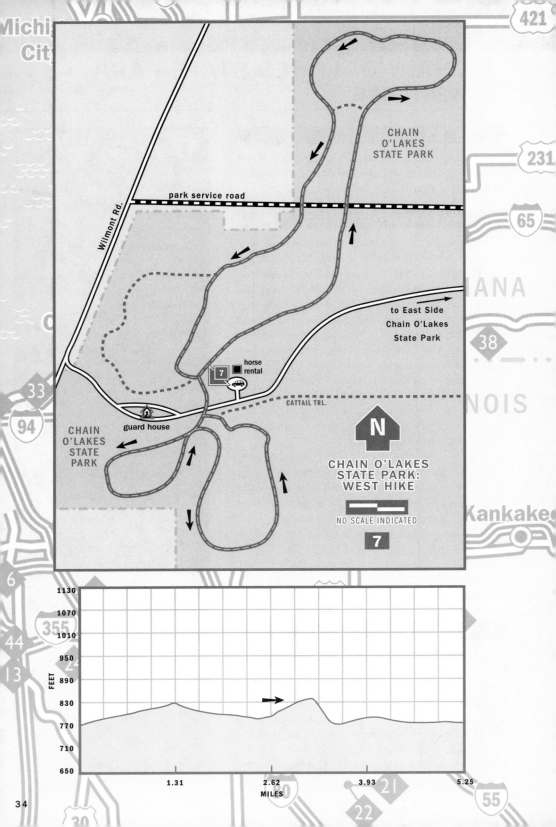

CHAIN O'LAKES STATE PARK

park service road

Wilmont Rd.

CHAIN O'LAKES STATE PARK

to East Side Chain O'Lakes State Park

horse rental

7

CATTAIL TRL.

guard house

CHAIN O'LAKES STATE PARK

N

CHAIN O'LAKES STATE PARK: WEST HIKE

NO SCALE INDICATED

7

intersection, the trail begins a winding 3-mile stretch through lush, dense woods. As the trail takes tight turns and passes over small, steep hills, watch for fleet-footed wild turkeys on the trail ahead. Since they were wiped out of the Midwest a century ago, groups of wild turkeys have been successfully reintroduced to a handful of parks and preserves in the Chicago region.

After crossing a dirt service road at 1.25 miles, a cutoff trail soon appears on the left (if you take the cutoff, you can trim 0.8 miles off the total hiking distance). After the cutoff, you'll see a sizable prairie through the trees on the right, as well as a section of the trail in the eastern side of the park, described on pages 29–32. Proceeding ahead, the trail takes a steep climb. At the top of the hills on this section of the hike, the gravel mining operation just north of the park becomes more audible. You'll also hear traffic from IL 173 and Wilmot Road in the distance.

Through much of this part of the hike, the landscape is continuously dropping or rising. At 1.9 miles, watch your step on loose gravel while climbing one of the highest hills in Lake County. Reaching the top of the hill, the trail runs along a ridge overlooking a steep, tree-covered ravine on the left. You'll see some open spaces on the right before meeting up with the other end of the connecter trail at 2.3 miles. After crossing the dirt road again at 3 miles, the trail proceeds through a bottomland forest, decorated in spots with lovely moss-covered deadfall. Gradually rising from the bottomland, the trail eventually pulls alongside an agricultural field. Coming to a prairie at 3.6 miles, the trail splits. If you're hiking for mileage, take the 0.9-mile path to the right; it runs next to Wilmot Road before dropping you off at the intersection you passed near the start of the hike. I recommend the quieter route to the left, which winds through a rolling tallgrass prairie for 0.3 miles before reaching the same intersection.

In late summer and early fall, this prairie is a sight to behold with the big bluestem grass reaching heights of 8 to 10 feet. Named for its mauve stalks, big bluestem is the dominant grass of tallgrass prairies—the type of prairie that originally existed throughout the northern three-quarters of Illinois. Just before reaching the trail junction you passed near the start of the hike, the trail leads to a hilltop that offers a pleasant vista of a low-lying forest and savanna on the left. At the intersection, follow the middle trail for 0.2 miles back toward the parking lot.

Just before reaching the parking lot, take the trail to the right to finish the remaining 1.6 miles of the hike. Immediately, you'll cross the park road, alongside which is the Cattail Trail, providing access by foot to 7 miles of hiking in the eastern section of the park. Stay to the right at two successive trail junctions. After the second junction, the trail rises through dense woods, and leads you along the top of a small ridge for a quarter mile. Leaving the ridge, the trail arrives at an open area with a view of Wilmot Road to the west and a few houses to the south beyond the agricultural field. Complete the loop at 0.7 miles after crossing the park road, and then stay to the right as you begin another loop immediately ahead.

This section of the hike alternates between dense woods, lightly wooded savannas, and grassy prairie. At 0.1 miles beyond the last junction, you'll climb a hill and then see a sizable ravine on the left. Just ahead, the trail takes a hairpin left turn as it enters an area thick with oaks. When the trail reaches a small pond, you'll have a great view of a wetland in the middle of the park. Most of the year, ducks are feeding and floating about in this small pond. The trail skirts the outer edge of the big wetland for 0.2 miles until reaching the junction that leads back to the parking lot.

CHANNAHON STATE PARK:
I & M CANAL TRAIL

KEY AT-A-GLANCE INFORMATION

LENGTH: 6.4 miles

CONFIGURATION: Out-and-back

DIFFICULTY: Easy

SCENERY: I&M Canal and locks, Des Plaines River, bluffs, and dense woods

EXPOSURE: Mostly exposed

SURFACE: Crushed gravel

HIKING TIME: 3 hours

ACCESS: The Channahon State Park parking lot is open from dawn to dusk

FACILITIES: Water, restrooms, park office, picnic tables

MAPS: Pick up a map in the park office; USGS topo Channahon, IL

SPECIAL COMMENTS: This hike follows a segment of the 61-mile I&M Canal Trail, which runs between Joliet and LaSalle. At the turnaround point for this hike, you have the option to continue hiking through McKinley Woods (see pages 161–163 for all you need to know about hiking at McKinley Woods). There's tent camping at the beginning of the hike and at the turn-around point. For camping at Channahon State Park and for the much more secluded sites along the Des Plaines River near McKinley Woods, pay fees at the Channahon State Park office. For information about camping at McKinley Woods, contact the Will County Forest Preserve at (815) 727-8700. To reach Channahon State Park, call (815) 467-4271.

UTM Trailhead Coordinates for Channahon State Park: I&M Canal Trail

UTM Zone (NAD27)   16T

Easting   397363

Northing   4586318

IN BRIEF

This historic towpath follows a sliver of land that runs between the mighty Des Plaines River and the much narrower Illinois and Michigan Canal. The surrounding landscape is wooded and hilly, with bluffs and patches of farmland.

DESCRIPTION

In 1848, the Illinois and Michigan Canal provided the final shipping link between the East Coast of the United States and the Gulf of Mexico. From Chicago, the canal went southwest, running beside the Des Plaines River and the Illinois River halfway across the state to where the Illinois River was deep enough for boat traffic. Thanks to the 96-mile-long canal, Chicago quickly became the largest and most efficient grain market in the world. Channahon, which once claimed six grain elevators along the canal, is one of the many towns that were built up alongside this waterway. From 1848 until 1900, the canal bustled with commerce. For most of that time, the 150-ton canal boats were pulled along the towpath by mules or horses, usually guided by boys.

Now, the I&M Canal and the accompanying towpath are owned by the Illinois Department of Natural Resources. Running from the outskirts of Joliet to the town of LaSalle, the 61-mile, crushed-limestone path generally runs straight and flat alongside the canal. From end to end, the route wanders through a variety of landscapes: dense woods, marshes, prairies, riverbank, agricultural

DIRECTIONS

Take I-55 2 miles south of I-80 to Exit 248. From this exit, head southwest on US 6 for 2.7 miles. Turn left (south) on South Canal Street. The entrance to Channahon State Park is three blocks ahead on the right.

CHANNAHON
STATE PARK:
I&M CANAL
TRAIL

0.5 MILE

8

N

Michigan
City

6

locktender's
house

CHANNAHON
STATE PARK

Canal St.

Bridge St.

DuPage River

I & M Canal

I&M CANAL TRL

Moose
Island

Des Plains River

Hansel Rd.

McKinley Woods Rd.

McKinley
Woods

I & M Canal

I&M CANAL TRL.

CANA

NOIS

Kanka

830
770
710
650
590
530
470
410
350

FEET

1.6

3.2

4.8

6.4

MILES

One of the only locktender's houses that remain along the I&M Canal.

land, and small towns. The Channahon-to-McKinley-Woods segment described here is one of my favorite parts for its scenic beauty and its proximity to Chicago.

From the parking lot, head up a small hill to the white house that is one of only two locktender's houses remaining along the canal. Locktenders had to be available day or night to keep the boat traffic moving. Their all-important procedure was to open the gate for the canal boat to enter the 12-by-100-foot lock, close the gate, and then fill or drain the lock to raise or lower the boat so that it left at a new water level. Fifteen locks were needed along the canal to raise and lower boats for 141 feet of elevation change between Chicago and the Illinois River. The Channahon locks were constructed of limestone block walls recessed about 12 feet into the ground.

From the locktender's house, head left toward lock 7 by crossing a footbridge that spans a small dam in the DuPage River. To the right is the dam's backwater, fringed with cattails. In several places along the canal, when builders encountered another waterway, they constructed aqueducts for the canal to flow over streams. In Channahon, the builders had a different solution: here, the canal runs right through the DuPage River, with locks 6 and 7 on either side. Beyond lock 7, the trail accompanies the canal under Bridge Street, and then passes a parking area with restrooms. For a half mile after the parking area, the path shares its route with a limited-access paved road. On the other side of the canal, you'll see a few houses, a small stream that empties into the canal, and pastures for sheep and cows. At 0.6 miles into the hike, the woods on the left are interrupted by a short stretch of the DuPage River just before it empties into the Des Plaines River. Next, you'll come upon the northern end of a 0.8-mile-long wooded peninsula—known as Moose Island—that juts out into the Des Plaines River. At the gated entrance to Moose Island, the trail surface becomes crushed limestone.

For the next 2.25 miles—until you reach the turnaround point at McKinley

Woods—you'll follow an 8–10-foot-wide strip of land between two bodies of water: the 20-to-30-foot-wide canal is on the right, and the broad and mighty Des Plaines River is on the left. Continuing ahead, the trail passes by the eddy created by Moose Island. The eddy is a good spot to look for water birds such as egrets and great blue herons, as well as for signs of beaver activity. After passing under a set of power lines and seeing an industrial plant on the far shore of the Des Plaines, another wooded island appears (this one is an actual island). This is also where you'll start to see the wooded bluffs rising on the right.

Every half mile or so, little pulloffs bordered by squat limestone ledges appear on the left; these are great places to have a seat and rest. With good weather, expect to see plenty of pleasure boats on the Des Plaines. Barges may come lumbering by, too, some as long as a couple of city blocks. Getting closer to McKinley Woods, you'll pass a boat landing on the opposite shore of the Des Plaines, and the bluffs on the right become more dramatic.

McKinley Woods is situated at a large bend in the river. Reaching the tip of the bend at 3.2 miles into the hike, you'll see a stone observation platform at the edge of the river. As one of the more popular stopping points along the 60 miles of the I&M Canal Trail, this little viewing platform is a great place to meet people and learn about other sights along the canal. To the right is a bridge over the canal leading to the McKinley Woods picnic area.

Once you reach McKinley Woods, you have a few options. Continuing ahead along the towpath for 2.6 miles brings you to the Dresden Dam and the only mule barn left standing along the canal (when the canal was built, mule barns were situated every 10 to 15 miles, so the mules and horses could eat and rest before their next haul). The bluffs you see at McKinley Woods continue along the canal nearly all the way to the Dresden Dam. If you'd like to ramble through those bluffs, head across the canal for an exceedingly pleasant 1.8-mile hike through McKinley Woods, described on pages 161–163.

Of course, the final option is to simply retrace your footsteps back to Channahon. On your return trip, be sure to take the trail branching to the right just after passing the driveway to Moose Island. Mostly used by fishermen, this half-mile trail runs between the DuPage River on the right and a bottomland forest on the left. The trail ends at the picnic area alongside the canal, just before it runs under Bridge Street. From the picnic area, the parking lot is 0.3 miles ahead.

▶ NEARBY ACTIVITIES

In the Channahon State Park office, ask for the I&M Canal Corridor Driving Tour map. It offers a concise history of the canal and points out notable landmarks and parks along the way. History and engineering buffs may want to ask in the office for photocopies of the official specifications used for building both the canal and the locks.

CHICAGO BOTANIC GARDEN HIKE

KEY AT-A-GLANCE INFORMATION

LENGTH: 2.7 miles

CONFIGURATION: Large loop with a few short loops attached

DIFFICULTY: Easy

SCENERY: Islands, prairie, oak woodland, marsh, and acres of pristine gardens of every stripe

EXPOSURE: Mostly exposed

SURFACE: Paved, gravel, woodchip

HIKING TIME: 1 hour

ACCESS: 8 a.m.–sunset, except December 25. Garden is free; parking is $10 per car.

FACILITIES: Visitor center, cafe, restrooms, gift shop, library, ATM, wheelchairs, and telephones

MAPS: Pick up a map at the visitor center; USGS topo Highland Park, IL

SPECIAL COMMENTS: No pets allowed. Two different tram tours run seasonally. Tickets and information are available at the booth outside of the visitor center. Check out www.chicagobotanic.org for more information.

UTM Trailhead Coordinates for Chicago Botanic Garden Hike

UTM Zone (NAD27) 16T

Easting   434704

Northing   4666365

▶ IN BRIEF

If you love to see carefully selected flowers, trees, and bushes growing in perfectly landscaped environments, the Chicago Botanic Garden is a slice of heaven. While the interior gardens are justifiably the main attraction here, many visitors miss the additional gardens, the prairie and woodland, and the striking views that accompany a walk through the outer perimeter of the garden, highlighted on this hike.

▶ DESCRIPTION

Among the Botanic Garden's 305 acres of artfully landscaped grounds, there are 23 distinct gardens, including Japanese- and English-style gardens, rose and bulb gardens, fruit and vegetable gardens, and gardens specially designed for children

▶ DIRECTIONS

Follow I-90/I-94 northwest, continuing on I-94 for 13.5 miles after I-90 splits off. At Exit 29, remain on the Edens Expressway (US 41), then take the next exit for Lake Cook Road. Turn right (east) and travel for a half mile to the botanic garden. Follow signs to the parking areas.

Alternate directions: Coming from the west on I-90, take I-294 north. Exit at Lake Cook Road and travel east 4 miles.

By bicycle from Chicago: Follow the North Elston Avenue bicycle lane until Elston Avenue turns to North Milwaukee Avenue. Catch a connector leading to the North Branch Trail from the Caldwell Woods Forest Preserve parking lot at the corner of North Milwaukee Avenue and West Devon Avenue. Turn left at the North Branch Trail and follow it 16 miles to the garden. Alternatively, bring your bike on the Blue Line to the Jefferson Park stop. Follow North Milwaukee Avenue to the connector trail at West Devon Avenue.

and for handicapped people. Along with this excess of gardens, there are attractive bridges, statues, fountains, and plenty of scenic spots situated among the nine islands and the surrounding shoreline. Owned by the Cook County Forest Preserve District and managed by the Chicago Horticultural Society, the gardens are just part of what goes on here. The botanic garden has programs in education and research, and offers a number of special events and services, such as classes, plant sales, opportunities to consult master gardeners, concerts, and speakers.

From the visitor center, start the hike by heading straight across the North Lawn to the service road leading over the lake at the far end of the garden. On the other side of the bridge, pine trees grow on the left and buckeye trees grow on the right. Take either the service road or the narrow, paved path to the left. In the lake is Spider Island, thick with alders, birch, and serviceberry trees. On the right, the Skokie River runs along the bottom of a shallow ravine. Also on the right is a newly added brick wall and 1,600 new tree plantings intended to block noise and pollution from I-94. Extending from Spider Island to the serpentine-shaped bridge that leads to Evening Island is the Sensory Garden, which hosts plants and trees that produce an array of colors, sounds, fragrances, and textures.

Just ahead on the left, take the gravel trail to Evening Island, added to the botanic garden in 2002 at a cost of $16 million. In gardening circles, the design of this 5-acre island is called the "new American" garden style, and is inspired by landscapes such as the meadow and the Midwestern prairie. Climbing the hill in the center of the island, watch how the placement of trees nicely frames the views of the nearby shoreline and prairie. Near the top of the hill, a circle of large stones provides a great place to relax. The square metal tower, called a carillon, contains 48 bronze bells that weigh between 24 pounds and 2.5 tons (check in the visitor center for information on regular carillon concerts). The bridges on the north side of the island provide a connection with the main gardens and complete the outline of a section of the lake called the Great Basin.

Back on the paved road, pass a few burr-oak trees and several purple martin houses attached to poles as you head into the 15-acre prairie. Entering the prairie, take the gravel trail left, and stay left at the next couple of junctions before crossing a bridge for a quick tour of Marsh Island. Botanic-garden staff maintain that Marsh Island (actually a wet prairie) is the best location on the grounds for spotting water birds and songbirds. Coming off Marsh Island, stay left as you pass a section of hilly prairie on the right—the dry, rocky soil is the reason that the grass is shorter at the top of the hill compared to the sides and bottom. After the small hills, take your pick of following the paved road, the dirt path, or the paved path, all of which lead to the bridge. On the way to the bridge, you'll pass compass plants (tall yellow flowers) and more burr oaks.

The bridge divides the botanic-garden lake on the left and the Skokie River on the right. On the other side of the bridge, turn left on the paved road and pass the plant-production area, which grows 420,000 plants annually. Next on the right is the children's garden, where kids can get involved in activities such as watering plants, digging in soil, and climbing through a plant maze. The garden on the left contains roses that are evaluated for qualities such as color, fragrance, novelty, and vigor. The next garden, featuring a big sundial surrounded by 7,000 herbaceous plants, also serves as an evaluation garden. Both of these evaluation gardens keep out deer by using solar-powered electric fencing that is turned on after hours.

After passing a stand of downy hawthorn trees next to the road, three islands come into view, each carefully landscaped and pruned in traditional Japanese styles. A low zigzag bridge connects the first and second islands. Off in the distance, between the second and third islands, a waterfall tumbles some 45 feet over granite boulders. The inaccessible third island contains smaller trees that are intended to present the optical illusion that the island is far off in the distance.

Finish up the hike with a brief stroll through the Mary Mix McDonald Woods, the only location at the botanic garden where the soil is undisturbed. Enter the oak woodland on the right before the road curves to the left. Stay to the left on the path as you pass over a series of footbridges spanning intermittent streams and several boardwalks. Along this path there's a steady progression of signs identifying plants and animals of the area and describing the basic concepts of woodland restoration in northeastern Illinois. As this trail crosses the park road, watch for traffic, especially on the weekends. In a number of spots you'll see that the botanic garden is engaged in a serious fencing campaign to keep deer out of the area. When finished with the hike through the McDonald Woods, continue along the paved road to the parking lots just ahead. Or if you wish to return to the visitor center or explore more of the interior gardens, follow the woodchip path that runs parallel to the lake and then take the service road left to the visitor center.

▶ NEARBY ACTIVITIES

At the southern edge of the Chicago Botanic Garden, visitors can connect with the 20.1-mile North Branch Trail. One of the great urban pathways of Chicagoland, the North Branch Trail runs through the Skokie Lagoons and along the North Branch of the Chicago River. To reach the trail from the botanic garden, head south on the service road on the east side of the lake. The path starts on the other side of Dundee Road. A section of the Skokie Lagoons and River Hike (page 207) runs along the North Branch Trail.

Another nearby opportunity for walking or bicycling is the Green Bay Trail/Robert McClory Bike Path, which runs for 36 miles from Kenilworth in Cook County north to Wisconsin. Pick up the trail 0.7 miles east of the botanic-garden entrance on Lake Cook Road. See the Chicago Bicycle Federation's "Chicagoland Bicycle Map."

CHICAGO LAKESHORE PATH:
NORTH HIKE

KEY AT-A-GLANCE INFORMATION

LENGTH: 5.75 miles

CONFIGURATION: A linear shoreline path

DIFFICULTY: Easy

SCENERY: Lake Michigan shoreline, city parks, beaches, harbors, Navy Pier, and the Chicago skyline

EXPOSURE: Open

SURFACE: Paved path; a gravel shoulder runs along much of this section

HIKING TIME: 3–4 hours

ACCESS: Except for the busiest summer weekends, parking is no problem at Montrose Harbor. Footbridges and pedestrian underpasses provide access across Lakeshore Drive every half mile or so.

FACILITIES: Snack shops, cafes, beaches, bike rentals, restrooms, and picnic tables. Drinking fountains every mile or so.

TRAFFIC: Travel on the right side of the path, and watch for path users who may not be paying attention. On summer weekends, this section can be clogged with bicyclists, in-line skaters, runners, and walkers. Avoid the crowds by going early.

MAPS: Call the Chicago Park District at (312) 742-7529 for Chicago's Lakefront Path Map. USGS topo Chicago Loop, IL

SPECIAL COMMENTS: Once you've finished the hike, you have the option of using the L to get back to your starting point (see the directions box). While walking in an urban area such as this, stay aware of your surroundings.

UTM Trailhead Coordinates for
Chicago Lakeshore Path: North Hike

UTM Zone (NAD27)   16T

Easting   447200

Northing   4645662

IN BRIEF

Harbors, beaches, and the lake itself serve as the backdrop for a dazzling skyline. Some sections of this path provide just a seawall with a walkway, while other parts run through wide grassy parks. There are numerous options for combining this hike with other activities, such as renting bicycles or in-line skating or a trip to Navy Pier, the zoo, or one of the nearby theaters.

DESCRIPTION

Especially during the summer, this stretch of the Lakeshore Path· serves as a place where many parts of the city come together. Beneath the high rises and along the beaches, elderly couples stroll with their poodles, teenagers zoom by on in-line skates, fishermen cast into the harbors, and the yacht owners gather on their docked boats. Along with top-notch people-watching, the path offers stellar views of the skyline and the lake.

DIRECTIONS

From downtown, head north on North Lakeshore Drive. Exit at Montrose Avenue and turn right (east) toward the lake. Proceed for 0.3 miles and park in the large lot. Start the hike on the gravel path that runs south along the seawall between the golf course and the mouth of the harbor.

Public transportation: Once you reach Navy Pier, you can return to your starting point by taking the L. From Navy Pier, follow East Grand Avenue 0.8 miles to the Red Line stop at East Grand Avenue and North State Street. Take the Red Line north to either the Irving Park or the Sheridan stops. The Lakeshore Path is several blocks west. For Chicago Transit Authority scheduling information and a map, call (888) 969-7282 or visit www.transitchicago.com.

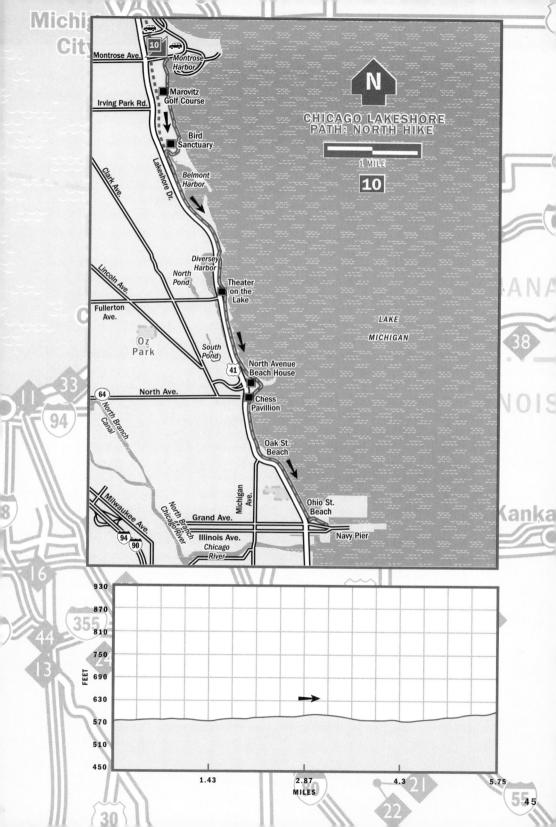

N

CHICAGO LAKESHORE
PATH: NORTH HIKE

1 MILE

10

Michigan
City

Montrose Ave.
Montrose Harbor

Irving Park Rd.

Marovitz Golf Course

Bird Sanctuary

Lakeshore Dr.

Belmont Harbor

Clark Ave.

Lincoln Ave.

Diversey Harbor
North Pond

Theater on the Lake

Fullerton Ave.

Oz Park

South Pond

41

North Avenue Beach House

64
North Ave.

Chess Pavillion

North Branch Canal

Oak St. Beach

Michigan Ave.

Milwaukee Ave.

94 **90**

North Branch Chicago River

Grand Ave.

Illinois Ave.
Chicago River

Ohio St. Beach

Navy Pier

LAKE
MICHIGAN

ANA

38

NOIS

Kanka

FEET

930
870
810
750
690
630
570
510
450

1.43   2.87   4.3   5.75
             MILES

94

355

44

13

16

30

22

55

Start the hike near the mouth of Montrose Harbor on a wide crushed-gravel path that runs for 0.7 miles between the Sydney R. Marovitz Golf Course and the seawall. This is not the actual Lakeshore Path, but is a quieter, more scenic alternative to a section of the Lakeshore Path that runs very close to North Lakeshore Drive. Keep straight ahead as you pass the golf course and the clock-tower building, which has restrooms and a snack shop. Just ahead, bear right toward the observation deck at the edge of the fenced-in Addison Street Bird Sanctuary. Although I haven't seen much bird activity in this sanctuary, I've heard the call of the eastern screech owl here. Follow the gravel path left around the sanctuary, cross the park driveway, and then turn left at the Lakeshore Path, with the northern tip of Belmont Harbor on the left.

For the next 0.7 miles, as the path runs between Belmont Harbor and North Lakeshore Drive, you'll see a series of exercise stations on the right. If you have your dog along, take it for a swim at the special doggie beach on the left (dogs may swim at the regular beaches only during the off season). Not long after passing a yacht club and the Belmont Avenue underpass, you'll see two life-size statues depicting unnamed Native Americans. Just before West Fullerton Avenue meets the lakeshore, you'll pass by the Fullerton Pavilion, a prairie-style structure built in the early twentieth century as a "fresh air sanitarium" to promote health among the infirmed. Now the building is home to a restaurant and a summer theater that has been active for 50 years. From Fullerton, the path runs along the shoreline to North Avenue Beach, which is elbow to elbow with volleyball games during the summer. Also at this beach is an outdoor gym, complete with a floor-hockey rink.

Bear left just before North Avenue Beach House, which was designed to look like an ocean liner that has been parked in the sand. This large beach house offers bicycle and in-line skate rentals, as well as restrooms, showers, and a cafe. After passing by the front of the beach house, turn right on the sidewalk that goes toward the shore on the opposite side of the jetty. Turn right again at the water and head toward the small Chess Pavilion that looks like it was inspired by the futuristic designs in the Jetsons TV cartoon. First, though, you may be forced to take a seat on the little wall that accompanies this walkway and enjoy one of the best views of the Chicago skyline.

From the Chess Pavilion, stay close to the shore as you head south toward Oak Street Beach. In the warmer months, Oak Street Beach always has plenty going on, whether that's jugglers, BMX trick riders, or in-line skaters whizzing through a slalom coarse. There's also a small seasonal restaurant. For the next 0.8 miles, the path continues right alongside North Lakeshore Drive, swerving left and then right, until it arrives at the Ohio Street Beach.

Just east of Ohio Street Beach, be sure to visit Milton Lee Olive Park, a pleasant little park with benches, water fountains, and great views. Just a bit farther east, this hike ends at Navy Pier, the most popular tourist attraction in Chicago. The pier offers oodles of tourist-oriented shops and restaurants, as well as the Chicago Children's Museum, a 3-D Imax theater, the Chicago Shakespeare Theatre, a concert venue, a museum of stained-glass windows, and a monster Ferris wheel. Moored along the south section of the pier are a half dozen tour boats in a range of sizes. While Navy Pier can be annoyingly commercial, it does offer a nice place for an open-air stroll out on to the lake.

A view of the skyline as it appears near North Avenue Beach.

▶ NEARBY ACTIVITIES

Spring and fall migrations bring an abundance of birds to the Montrose Nature Sanctuary, which is a lightly wooded area on a small hill at the eastern tip of the jetty that forms Montrose Harbor. Heading toward the lake on the north side of the harbor, bear left as the harbor curves right. Across the park road, you'll see signs for the sanctuary. On the north side of the jetty, be sure to visit Montrose Beach, which is perhaps the best beach in the city.

West Fullerton Avenue provides quick access to two great spots that offer free admission: the Lincoln Park Zoo, at 2200 North Cannon Drive, and the Lincoln Park Conservatory and Gardens, at 2400 North Stockton Avenue. To reach the zoo, follow West Fullerton Avenue west for 0.2 miles, and then turn left on North Cannon Drive. The zoo entrance is 0.3 miles ahead. Zoo summer hours are Monday–Friday, 10 a.m.–5 p.m.; weekends, 10 a.m.–7 p.m.; fall to spring, daily 10 a.m.–5 p.m. Call the zoo at (312) 742-2000 or visit www.lpzoo.com. The conservatory is 0.3 miles west of the lakeshore on Fullerton Avenue. Conservatory hours are 9 a.m.–5 p.m. Contact the conservatory at (312) 294-4770. Fullerton Avenue and the lakeshore are also where you'll find Theater on the Lake. Call (312) 742-7994 for information about shows.

Navy Pier summer hours are Sunday–Thursday, 10 a.m.–10 p.m.; Friday and Saturday, 10 a.m.–midnight. Fall to spring hours are Monday–Saturday, 10 a.m.–10 p.m.; Sunday, 10 a.m.–7 p.m. Contact Navy Pier at (800) 595-PIER or at www.navypier.com. The Shoreline Sightseeing boats can take you from Navy Pier to the Sears Tower or to the Shedd Aquarium and the Field Museum. Call (312) 222-9328 for more information. For the schedule of productions at the Chicago Shakespeare Theatre, call (312) 595-6600. The Chicago Children's Museum can be reached at (312) 527-1000 or www.childrensmuseum.org.

CHICAGO LAKESHORE PATH:
SOUTH HIKE

KEY AT-A-GLANCE INFORMATION

LENGTH: 4.4 miles

CONFIGURATION: A linear path along the shoreline

DIFFICULTY: Easy

SCENERY: Chicago shoreline parks, city skyline, a beach, Field Museum, Soldier Field, Shedd Aquarium, Buckingham Fountain

EXPOSURE: Open

SURFACE: Paved path. For much of this route, you can walk on the grass near the water or on the concrete revetments that protect the shoreline.

HIKING TIME: 2.5 hours

ACCESS: Parking is available at the 31st Street Beach

FACILITIES: Snack shops, beach, bike rentals, benches, restrooms, and picnic tables; drinking fountains every mile or so

TRAFFIC: Always travel on the right side of the path. On warmer days, this south section of the Lakeshore Path is less crowded than the north section.

MAPS: Call the Chicago Park District at (312) 742-7529 for Chicago's Lakefront Path Map. USGS topos Jackson Park, IL and Chicago Loop, IL

UTM Trailhead Coordinates for
Chicago Lakeshore Path: South Hike

UTM Zone (NAD27)   16T

Easting   449616

Northing   4631820

IN BRIEF

Enjoy stunning views of the downtown skyline as you hike along this strip of parkland that links the city and the lake. Pass Chicago landmarks such as Soldier Field, the Field Museum, and Buckingham Fountain.

DESCRIPTION

Chicago would be unthinkable without the great expanse of Lake Michigan at its doorstep. The Lake Michigan shoreline not only offers city dwellers refuge from the relentless concrete grid, but if you live in Chicago, it's probably the most accessible place where you can run, walk, cycle, and skate uninterrupted for miles. Indeed, for a great number of Chicagoans, a trip to the lake is synonymous with following this path as it snakes by harbors, museums, high rises, and acres of moored boats.

DIRECTIONS

From downtown Chicago, take South Lakeshore Drive south to the 31st Street exit. Turn left (east) on East 31st Street and follow the driveway to the parking lot on the right. Alternatively, if you're approaching via I-90/I-94, exit on West 31st Street and head east toward the lake. Proceed to the 31st Street Beach parking lot 1.2 miles ahead.

Public transportation: When you reach North Michigan Avenue and East Wacker Drive, instead of hiking back the way you came, it's fairly easy to take a bus back to the beginning of the hike. Catch the 3, X3, or X4 bus on North Michigan Avenue and get off at the corner of South Dr. Martin Luther King Drive and East 31st Street. Head east for 0.5 miles to reach the 31st Street Beach. For Chicago Transit Authority scheduling information and a map, call (888) 969-7282 or visit www.transitchicago.com.

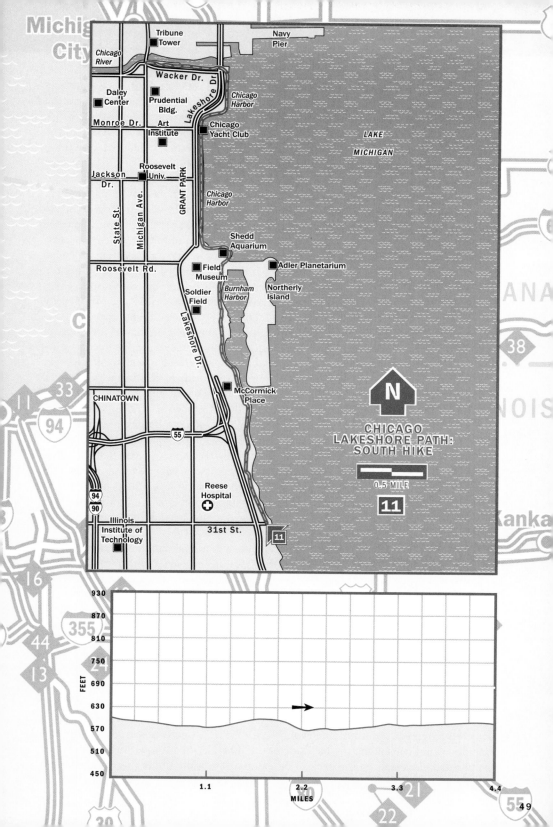

Michigan City

Chicago River

Tribune Tower

Navy Pier

Wacker Dr.

Daley Center

Prudential Bldg.

Chicago Harbor

Monroe Dr.

Lakeshore Dr.

Art Institute

Chicago Yacht Club

LAKE MICHIGAN

Jackson Dr.

Roosevelt Univ.

State St.

Michigan Ave.

GRANT PARK

Chicago Harbor

Shedd Aquarium

Roosevelt Rd.

Field Museum

Adler Planetarium

Burnham Harbor

Northerly Island

Soldier Field

Lakeshore Dr.

McCormick Place

CHINATOWN

55

N

CHICAGO
LAKESHORE PATH:
SOUTH HIKE

0.5 MILE

11

94

90

Reese Hospital

Illinois Institute of Technology

31st St.

11

INDIANA

38

ILLINOIS

Kankakee

33

94

16

44

13

355

21

22

55

49

930
870
810
750
690
FEET
630
570
510
450

1.1

2.2
MILES

3.3

4.4

For those who prefer a less busy ramble on the Lakeshore Path, this south section is the place to go. This hike also offers a nice way to combine a shoreline stroll with a visit to one of the world-class museums along the way. (This strategy also allows you to avoid the high cost of parking downtown or near the museums.) Thirty-first Street Beach, where this hike begins, hosts a playground, beach, beach house, restrooms, and a snack shop. North of the beach house, Burnham Park is fairly open and grassy with plenty of new trees planted. In recent years, the city has relandscaped parts of the park and rerouted this and other sections of the south path. These changes have been happening in conjunction with a multiyear citywide effort to replace the revetments—the structures on the shoreline that protect the land from the pounding of the waves. Some people who walk this section of the lakeshore stay close to the shoreline on the grass or on the new concrete revetments rather than following the path. When the path is busy with bikers and in-line skaters, this is a good option.

Just before reaching McCormick Place, the world's largest convention center, you'll see a small bird sanctuary that occupies a fenced-in prairie. Nearby, several small sculptures and a garden are part of a memorial to Chicago firefighters and paramedics who died in the line of duty. The mammoth horizontal presence of McCormick Place is softened a bit by the waterfall that seems to tumble from its interior and the many limestone blocks scattered about, providing places to sit.

McCormick Place is situated at the mouth of Burnham Harbor, which is well stocked with private boats in the warmer months. Across the harbor, you'll see Northerly Island. Built in 1925, Northerly Island was conceived by the park's namesake, Daniel Burnham, an architect and urban planner known for helping to plan the 1893 World's Columbian Exposition in Chicago and known for his Plan of Chicago, a comprehensive design for the city. Northerly Island was to be the first of a five-island chain of parks heading south, but the Depression came and the other four islands were never built. Some years later, the city turned it into a little peninsula by building a roadway to the island. A private airport that operated on Northerly Island for 55 years was recently shut down, and now the city is planning on providing a concert venue on the property.

Coming up on the left is Soldier Field, a national landmark dedicated to Chicago's fallen soldiers. Built in 1922, the stadium received a controversial facelift in 2003 when a glass-and-steel top section was added to the existing neoclassical structure. Sandwiched between Chicago Harbor and Soldier Field is a sledding hill on the left and a harbor parking lot on the right. Just north of the Chicago Bears' home turf is the Field Museum, one of the most prominent natural-history museums in the world. This enormous marble structure, also designed by Burnham, houses a vast collection of exhibits on anthropology, zoology, botany, and geology. The main floor lobby contains the skeleton of the largest and most complete T-rex ever found.

Continuing ahead through the museum campus, the trail gains a bit of elevation and then crosses East Solidarity Drive, which leads out to Adler Planetarium and Northerly Island. On East Solidarity Drive's median strip is a bronze statue of a horse-mounted general from the Revolutionary War, Thaddeus Kosciusko. As the trail dips down and runs along the backside of the John G. Shedd Aquarium, you can see the paneled glass wall on the back of the oceanarium. Containing the world's largest indoor saltwater pool, the oceanarium is home to a family of beluga whales and a handful of dolphins.

As the path winds around the aquarium, you'll likely notice seagulls fishing from the long thin breakwater that protects Chicago Harbor. Coming out from behind the aquarium, instead of following the path up the hill and walking beside the traffic on North Lakeshore Drive, stay to the right and walk along the water. About halfway along this harbor walkway, you'll see the grand Buckingham Fountain in the midsection of Grant Park on the left. Passing the Chicago Yacht Club, continue alongside the shoreline as it bends right and runs alongside acres of moored boats and a large passenger ship. At the first set of sculptures that look like enormous pieces from a game of jacks, the Lakeshore Path forks. The path heading left crosses the Chicago River and then runs near Navy Pier (which is the end point for the Chicago Lakeshore Path: North Hike profiled on page 44).

To finish the south hike, stay right at the fork, following the path as it swings left alongside the Chicago River and then heads through an art deco–style passageway with scenes from Chicago history painted on tiled walls. At certain times along this stretch of path you'll see a giant arc of water that shoots across the river from the other side. Just after passing a small seasonal restaurant and a spot where several tour boats operate, the path ends at a staircase leading up to the corner of North Michigan Avenue and East Wacker Drive.

▶ NEARBY ACTIVITIES

Combine this hike with a visit to an attraction or two downtown. Instead of retracing your steps at the turnaround point, you can take public transportation back to the 31st Street Beach (see directions box). The 5.5 miles of the Lakeshore Path south of East 31st Street is a popular bicycling route with far fewer people walking. Because this stretch is less populated, it seems less safe than northern parts of the path. If you do decide to continue walking south of 31st Street Beach, consider bringing a companion and going earlier in the day. Of course, while walking in any urban area, stay aware of your surroundings and be on the lookout for suspicious individuals.

The Field Museum, 1400 South Lakeshore Drive, is open daily 9 a.m.–5 p.m. (June 17–August 26, open until 8 p.m. on Thursdays). Admission is $8. Admission is free on Wednesday. Call (312) 922-9410 or visit www.fmnh.org.

The John G. Shedd Aquarium, 1200 South Lakeshore Drive, is open in summer Friday–Wednesday, 9 a.m.–6 p.m.; Thursday, 9 a.m.–9 p.m.; fall through spring, Monday–Wednesday, 9 a.m.–5 p.m.; Saturday and Sunday, 9 a.m.–6 p.m. Admission is $13; $8 for aquarium and oceanarium on Monday. Call (312) 939-2438 or visit www.sheddaquarium.org.

Adler Planetarium, 1300 South Lakeshore Drive, is open Labor Day to Memorial Day: Monday–Thursday, 9 a.m.–5 p.m.; Friday, 9 a.m.–9 p.m.; weekends, 9 a.m.–6 p.m.; Memorial Day to Labor Day: Saturday–Wednesday, 9 a.m.–6 p.m.; Thursday–Friday, 9 a.m.–9 p.m. Admission is $5; theater presentations are an additional $5. General admission is free on Tuesday. Call (312) 922-7827 or visit www.adlerplanetarium.org.

CRABTREE NATURE CENTER HIKE

KEY AT-A-GLANCE INFORMATION

LENGTH: 2.8 miles

CONFIGURATION: 2 connected loops

DIFFICULTY: Easy

SCENERY: Ponds, marshes, lake, woodland, prairie, and plenty of bird life

EXPOSURE: The prairie is exposed while the rest of the hike is mostly shaded

SURFACE: Wood chip, dirt, mowed grass

HIKING TIME: 1.5 hours

ACCESS: 8 a.m.–5 p.m.

FACILITIES: Exhibit building, restrooms, water

MAPS: Maps available at trailhead; USGS topo Streamwood, IL

SPECIAL COMMENTS: Recently, the Phantom Prairie Trail was closed due to a boardwalk in need of repairs. The trail is expected to reopen by the summer of 2005 once the boardwalk is repaired or the trail is rerouted.

UTM Trailhead Coordinates for
Crabtree Nature Center Hike

UTM Zone (NAD27)   16T

Easting   403982

Northing   4662879

IN BRIEF

Situated among the rolling hills of far northwest Cook County, Crabtree Nature Center is a place that invites you to linger while admiring wildflowers, spotting waterfowl, and relishing the rapid shifts from prairie to woodland to wetland.

DESCRIPTION

The Cook County Forest Preserve District added an attractive parcel to its holdings in the mid-1960s when it bought a country estate and adjoining farmlands and transformed these into the Crabtree Nature Center. Over the years, the county restored the prairie and the scattered plots of woodland that once adorned this 1,100-acre plot. This hike takes place in the western side of the preserve, notable for its varied landscape: prairie, savanna, woodland, ponds, marshes, and a lake are all packed into a small area. Another attraction here is the exhibit building, which offers a collection of handmade displays, as well as a live screech owl, a snapping turtle, plenty of fish, and an enormous bullfrog.

From the parking lot, follow the paved path to the back of the nature center. At the trail board, stay to the right as the trail skirts the edge of Sulky Pond (formerly a sulky track sunken in the

DIRECTIONS

Take I-90/I-94 northwest from Chicago. Continue on I-90 for 19 miles after I-94 breaks off. Exit at North Roselle Road and head to the right (north) for 0.9 miles. Turn left (northwest) on IL 62 (Algonquin Road) and drive for 5.3 miles. Turn right (east) on East Palatine Road and go for 0.6 miles. The entrance to Crabtree Nature Center is on the left. From the parking lot, look for signs to the exhibit building.

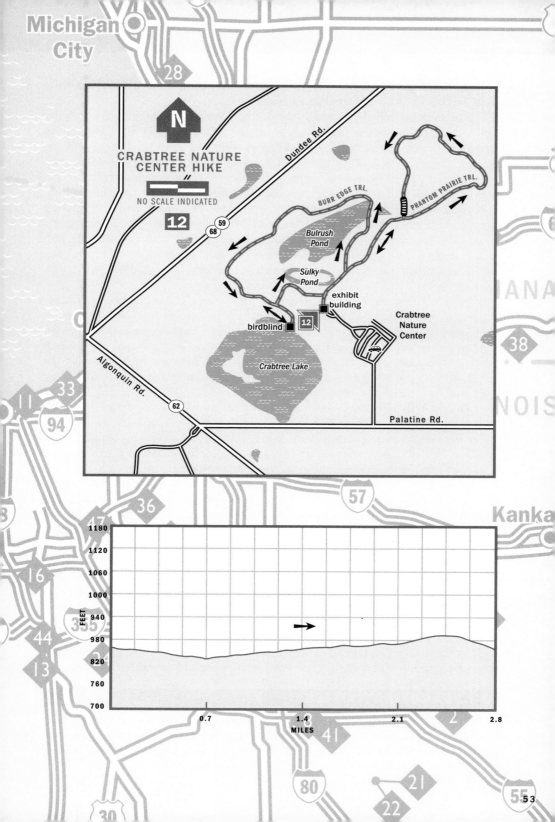

N

**CRABTREE NATURE
CENTER HIKE**

NO SCALE INDICATED

12

59
68

Dundee Rd.

BURR EDGE TRL.

PHANTOM PRAIRIE TRL.

*Bulrush
Pond*

*Sulky
Pond*

exhibit
building

12

birdblind

Crabtree
Nature
Center

Crabtree Lake

Algonquin Rd.

62

Palatine Rd.

FEET				
1180				
1120				
1060				
1000				
940				
880				
820				
760				
700				

0.7   1.4   2.1   2.8
MILES

ground). The oaks hanging out over the water, the lightly wooded island, and the geese and ducks make this pond an enjoyable spot.

Continue the hike by turning right on the Phantom Prairie Trail. An amusing sign at the beginning of this trail stirs some interest with a warning that this prairie is "not for the meek" because of the harsh winter wind and a lack of shade during the summer. Initially, this trail runs between a woodland on the left and a vast cattail marsh dotted with black willows on the right. Then it winds through a grassy scrubland mixed with goldenrod, staghorn sumac, and cherry trees before reaching a fork. At the fork, head to the right through the wet prairie toward the stands of quaking aspen and buckthorn trees. Cross an intermittent stream and then you'll emerge in a rolling tallgrass prairie. After brushing against stands of maple and white oak, the trail runs through an area rife with rattlesnake master (round heads dense with little flowers), a member of the parsley family, which at one time was thought to cure rattlesnake bites.

Keep watch at the edges of the prairie for raptors—either perched or soaring. Higher up, you're likely to see (and occasionally hear) a progression of airplanes on the flight path to O'Hare Airport. After passing several small sections of wet prairie, look for honey-locust trees on the right. These trees are unmistakable due to their clusters of thorns—up to eight inches long—growing from the bark. Crossing the boardwalk over the wet, grassy area brings you to the fork that leads back to the Bur Edge Trail.

On the Burr Edge Trail, continue circling the marsh, passing by pasture rose, buckthorn trees, as well as walnut and hickory trees wrapped in vines. As you pass under the enormous weeping willows, you'll come upon a pleasant cattail-fringed pond on the left. Along with plenty of waterfowl, the pond is home to muskrats, kingfishers, and, according to park staff, a 40-pound snapping turtle.

From the pond, the trail swings left, passing several silver maples on the way to a grassy area interrupted with stands of black willow and walnut. After catching a few more fleeting views of the pond through stands of willow shrubs, the trail enters a dense grove of buckthorn followed by a cluster of cattails on one side of the trail and box elder trees on the other side.

Leaving the pond, the trail enters a prairie dominated with big bluestem grass and prairie dock, and dotted with quaking aspen. From the prairie, the trail runs alongside split-rail fence through a woodland with specimens of maple, pine, shagbark hickory, and burr oak. For now, continue past the Giants Hallow Trail on the left while you pay a visit to the bird blind on Crabtree Lake. Inside the little blind are some handy, hand-painted signs identifying the lake's ducks and geese in flight and at rest. Back on the Giants Hollow Trail, you'll return to the Sulky Pond and then pass through a savanna with sprawling oaks on your way back to the exhibit building.

▶ NEARBY ACTIVITIES

To the west of Crabtree Nature Center are a couple of hiking opportunities within other Cook County forest preserves. Located a few miles southwest of Crabtree, and south of I-90, the Poplar Creek Forest Preserve offers a large expanse of woods, prairies, savannas, and wetlands. Follow the trail from the parking lot to the lake and along the top of the dike. After the dike, keep straight ahead until you reach a major trail junction. Hanging a right at the junction takes you on a longer hike through mostly grassland and eventually back to the park road. Heading to the left takes you on a shorter hike through woodland and marsh and back to the lake. From Crabtree, take a right on East Palatine Road (IL 62), then turn left on New Sutton Road (IL 59). Follow New Sutton Road until you reach Shoe Factory Road Prairie parking lot, 0.6 miles south of Shoe Factory Road, on the right.

Northwest of Crabtree, trails also can be found among the lakes, grasslands, woods, and marshes at the Spring Creek Valley Forest Preserve. In the southern section of the preserve, 2.4 miles of established trails are accessible from the Beverly Lake parking area. Starting from the shore of Beverly Lake, the loop begins after a half mile of hiking. Follow the entire loop or shorten the hike via connector trails. Several hiking and bridle trails are accessible from the dog-training area to the west along Higgins Road. Bring a GPS device, however, because these trails can be confusing. To reach Beverly Lake, follow the directions to Poplar Creek Forest Preserve. As you're heading south on New Sutton Road, turn right on West Higgins Road (IL 72). The parking area is 2.1 miles ahead on the right.

DANADA FOREST PRESERVE HIKE

UTM Trailhead Coordinates for Danada Forest Preserve Hike

UTM Zone (NAD27) 16T

Easting   407884

Northing   4630038

IN BRIEF

Nestled in an unlikely spot between subdivisions and I-88, Danada Forest Preserve offers some terrific hiking through wide-open prairies and gently sloping savannas. Once a training ground for top racehorses, Danada still caters to equestrians, with an array of programs.

DESCRIPTION

Before the county acquired this 753-acre forest preserve, the land hosted a farm and a racehorse training facility owned by commodity trader Daniel Rice and his wife, Ada. After buying the property in 1929, they began raising wheat, corn, and livestock. Over the years, they built a 19-room mansion, a greenhouse, an employee boarding house, a swimming pool, formal gardens, a 26-stall Kentucky-style horse barn, and a half-mile horse-exercise track. The Rices entered their first horse in the Kentucky Derby in 1949. Fourteen years later, their horse Lucky Debonair won the Derby with the third fastest time in the history of the race. The following year their horse Abdicator took second place. The Rices sold their racehorse interests in the early 1970s for an estimated $5 million.

Once DuPage County bought Danada in 1980, it was reborn as a hiking and biking destination, as well as a place for beginning and intermediate equestrians to learn horse care and riding. Today, the Danada Equestrian Center offers an assortment of classes, lectures, trail and sleigh rides, and even a summer riding camp for kids.

Start the shorter 1.25-mile section of this hike on the wide gravel path known as the Regional

DIRECTIONS

From Chicago, take I-290 west to I-88. Follow I-88 for 12 miles until reaching Naperville Road. Follow Naperville Road to the left (north) for 0.8 miles; turn right at the sign for Danada.

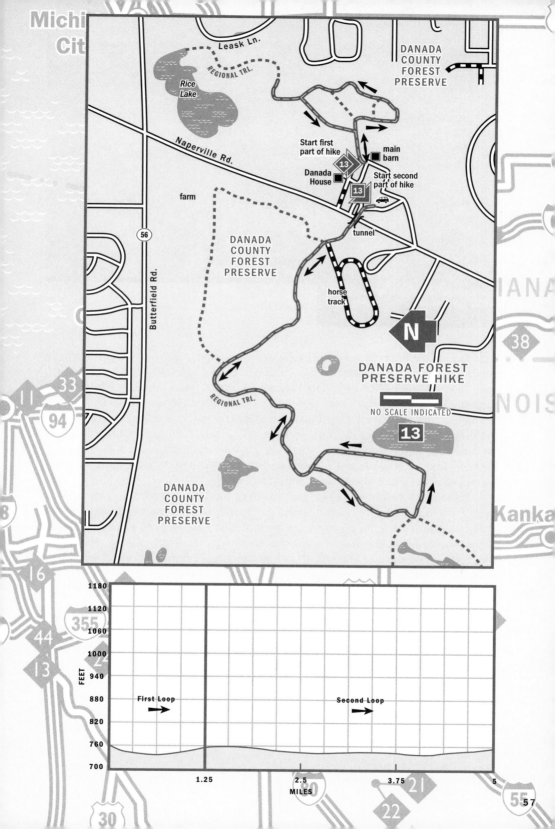

DANADA COUNTY FOREST PRESERVE

Rice Lake

Leask Ln.

REGIONAL TRL.

Naperville Rd.

Start first part of hike

main barn

Danada House

Start second part of hike

farm

56

DANADA COUNTY FOREST PRESERVE

Butterfield Rd.

tunnel

horse track

REGIONAL TRL.

N

DANADA FOREST PRESERVE HIKE

NO SCALE INDICATED

13

DANADA COUNTY FOREST PRESERVE

First Loop

Second Loop

1180
1120
1060
1000
940
880
820
760
700

FEET

1.25   2.5   3.75   5
                MILES

Rice Lake is tucked away in the northeast corner of Danada Forest Preserve.

Trail. Pick up the Regional Trail to the right of the mansion, and head east past the main barn and past trail marker 15. At marker 16, take a narrow trail on the right, which leads into a beautiful lightly rolling savanna known as Parson's Grove. To hike the perimeter of the grove, stay to the right at the next four trail intersections. Once in the savanna, it's difficult to miss the birds chattering continuously among the tall grasses and the abundant oaks. As the trail proceeds, the savanna undergoes subtle changes in the concentration of oaks and the varieties of grasses. On the trail surface, look for coyote scat—four inches long and usually consisting of fur (coyotes are known for marking trails and even trail intersections with their scat).

The narrow path meets again with the Regional Trail 0.7 miles into the hike, at marker 17. Turn right and continue straight ahead, beyond the mapboard and the two-track intersection, for an expansive view of Rice Lake and the surrounding suburban development. Also visible is the continuation of the Regional Trail, which runs a mile along the shore of the lake to the intersection of Butterfield Road and Leask Lane. To the left is a trail leading up a small hill that provides an even better view of the prairie and the 40-acre man-made lake. After taking in the view, head back along the Regional Trail for 0.4 miles to the trailhead.

The longer 3.75-mile section of this hike begins by following the Regional Trail through the tunnel under Naperville Road, west of the parking lot. Coming out of the tunnel, the DuPage County Forest Preserve District Headquarters is on the left. Also on the left is Heroes' Grove, a planting of 9 burr oaks and 11 white oaks dedicated to American heroism demonstrated on 9/11. After passing a gravel service road, the trail runs by horse-racing starting gates and the beginning of the horse exercise track. After the gates, there's another gravel service road on the right, which leads a half mile north to a small, 1950s-style model farm that operates in the northeastern section of the preserve.

As the trail enters Danada's wide-open prairie, hikers may want to refer to a sign along the way that will help them identify common prairie grasses such as goldenrod, big bluestem, compass plant, and Indian grass. This flat, grassy landscape draws in the birds, particularly swallows, goldfinches, and sparrows. Also common are brown-headed cowbirds, a member of the blackbird family known as a "brood parasite" because the female lays its eggs in the nests of the other birds, often to the detriment of the host's young.

At 1.2 miles from the parking lot, a marshy area appears on the right. Just after the mileage board, take the fork to the right. Clusters of trees and shrubs start to interrupt the grassy prairie just before reaching an intersection at 1.7 miles. At the intersection, stay left. Finish the loop at 2.3 miles and turn right, heading back the way you came. Follow the Regional Trail for 0.9 miles back through the savanna and prairie. After passing through the tunnel, the parking lot is straight ahead.

▶ NEARBY ACTIVITIES

For those who want more of the open vistas seen on the prairie hike, continue beyond the final loop to the Herrick Lake Forest Preserve, which offers several miles of hiking.

DEEP RIVER HIKE

KEY AT-A-GLANCE INFORMATION

LENGTH: 2.9 miles

CONFIGURATION: Out-and-back with loop

DIFFICULTY: Easy

SCENERY: River, woodland, grassland, restored gristmill

EXPOSURE: Mostly shaded

SURFACE: Dirt

HIKING TIME: 1.5 hours

ACCESS: 7 a.m. to dusk

FACILITIES: Restrooms, picnic area, gift shop/visitor center, historic gristmill and sawmill

MAPS: USGS topo Plamer, IN; ask for a map in the gift shop/visitor center

SPECIAL COMMENTS: The mill and the gift shop/visitor center are open 10 a.m. to 5 p.m. from May 1 to October 31. For more information, call (219) 947-1958 or (219) 945-0543. For information about the vintage baseball games played by Deep River Grinders, call (219) 947-1958.

UTM Trailhead Coordinates for
Deep River Hike

UTM Zone (NAD27)   16T

Easting   481440

Northing   4591476

▶ IN BRIEF

This hike takes you along the edge of the Deep River as it meanders through a large, diverse hardwood forest. At some point during your visit, stop in at the gristmill that was first built next to the river in 1837.

▶ DESCRIPTION

At the entrance to Deep River County Park sits an old church that now serves as the park's visitor center/gift shop. Built in 1904, the inside of this former church now looks like an old-style general store, with jars of candies and preserves, wooden toys, maple syrup, handcrafted items, and various souvenirs stacked high up on shelves. After picking up a map and perhaps a few pieces of hard candy for the hike, take a walk next door to the brick gristmill.

In 1837, John Wood built his gristmill on the banks of the Deep River using native white oak. He also built a sawmill that still stands on the other side of the river. After grinding grain into flour for nearly 20 years, 56-year-old Wood decided to sell the operation to his sons Nathan and George. Several years later, Nathan bought out his brother George, and 16 years later, Nathan decided to tear down the wooden mill and erect

▶ DIRECTIONS

Driving from Chicago, take I-90/I-94 south until reaching the Chicago Skyway (I-90), Exit 59A. After traveling 23.7 miles southeast on the Skyway, take Exit 17 to I-65. Proceed south on I-65 for 8.5 miles until reaching Exit 253. Follow US 30 (East Lincoln Highway) to the left (east) for 4.5 miles, and then turn left (north) on Randolph Street. Proceed along Randolph Street for 0.3 miles before taking another right (east) on Old Lincoln Highway (East 73rd Avenue). The park is 0.9 miles ahead on the left.

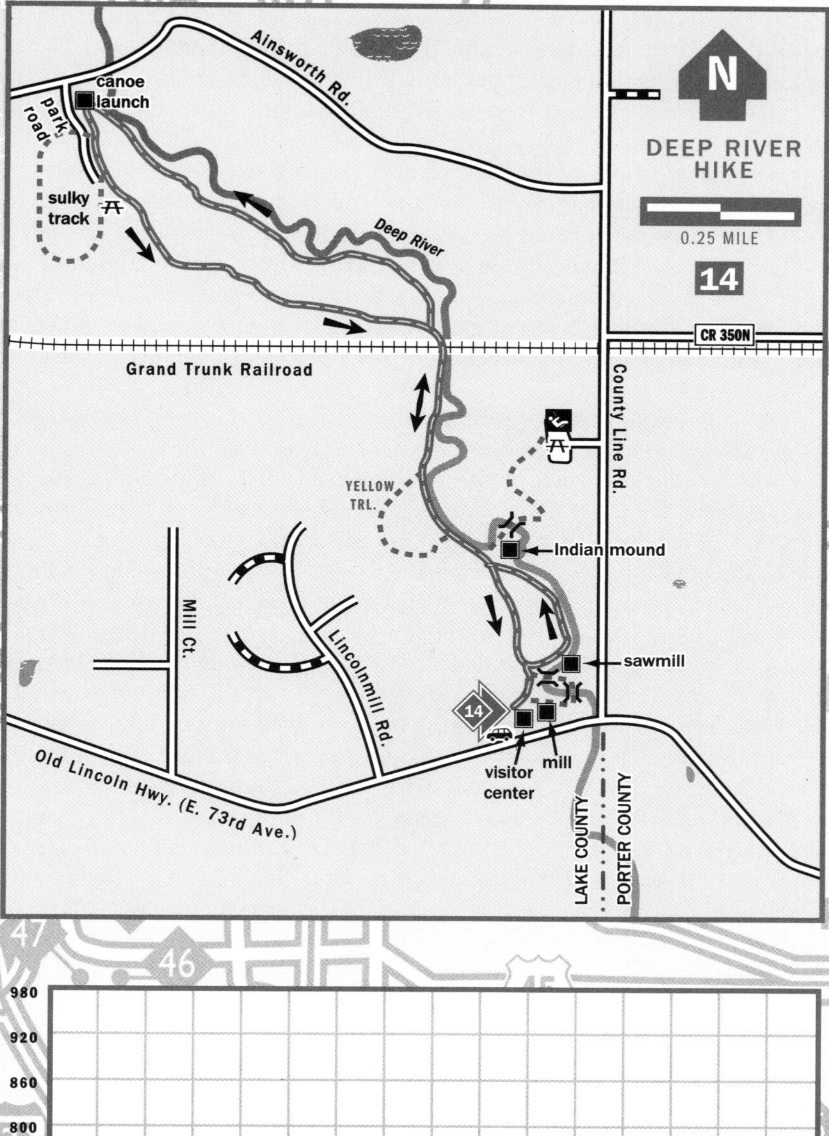

Michigan
City

N

**DEEP RIVER
HIKE**

0.25 MILE

14

CR 350N

canoe
launch

park
road

sulky
track

Ainsworth Rd.

Deep River

Grand Trunk Railroad

YELLOW
TRL.

Indian mound

sawmill

Mill Ct.

Lincolnmill Rd.

14

visitor
center

mill

Old Lincoln Hwy. (E. 73rd Ave.)

County Line Rd.

LAKE COUNTY

PORTER COUNTY

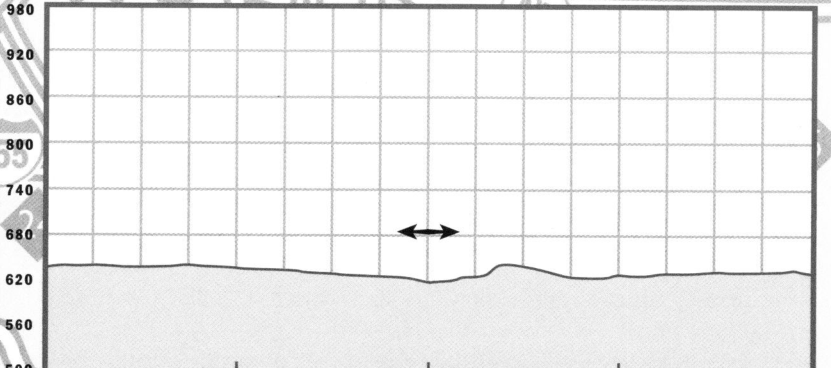

IANA

NOIS

Kanka

980
920
860
800
740
680
620
560
500

FEET

0.72   1.45   2.17   2.9
MILES

one of the finest mills in the county. This new brick mill could grind 12 bushels of corn, wheat, rye, or buckwheat per hour. Nathan sold the mill in 1908, and it passed through the hands of many owners. By 1930, the mill lay abandoned and forgotten until it was renovated by the county and opened to the public in 1977.

On the first floor of the mill, you can watch the 4,000-pound millstone (now powered by electricity rather than the river) pulverizing various grains that are loaded into cotton bags and offered for sale. A volunteer is on hand to demonstrate the grinding process and describe how it worked. In front of the grinding platform, a drawing shows which millstones—each with a different pattern etched in the stone—were used for grinding different grains. Upstairs, quilts and nineteenth-century furniture and fashions are on display, and the third floor contains a gallery for local artists.

A picturesque gazebo surrounded by plantings of flowers and prairie grasses sits next to the gristmill. From the gazebo, head left across the footbridge to the open area, which is the home field to the Deep River Grinders, a vintage baseball team that takes on teams from across the Midwest, playing in accordance with 33 rules in effect in 1858. Before the Grinder's season starts, during the second and third weekends in March, the building on the right hums with activity as park staff and volunteers use the wood-fired evaporator to create maple syrup from sap collected in the park. Just before my visit in the summer of 2004, a violent storm swept through the park, blowing down about 100 trees. One benefit of the storm, commented a park volunteer, is that the downed trees will provide plenty of fuel for maple-syrup production in coming years. To the left of the sugar shack is the sawmill built by John Wood in 1837.

Continuing left, across another footbridge, follow the dirt trail to the right as it weaves alongside the sandy-bottomed river. From the footbridges and the trailside observation platform overlooking the river, it may be apparent that this is not a particularly deep river. Its name, Deep River, was inspired by deeper stretches of water downstream. Stay to the right at the junction at 0.3 miles. After the junction, an Indian mound marked with a sign rises on the bank of the river. The mound—70 feet long and 30 feet high—is likely the handiwork of Potawatomi Indians who set up summer encampments along Deep River before white settlers came to the area. John Wood reportedly paid much more than the going rate for this land because it was under the ownership of the Potawatomi. After the Indian mound, a trail breaks off to the right, heading over a footbridge toward a playground and picnic area on the other side of the river. Continuing ahead on the main trail, you'll pass an open field and a grassy marsh on the left, and signs for the two ends of the short loop called the Yellow Trail.

After the railroad underpass at 0.6 miles, take the narrow trail on the right as it continues near the river. In this more remote section of the park, the river winds through a deeper channel. For anyone who likes to admire and identify trees, hiking along the Deep River is a treat: substantial cottonwoods, sycamores, basswood, swamp white oak, sweetgum, shagbark and bitternut hickory, and Kentucky coffee trees all grow in the moist riparian soil. While it's not the largest of Lake County's parks, Deep River's 1,400 acres easily take the prize for the greatest variety of trees.

At the hike's halfway point, the trail ends at the canoe launch alongside the park driveway that leads to the sulky track. (If you're in the mood for exploring a less-used section of the park, check out the trails north of Ainsworth Road near the entrance to the sulky track. While these trails can be overgrown in places, the hiking is pleasant, and, with a little exploration, you'll find a scenic overlook.) For the next part of this hike, take a left at the canoe launch, following the park road toward the sulky track. When you reach the small picnic area on the left, look for the trail leading into the woods.

Now heading back toward the mill, the trail runs next to a marsh before reaching an agricultural field flanked by train tracks on the far side. After walking for 0.2 miles between the agricultural field on the right and stands of cottonwood and apple trees on the left, the trail re-enters woodland. This hilly swath of woodland is dense with large oak, walnut, and hickory trees—many with vines hanging from their branches or snaking around their trunks. During the summer, look for wildflowers such as white and purple asters. After finishing the loop, passing underneath the train tracks, and going by the Indian mound, take the fork to the right marked "loop." This short trail takes you next to a large grassy field and through a picnic area on the way to the parking lot.

DEER GROVE LOOP

KEY AT-A-GLANCE INFORMATION

LENGTH: 5.6 miles

CONFIGURATION: Loop

DIFFICULTY: Easy

SCENERY: Rolling woodland, ravines, streams, and wetland.

EXPOSURE: Shaded

SURFACE: Old pavement, dirt, and some gravel

HIKING TIME: 2 hours

ACCESS: 6:30 a.m.–sunset

FACILITIES: Restrooms, picnic tables, and shelters

MAPS: The Deer Grove Natural Areas Volunteers offer a map on its website: www.enviroporium.com/deergrove/deergrv.html. USGS topo Lake Zurich, IL

SPECIAL COMMENTS: Sections of this trail drain poorly. If you're visiting after a rain, plan on getting some mud on your shoes. During summer, bring mosquito repellent. In winter, Deer Grove is popular with cross-country skiers.

UTM Trailhead Coordinates for
Deer Grove Loop

UTM Zone (NAD27)   16T

Easting   411201

Northing   4666486

IN BRIEF

The rolling landscape at Deer Grove is blanketed with thick groves of oak, hickory, and maple. Mixed in with the dense forest are ravines, marshes, ponds, and the occasional stream straddled by picturesque old limestone bridges.

DESCRIPTION

In 1916, Cook County started acquiring land to create one of the nation's first networks of county forest preserves. The county's first parcel—500-acres that is now part of Deer Grove—was prized for its wooded ravines, winding streams, and countless marshes and ponds. Over the years, as the size of Deer Grove nearly quadrupled, the preserve was split into two sections. The west section of the preserve, the destination for this hike, encompasses a larger, more heavily forested area, while the east section offers more open space and fewer trails (read about the east section in the "Nearby Activities" section).

While Deer Grove claims some of the best hiking in Cook County, the charm of this place has not always been guaranteed. In recent years, sections of the preserve have been plagued by illegal bicycle trails crisscrossing the forest and eroding

DIRECTIONS

From Chicago, follow I-90/I-94 northwest. After I-94 splits north, follow I-90 for 16 miles to IL 53. Head north for 6.3 miles on IL 53. At North Dundee Road (IL 68), turn left (west) and proceed for 2.9 miles to North Quentin Road. Turn right (north) on North Quentin Road and continue for 0.4 miles until you see the entrance to the preserve on the left. Follow the forest-preserve road for 0.2 miles until coming to the first right. Follow this second unnamed forest-preserve road for 0.6 miles, and then park at the first parking spaces you see on the right, next to the mapboard.

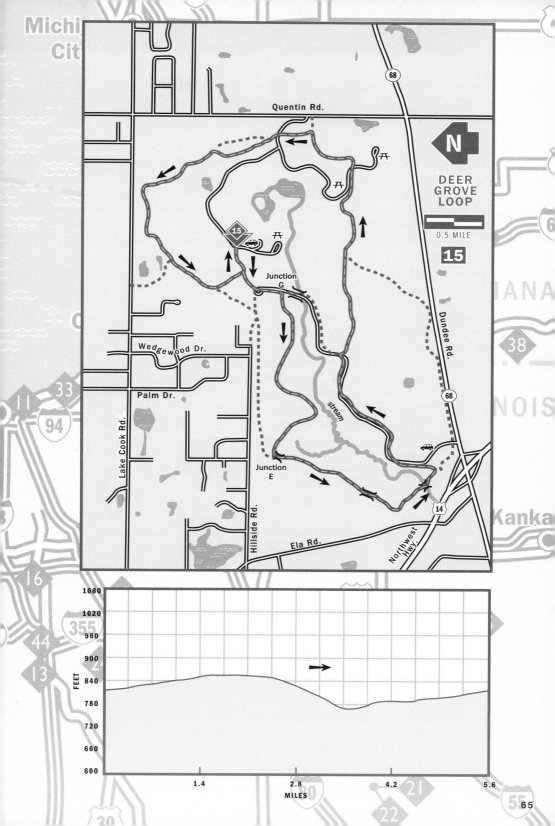

Michi
Cit

Quentin Rd.

68

N

DEER
GROVE
LOOP

0.5 MILE

15

15

Junction
G

Dundee Rd.

68

Wedgewood Dr.

Palm Dr.

Lake Cook Rd.

stream

Junction
E

14

Kanka

Hillside Rd.

Ela Rd.

Northwest Hwy.

94

33

355

44

13

76

1080
1020
960
900
840
780
720
660
600

FEET

1.4   2.8   4.2   5.6
MILES

65

hillsides. While new restrictions have reduced the damage by knobby tires, the existing side trails can make hiking at Deer Grove confusing at times. If you're unsure which way to continue at a particular junction, choose the wider trail. Also, consider packing a compass and map or a GPS device to keep your bearings.

The first section of this hike follows an old—sometimes crumbling—paved road that cuts diagonally through the preserve. After passing a couple of trails on the right, the narrow paved path turns wider at 0.2 miles. At 0.4 miles, turn right on the dirt path that appears at Junction G. But before following this trail, I suggest continuing straight ahead for 100 feet down the small hill to a scenic spot where a rocky creek winds under a limestone bridge. This bridge is where I met a husband and wife who showed me a hatful of edible chanterelle mushrooms they had gathered in the woods. They claimed Deer Grove was one of the better spots in the area for finding specimens sought after by their mycology club. (Novice mushroom hunters should always have the edibility of a specimen confirmed by someone with authoritative knowledge.)

Taking the trail at Junction G, you'll immediately pass over a small stream running through a culvert. After the culvert, stay left at the fork, and soon the trail winds along the edge of a shallow ravine containing a tranquil stream. Here and there, dead trees have fallen across the ravine. Farther along, watch your footing as you step over a trickling stream that has carved a small trough in the ground. Stay to the right at the next fork, and then at 1.3 miles into the hike, take a left at a major trail junction. After this junction, cross another one of the preserve's limestone bridges.

While hiking, keep an eye peeled for buckthorn, an invasive shrub that has been the source of many headaches for the volunteers and county employees who maintain Deer Grove and other natural areas in the region. Since it was imported from Europe in the early twentieth century for use on the lawns of lakefront mansions, buckthorn has spread widely throughout Chicagoland. Requiring constant vigilance to keep it under control, buckthorn grows quickly to a height of 20 feet, taking over wooded areas while blocking sunlight for all underlying plants (the oval-shaped leaves are one- to two-and-a-half inches long with fine wavy-toothed edges).

As you approach a large marshy pond on the right, the trail crosses another bridge spanning a small ravine. Staying to the left at the next two major junctions brings you back on the old paved road on which the hike started. As the paved trail dips and rises, you'll pass a parking area on the right. At 2.9 miles into the hike, turn right on the dirt trail at Junction J. This wide and fairly flat trail runs through a pleasant oak forest and passes a major junction on the right. As the trail descends a gradual hill, you'll cross a park road and a parking area on the left. On the other side of the park road, the trail accompanies a paved bicycle trail for a bit and crosses a stream. Just after the hiking trail splits from the paved trail, turn left at the junction and then cross the paved path. To the right, the paved path crosses Quentin Road and provides access on foot to the east section of Deer Grove. At 4.2 miles into the hike, a trail mapboard appears where the trail crosses the park road.

As the trail arcs toward Lake-Cook Road, ignore several side trails on the right. Through this section, the woods are dense and the landscape remains flat; if rain has fallen recently, get ready to encounter some mud. Taking the first junction on the left

(1.2 miles after your last crossing of the park road), you'll hike by open pond, and then cross a wide board that serves as a bridge over a creek. At the paved trail, turn left, and the parking lot is just ahead.

▶ NEARBY ACTIVITIES

On the other side of Quentin Road, the east section of Deer Grove contains wooded areas, marshes, and an ample amount of gently rolling open space. There are a couple of miles or so of dirt trails and a 2.5-mile loop of smooth pavement. Park at the picnic area 1 mile east of Quentin Road on Dundee Road or at the Camp Reinberg lot on the east side of Quentin Road, just south of the main entrance for the west side of Deer Grove. You can also walk across Quentin Road on the paved connector trail that accompanies this hike near the main entrance.

FULLERSBURG WOODS FOREST PRESERVE LOOP

KEY AT-A-GLANCE INFORMATION

LENGTH: 3.25 miles

CONFIGURATION: Loop that includes a couple of short loops

DIFFICULTY: Easy

SCENERY: Salt Creek, woodland, marshes, islands, footbridges, and a mill that is now a museum

EXPOSURE: More exposed than shaded

SURFACE: Crushed gravel

HIKING TIME: 2 hours, including a visit to the Graue Mill

ACCESS: 1 hour after sunrise to 1 hour after sunset

FACILITIES: Visitor center, restrooms, water, benches, and numerous log picnic shelters alongside the trail

MAPS: Maps available outside the visitor center; USGS topo Hinsdale, IL

SPECIAL COMMENTS: If you're at the park in April or May, ask at the visitor center for the forest preserve's wildflower guide, and then head over to the 0.1-mile-long wildflower trail, just west of the visitor center. The visitor center is open 9 a.m.–5 p.m., except for major holidays, and can be reached at (630) 850-8110. The mill is open mid-April–mid-November, Tuesday–Sunday, 10 a.m.–4:30 p.m. Admission to the mill is $3.50 for adults. Call (630) 655-2090 for more information.

IN BRIEF

You may be surprised to find this much natural beauty just 20 miles from the Loop. Nearly this entire hike accompanies Salt Creek as it meanders next to a bluff and winds around a couple of islands on its way to the historic watermill at the south tip of the park.

DESCRIPTION

Nestled against the communities of Hinsdale, La Grange, and Oak Brook, the 222 acres of Fullersburg Woods Forest Preserve have been a popular spot since opening to the public in 1920. While visitors have always been drawn to the creek and its environs, more recently the historic mill and visitor center have served as added attractions. When you pick up a map at the door of the visitor center, be sure to duck inside to see the 13,000-year-old wooly mammoth skeleton. The skeleton was uncovered in 1977 at the Blackwell Forest Preserve, about 15 miles west of Fullersburg. The accompanying signs describe how researchers determined the animal's age at death and gender, and why researchers disagree about whether the mammoth was killed by humans. Along with the mammoth skeleton, there are a few mounted animal specimens and interactive displays that kids will enjoy, as well as spotting scopes pointed toward Salt Creek.

To start the hike, look for the crushed-gravel trail on the north side of the visitor center. After

UTM Trailhead Coordinates for Fullersburg Woods Forest Preserve Loop

UTM Zone (NAD27) 16T

Easting 422583

Northing 4630735

DIRECTIONS

From Chicago, take I-290 west to I-88. Follow I-88 for 3.5 miles until reaching IL 83 (Kingery Highway). Follow IL 83 south for 0.8 miles. Turn left (east) on 31st Street and travel 0.5 miles until turning right (south) on Spring Road. Turn left 0.6 miles ahead at the sign for Fullersburg Park. The visitor center is at the north end of the parking lot.

passing a wide point in the creek, continue straight ahead over the bridge that leads to a part-time island. Heading to the left, the trail passes under a large tree trunk, riddled with woodpecker holes; nearby, you'll also see tree stumps sculpted by beavers. During the short stroll around the island, you'll pass a picnic shelter and a dried pond bed on the right.

Crossing the bridge again, turn right, passing a water pump and restrooms on the left. Here, the trail meanders beside an attractive stretch of Salt Creek: trees hang lazily over the water, and, on the opposite bank, a small bluff rises above the creek. Just ahead, the trail passes an impressive stone picnic shelter with benches and a fireplace. Many of the Fullersburg picnic shelters, as well as the log visitor center and the Graue Mill, were built or restored by the Civilian Conservation Corps, which had a camp here in the 1930s. Beyond the large boulders on the left, stay to the right at the next five trail junctions.

After crossing Salt Creek again, you'll pass a trail heading left into the Paul Butler Nature Area. If you wish to add an extra mile or so to your hike, take this narrow footpath as it follows the creek upstream to a small dam. Reaching the pond beyond the dam, I suggest turning around and heading back to the main trail (the remainder of this trail can be flooded in spots and is noisy due to traffic on 31st Street).

Continuing on the main trail, the path curves left, away from Salt Creek, and then rises up a small hill. As the path returns to the side of the creek, look for the trail you just hiked on the other side of the creek. On the left, you'll soon pass the other end of trail for the Paul Butler Nature Area. Not long after the landscape drops down to creek level, you'll pass over a couple of small streams; the first is intermittent, and the second looks as though it runs year-round. As you pass the island you hiked earlier, you'll start to see backyards of houses on the left. At 1.9 miles into the hike, a picturesque log bridge leads over Salt Creek to the visitor center.

After the bridge, the path runs straight south as the creek slowly curves to the right. When you meet back up with the creek, the water grows wider, until you reach the dam, which is flanked by the brick Graue Mill and its giant waterwheel. For anyone with an interest in local history and water mills, the Graue Mill is well worth a visit. Cross York Road on the footpath, and head over to the front door of the mill, which faces the former Graue House, where the owner of the mill, Frederick Graue, once lived with his family.

For a small admission fee, you can hear a 20-minute presentation in which a white-aproned miller explains the 15,000-year-old practice of grinding grain and how it was done here. After Fredrick Graue built the mill in 1852, three generations of his family operated the mill until 1912, and it continued as a working mill until 1929. At the end of the presentation, the miller grinds a half bucket of cornmeal using the mill's original millstones, which are made from a type of quartz—known as buhrstone—imported from France. While the millstones are now powered by electricity, sets of giant wooden gears in the basement are set up as they would have been when the waterwheel powered the millstones.

In the basement, you'll learn that the mill was also a stop on the Underground Railroad. Along with other local stops in Plainfield, Aurora, Sugar Grove, Joliet, and Hinsdale, the Graue Mill was a part of the clandestine network of places where escaped slaves could rest and be fed on their way to Chicago, from which they could travel across the Great Lakes to Canada. On the second and third floors of the mill is a collection of artifacts from the period of 1850 to 1890, including room settings, farm implements, and a re-created general store.

From the mill, the path runs back to the visitor center between the dam's backwater and Spring Road. Along the way, you'll pass a sign explaining that Salt Creek got its name when a farmer's wagon was stuck in the creek while hauling a barrel of salt. Leaving the wagon in the creek overnight, the farmer returned the next morning and found the salt had dissolved. Farther ahead, follow the trail branching to the right. Then take the short bridge to the right for a short loop around this little piece of land—sometimes an island—that sticks out into the water. Crossing back over the bridge, continue to the right until you see the parking lot on the left.

A trailside sculpture chiseled by Fullersburg's dam-building inhabitants.

▶ NEARBY ACTIVITIES

If you'd like to see more of Salt Creek, head over to Bemis Woods Forest Preserve, a mile directly east of Fullersburg Forest Preserve. Bemis Woods offers several miles of multipurpose trails, a toboggan slide, and the western end of the Salt Creek bicycle path. This paved path runs for 6.6 miles east, ending at the doorstep of the world-renowned Brookfield Zoo. To reach Bemis Woods, turn left (southeast) on Spring Road as you're leaving Fullersburg Park. After passing the Graue Mill, turn left (south) on York Road. Turn left (east) on Ogden Avenue and proceed for 1.2 miles. The driveway for Bemis Woods is on the left. The bicycle trail starts on the right just before the toboggan slides. You can catch one of the hiking trails just after the slides. Unfortunately, all the toboggan slides in Cook County were closed indefinitely in January 2005.

GENEVA LAKE: BIGFOOT BEACH
HIKE

KEY AT-A-GLANCE INFORMATION

LENGTH: 4.9 miles

CONFIGURATION: Out-and-back with loop on the end

DIFFICULTY: Moderate difficulty because of a couple of rugged sections along the lake

SCENERY: Downtown Lake Geneva, historic mansions on lakefront, beach, lagoon with footbridges, bottomland forest, large pine plantation, camping and picnic areas

EXPOSURE: Geneva Lake section is mostly exposed, while Big Foot Beach section is mostly shaded

SURFACE: Dirt, mowed grass, concrete, stone. The surface on the Geneva Lake section changes frequently.

HIKING TIME: 2 hours

ACCESS: Sunrise to sunset

FACILITIES: Picnic areas, restrooms, camping, water fountains, swimming beach, payphones, and restaurants and shops in Lake Geneva

MAPS: Maps for the Big Foot Beach section of the hike are available at the guardhouse and posted at most of the major trail intersections; USGS topo Lake Geneva, WI

SPECIAL COMMENTS: This hike can easily be divided into 2 sections. If you're hiking only at Big Foot Beach State Park, park in the large lot next to the guardhouse. During the winter, use the park's east entrance on South Wells Street.

UTM Trailhead Coordinates for
Geneva Lake: Bigfoot Beach Hike

UTM Zone (NAD27) 16T

Easting 382185

Northing 4716068

IN BRIEF

The first section of this hike runs through downtown Lake Geneva before taking you past a series of historic mansions overlooking the lake. The second part takes you on a 1.5-mile loop along the shore of a scenic lagoon and through a bottomland forest and a large pine plantation at Big Foot Beach State Park.

DESCRIPTION

While half of this hike is an out-and-back along a section of the 20.2-mile Geneva Lake Shore Path, the other half runs through a 271-acre state park named after a local Potawatomi chief. Chief Maunk-suck—"Big Foot" in English—lived with his people in the Lake Geneva area from the late 1700s until 1836, when they were removed by the United States government and relocated to Lawrence, Kansas. In downtown Fontana, on the other side of Geneva Lake, a bronze life-size statue depicts a somber Chief Big Foot as he looks toward the lake for the last time before departing for Kansas.

DIRECTIONS

Take I-90/I-94 west, proceeding along I-94 as it splits off northward. Exit I-94 at IL 173 (Rosecrans Road). Follow IL 173 west for 17.8 miles until reaching US 12. Turn right (north) on US 12 and follow it for 10 miles to WI 50. Turn left (west) and drive for 1 mile to downtown Lake Geneva. Since parking spots near the lake are metered, I suggest parking on one of the side streets just north of WI 50. After passing Broad Street, turn right (north) on Cook Street. Then turn left (west) on Geneva Street as it runs beside the school and look for a spot. After parking, follow Cook Street toward the lake where it turns into Wrigley Drive. The Riviera Ballroom is on Wrigley Drive, where Broad Street meets the lake.

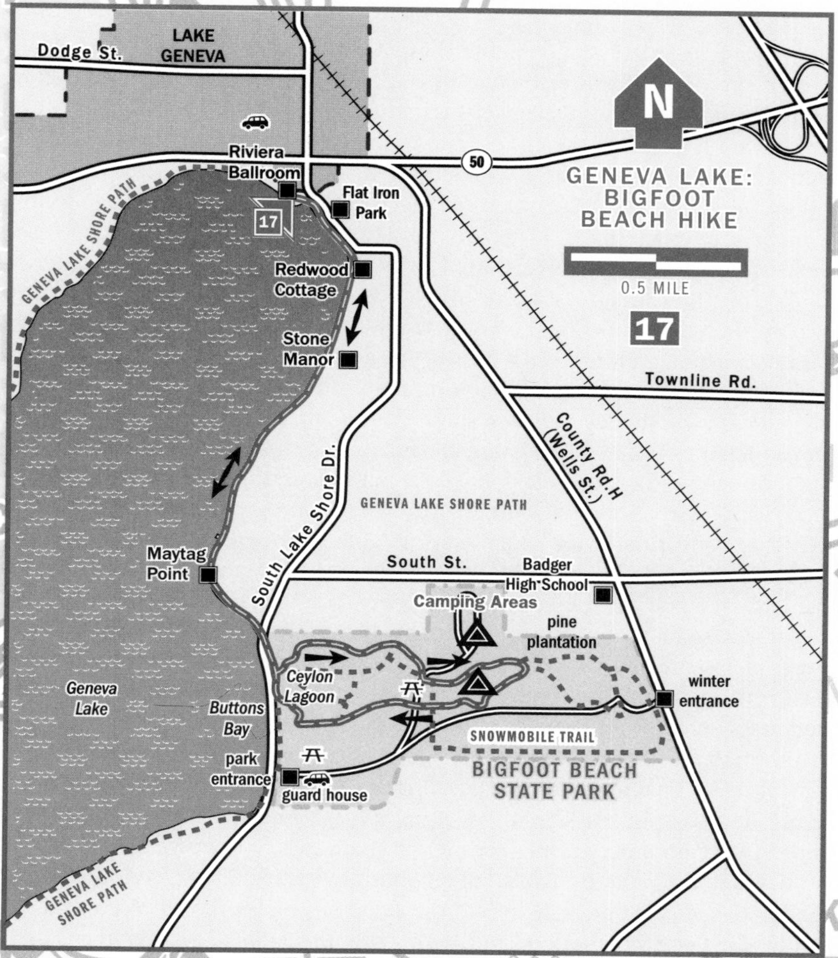

Michigan City

LAKE GENEVA
Dodge St.

Riviera Ballroom

Flat Iron Park

17

Redwood Cottage

Stone Manor

N

GENEVA LAKE: BIGFOOT BEACH HIKE

0.5 MILE

17

Townline Rd.

County Rd H (Wells St.)

GENEVA LAKE SHORE PATH

South Lake Shore Dr.

GENEVA LAKE SHORE PATH

South St.

Badger High School

Maytag Point

Camping Areas

pine plantation

Geneva Lake

Buttons Bay

Ceylon Lagoon

winter entrance

park entrance

guard house

SNOWMOBILE TRAIL

BIGFOOT BEACH STATE PARK

GENEVA LAKE SHORE PATH

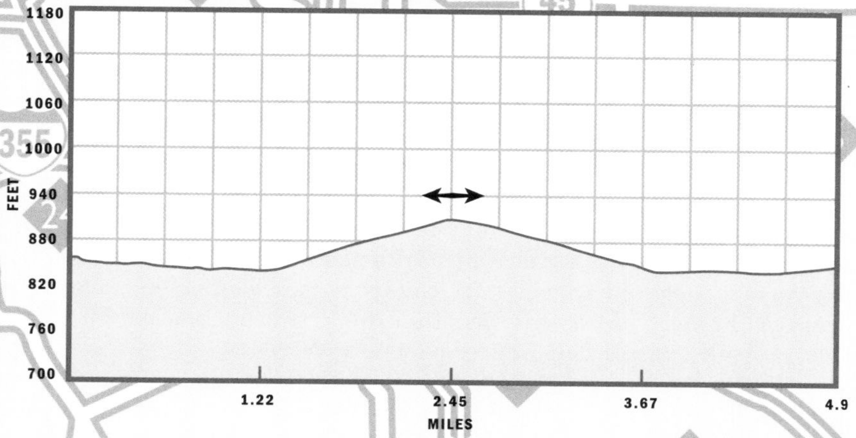

Kanka

IANA

INOIS

38

33

94

11

16

355

44

13

46

45

FEET

1180
1120
1060
1000
940
880
820
760
700

1.22   2.45   3.67   4.9
MILES

80

30

22   21

55

The hike starts in downtown Lake Geneva at the Riviera Ballroom, which is located on a man-made peninsula in Geneva Lake (the lake is called Geneva Lake, while the town is called Lake Geneva). The brick ballroom was built by the Civilian Conservation Corps in the 1920s, and in the 1940s hosted many popular big bands. Now, private parties and city events take place in the ballroom upstairs, while the ground level offers an assortment of snack and knick-knack shops. A fountain with an angel decorates the front of the building; the back of the building is where the Geneva Lake Cruise Line boats are docked.

With the lake on the right, follow the sidewalk along Wrigley Drive as it runs next to Flat Iron Park. In the park, you'll see a statue of the cartoon figure Andy Gump, whose creator, Sidney Smith, lived on the lake. According to the plaque, Andy Gump was the first daily cartoon strip in the *Chicago Tribune*. Farther ahead in the park is a gazebo, as well as a statue of the Three Graces—joy, charm, and beauty are depicted as lithe young maidens dancing in a circle.

As the road curves left, follow the path along the lakeshore through the yards of the impressive lakefront homes. Just ahead, situated between two new hotels, is the Redwood Cottage, an 1880s Queen Anne–style mansion that was added to the National Register of Historic Places in 1984. Several mansions later, you'll encounter the largest home on the lake, Stone Manor, built in 1901 by a Chicago real-estate investor. Also on the National Register of Historic Places, the four-floor, 50-room Italianate palace served as a private girls' school in the 1930s. In recent years, it was divided into six luxury condominiums. After Stone Manor, watch your step on the tree roots and loose dirt and gravel while navigating a couple of short, steep sections of the path. As the path follows a small promontory into the lake, you'll arrive at Maytag Point, named after the washing-machine manufacturer who once owned a house on this spot. Passing a few more modest homes brings you into Buttons Bay and into the boundary of Big Foot Beach State Park.

When the path drops you off on South Lakeshore Drive, continue alongside the road with the lake on the right and the small lagoon on the left. Enter the first opening in the fence on the left, and then cross the footbridge over the 7-acre Ceylon Lagoon, created as a miniature replica of Geneva Lake by the Maytag family. While the banks of the lagoon have changed slightly over the years, it retains the basic shape of Geneva Lake. The Maytag family, as well as the banker, John J. Mitchell, sold much of this land to the state for the creation of this park in the 1940s and 50s.

On the other side of the footbridge, follow the lagoon's wooded shore to the left. Just ahead, a posted park map shows your location (you can pick up a copy of the park map by following the shore of the lagoon to the right, and then continuing through the picnic area to the guardhouse). As the path curves away from the lagoon and enters a bottomland forest, the colored blazes on the trees indicate that you're on the red trail. The trail parallels the park's northern boundary as it passes through a powerline right-of-way and then crosses a rocky-bottom intermittent stream. Through the trees on the left, you'll see some structures belonging to the Lake Geneva Youth Camp, a Christian camp founded in 1948.

The landscape—mostly covered in oak and hickory—alternates between flat and gently rolling. Keep straight ahead as you pass a gate on the left and a trail junction on the right. Soon, the canopy breaks apart and the landscape becomes grassy and open,

Built in 1901, Stone Manor is the largest home on Geneva Lake.

with a sprinkling of cherry and locust trees. Not long after passing a spur trail on the left that leads to Wilmot Boulevard, the trail crosses the paved park road. On the other side of the park road, continue straight ahead alongside the pine trees through the grassy picnic area. Turn left as the trail cuts through the trees, following the blue blazes through another picnic area and another small grove of trees. The blue blazes guide you past a couple of pit toilets, and then through the camping area to the left. Near campsite 40, follow the blue blazes into the open grassy area, and then take an immediate left into the pine plantation. This wide, grassy, flat trail shoots straight through an enormous grove of bushy, 25-foot-high red pine trees. Getting closer to the Badger High School sports field, take a sharp right at the junction. (You can add another 0.7 miles to your hike by continuing straight ahead and staying to the right while following the blue blazes through more pines, another stretch of bottomland forest, and the park service area.)

Now heading back toward Geneva Lake, the red pines come and go as the trail takes a more meandering course. Soon, the last of the pine plantation is replaced by grasses and shrubs, and eventually, woodland. After passing a couple of trail junctions and crossing the park road at the picnic area, the blue trail dips, rises, and then passes under a few large oaks before reaching a junction where several trails come together. At the lagoon, cross the footbridge on the right and then look for the opening in the fence so that you can cross the road. From the road, hop on the lake path again as it guides you back to Lake Geneva.

▶ NEARBY ACTIVITIES

With adequate snow cover, the trails at Big Foot Beach are open for cross-country skiing. Call the park at (262) 248-2528 for information about camping. For another hike on the Geneva Lake Shore Path, see page 76.

GENEVA LAKE: NORTH SHORE HIKE

KEY AT-A-GLANCE INFORMATION

LENGTH: 10 miles (one way)

CONFIGURATION: Linear path

DIFFICULTY: Difficult

SCENERY: Geneva Lake, historic mansions, bluffs, woodland, public parks, and 3 pleasant lakeside villages

EXPOSURE: Mostly shaded

SURFACE: Surfaces include grass, dirt, brick, gravel, stone, and concrete. Be sure to wear good walking/hiking shoes.

HIKING TIME: 3-4 hours

ACCESS: Sunrise to sunset

FACILITIES: Restrooms, water, benches, public parks, beaches, parking, and restaurants available at each town along the way

MAPS: USGS topos Walworth, WI, and Lake Geneva, WI

SPECIAL COMMENTS: Consider taking two cars and parking one at each end of the hike or getting a lift back to Lake Geneva from a tour boat. Reservations are a must. The tour boat season runs from May 1 to October 31, depending on the weather. Call (800) 558-5911 or visit www.cruiselakegeneva.com for schedules and pricing.

Pets must be leashed. Hiking in late fall, winter, and early spring will require navigating your way around the many docks that are stacked up in homeowners' yards. Because of the steps and steep inclines, snow and ice would make this hike very difficult.

UTM Trailhead Coordinates for
Geneva Lake: North Shore Hike

UTM Zone (NAD27)   16T

Easting   382030

Northing   4716190

IN BRIEF

It's easy to see why so many wealthy Chicagoans built their opulent mansions on the shore of Geneva Lake during the late nineteenth and early twentieth centuries. The views from the wooded bluffs along this silvery lake are fantastic. While enjoying the lake and the historic estates on this hike, you'll encounter flower gardens, carefully landscaped lawns, boathouses, and pleasant little towns.

DESCRIPTION

In the early 1870s, following the Great Chicago Fire and the completion of a rail line connecting Lake Geneva with Chicago, sizable estates began springing up on the shores of this Wisconsin lake. Many of the homes served as summer resorts for wealthy families with familiar names such as Maytag, Swift, and Wrigley. After the turn of the century, a number of clubs, youth camps, and expensive subdivisions started squeezing in between the sprawling estates.

DIRECTIONS

Take I-90/I-94 west, proceeding along I-94 as it splits off northward. Exit I-94 at IL 173 (Rosecrans Road). Follow IL 173 west for 17.8 miles until reaching US 12. Turn right (north) on US 12 and follow it for 10 miles to WI 50. Turn left (west) and drive for 1 mile to downtown Lake Geneva. Since parking spots near the lake are metered, I suggest parking on one of the side streets just north of WI 50. After passing Broad Street, turn right (north) on Cook Street. Then turn left (west) on Geneva Street as it runs beside the school and look for a spot. After parking, follow Cook Street toward the lake where it turns into Wrigley Drive. Start the hike from the public library on the right.

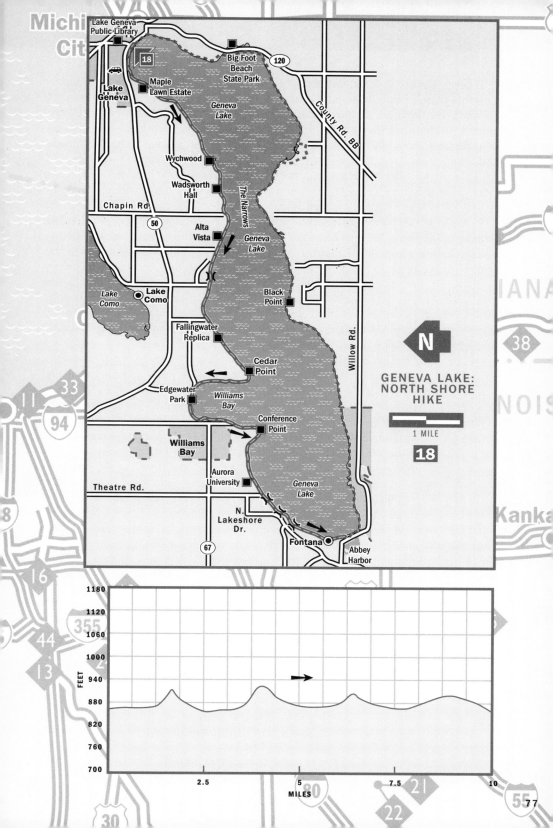

GENEVA LAKE: NORTH SHORE HIKE

1 MILE

18

Given the exclusive atmosphere at Geneva Lake, many people are surprised to learn that there's a public footpath circumnavigating the entire lake (the lake is called Geneva Lake; the town is called Lake Geneva). While not all landowners have been happy with the path, they've been legally obligated to leave their gates open since a court decision in the 1970s granted the public a "right of passage." The court made its decision based on the fact that the pathway existed before homeowners bought their property. Indeed, before European settlers arrived in the area, the local Potawatomi Indians regularly used a narrow dirt trail along the entire shoreline of Geneva Lake. Many signs are posted asking you to stay on the path.

While walking through people's yards may feel strange at first, this feeling diminishes once you see the many nice walkways installed by homeowners. Starting the hike from the park in back of the prairie-style library, follow the sidewalk to the right through Library Park. At the end of the park, the path turns to gravel and enters a yard. A sign just ahead identifies Maple Lawn, the oldest estate on the lake, dating from 1870. Next up are a number of newer homes, many with attractive flower bushes growing within carefully landscaped environments. After crossing a bridge over a rock-lined streambed, and passing the nice lawns of Covenant Harbor Bible Camp, wooded bluffs start to rise along the shoreline.

Just ahead is a green-trimmed Swiss-style mansion built in 1876 called North-woodside—once owned by the inventor of the paper milk-bottle cap. Between the estates on this section of the lake, the path runs through a number of brief wooded sections thick with weeping willows, sugar maple, and various oaks (since there are no public benches on the 7 miles between Lake Geneva and Williams Bay, consider discretely using the logs and tree stumps in the wooded areas for your rest breaks).

At 2.5 miles into the hike, the path runs by Wadsworth Hall, a stately red brick mansion from 1905 with six fluted columns in front. Near the House in the Woods (a large tan home with green shutters), there's a stretch of woods where someone has installed little signs identifying nearly all the trees that line the path. Just ahead, climb a set of stairs up the bluff past an attractive chalet-style home, and then follow signs as the path heads down a steep, paved ramp with switchbacks. At the bottom of the ramp, the path cuts through a sandy beach. Not long after passing the narrowest section of the lake—appropriately called the Narrows—the path climbs a bluff leading to Alta Vista, a white stucco mansion with a red tile roof and a huge porch. Coming down from the bluff, the path flattens out and then crosses a beautifully crafted iron footbridge with sides featuring ferns, flowers, and bluebirds. At 3.5 miles into the hike, the path crosses Chapin Road.

Beyond Chapin Road, the path runs next to a tight cluster of homes known as the Elgin Club. The closeness of the homes, the streetlamps, and the asphalt pathway makes this stretch feel like a city street. After passing a couple of private parks, you'll see a home that was intended to look like Frank Lloyd Wright's famous house, Fallingwater.

At 5.6 miles into the hike, on a promontory called Cedar Point, you'll climb a long flight of stairs up the bluff before taking in great views of Williams Bay. The dome of the Yerkes Observatory is visible on the other side of the bay. The path drops down as you get closer to the village of Williams Bay.

At 7 miles into the hike, across East Geneva Street from the boat launch in Edge-water Park, is one of the entrances to the Kishwauketoe Conservancy, which offers nearly 4 miles of trails through a marsh and bottomland. After traversing a couple of wooden footbridges and passing a statue of a Potawatomi Indian woman, you'll brush against the main business strip in Williams Bay. A few restaurants are located just to the right on WI 50.

Continuing on the trail, you'll soon pass through the boat yard at Gage Marine, the owner of the Geneva Lake tour boats. If boats are blocking the path, go around them and stay to the left. Passing a handful of old youth camps, the wooded bluffs rise steeply on the right as you get closer to Conference Point. From Conference Point, the path continues at the bottom of the wooded slope as it passes a big boulder called Kissing Rock. The cluster of brown cottages signals your arrival at Aurora University at 8.7 miles. The chairs and concrete wall on the veranda provide a nice place for taking a break. After the university, you'll catch glimpses of a series of houses perched high up on the bluff, followed by some pleasant wooded stretches and a number of attractive fieldstone footbridges. In the village of Fontana, the path runs between the boat launch and Pioneer Park. Farther ahead, after passing a restaurant, you'll see Reid Park, a beach, and Abbey Harbor.

To learn more about the historic houses, camps, and other sights along the way, send $7 to "Walk, Talk & Gawk: A map and guide of the Geneva Lake Shore Path," P.O. Box 413, Lake Geneva, WI, 53147. To receive "Touring the Geneva Lake Shore Path" ($5), call (800) 386-3228. Both guides are available at the Bread Loaf Bookshop (825 Wrigley Drive) located near the Lake Geneva Public Library.

▶ NEARBY ACTIVITIES

Considered one of the birthplaces of American astronomy, the Yerkes Observatory, on the outskirts of Williams Bay, has been operated by the University of Chicago since 1897. The observatory is open every Saturday for free public tours, beginning at 10 a.m., 11 a.m., and noon. There's also a small museum that's open at the same time as the tours. For more information, call (262) 245-5555, Ext. 832, or visit astro.uchicago.edu/yerkes/visiting.

While the southern shore of Geneva Lake may not have as many historic homes or as many wooded sections as the northern shore, it's still a fine location for a stroll. Continuing a counter-clockwise trip around the lake from Fontana, the path runs by a replica of a tugboat moored in the water and then passes by a series of exclusive clubs. As you get closer to the promontory called Black Point, the path becomes wooded, narrow, and occasionally steep. On the point, look high up on the bluff to see a four-story tower that is part of a Queen Anne Victorian mansion also called Black Point. At 5.2 miles, the Linn Pier boat launch offers weary hikers a picnic table and a restroom.

At 6.3 miles, after following several fairways at the Geneva Country Club Golf Course, watch carefully for signs directing you through a residential neighborhood and along a couple of quiet paved roads. On the second paved road, look for the sign posted on a tree directing you to the right through the grassy lawn. After passing through a gate, follow Burr Oak Road to Hillside Road. Take Hillside Road left to the boat launch, which has picnic tables, restrooms, and a water fountain. At 8.4 miles, Big Foot Beach State Park's lagoon appears on the right (see page 72 for information about Big Foot Beach and the final section of shore path).

GLACIAL PARK LOOP

KEY AT-A-GLANCE INFORMATION

LENGTH: 5 miles

CONFIGURATION: 2 connected loops with 1 brief out-and-back segment

DIFFICULTY: Easy

SCENERY: Savannas, prairies, a marsh, a bog, a creek, and expansive views from high spots

EXPOSURE: Mostly open

SURFACE: Hard-packed dirt, mowed grass, and woodchips

HIKING TIME: 2.5–3 hours

ACCESS: Sunrise to sunset

FACILITIES: Picnic areas, restrooms, water, sledding hill, and canoe launch

MAPS: Maps available at trail boards at the parking areas; USGS topo Richmond, IL

SPECIAL COMMENTS: For information on activities at the park such as the Trail of History event and cross-country skiing, call the McHenry County Conservation District at (815) 338-6223.

UTM Trailhead Coordinates for Glacial Park Loop

UTM Zone (NAD27)   16T

Easting   391298

Northing   4697409

▶ IN BRIEF

While hiking the trails of Glacial Park Conservation Area, you'll glide through open prairies, meander beside a lovely creek, and bound over hills that undulate like ocean waves. The star attraction, though, is a collection of curious mounds left by a receding glacier.

▶ DESCRIPTION

For those with an interest in learning the ways in which glaciers sculpted the landscape in northeastern Illinois, Glacial Park is a geologic jewel. The most eye-catching landforms in the park are mounds—called "kames"—that are formed when glacial meltwater deposits heaps of sand and gravel in depressions in the ice or at the edge of the glacier. The 100-foot-high Camelback Kame, which this hike passes over, is said to have formed at the edge of a glacier as it receded 15,500 years ago. The park's bog and marshes also offer a visual link to the area's geologic past. These wetlands began to take shape when large chunks of ice detached from a receding glacier: as ice melted, a pond formed in the depression, and eventually, vegetation overtook the pond.

But it's not just the geologic heritage that lends appeal to this 2,800-acre park: its variety—as well as its beauty and tranquility—make it a splendid place to stretch your legs and get a

▶ DIRECTIONS

From Chicago, head north on I-90/I-94. Follow I-94 as it separates from I-90. Continue on I-94 until you reach West Belvidere Road (IL 120). Turn left (west) on Belvidere Road and follow it for 18 miles until reaching IL 31 (North Richmond Road). Turn right (north) on IL 31 and travel for 6 miles. Turn left (west) on Harts Road and follow the signs for 1 mile until reaching the Wiedrich Education Center.

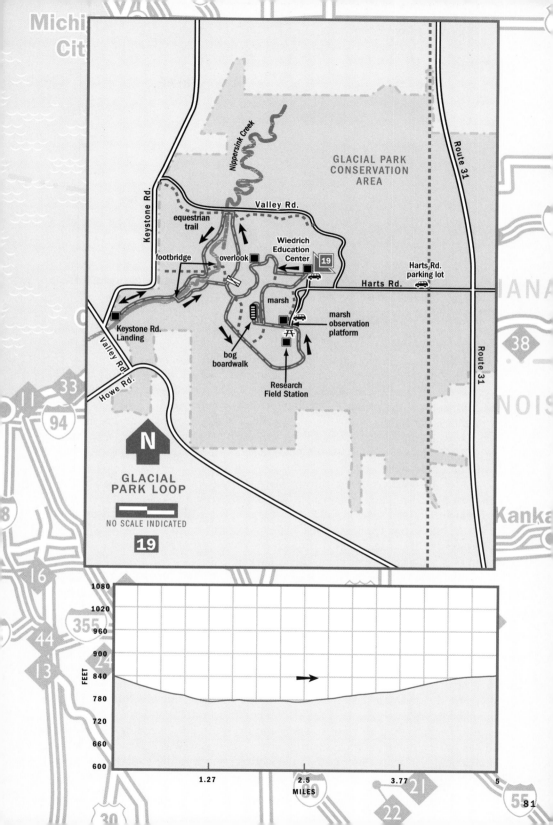

GLACIAL PARK
CONSERVATION
AREA

Nippersink Creek

Keystone Rd.

Valley Rd.

equestrian
trail

footbridge

overlook

Wiedrich
Education
Center

19

Harts Rd.
parking lot

Harts Rd.

marsh

marsh
observation
platform

Keystone Rd.
Landing

Valley Rd.

Howe Rd.

bog
boardwalk

Research
Field Station

Route 31

Route 31

N

GLACIAL
PARK LOOP

NO SCALE INDICATED

19

1080
1020
960
900
840
780
720
660
600

FEET

1.27   2.5   3.77   5
MILES

Horseback riders on the bank of Nippersink Creek.

concentrated dose of the natural world. Start the hike from the west side of the Wiedrich Education Center parking lot. Taking the trail on the right, marked by the sign for the Deerpath, Coyote, and Nippersink trails, you'll enter a rolling prairie fringed by oaks. After passing a small amphitheatre built into the hillside with large stone blocks, turn right at the first intersection. At a quarter mile into the hike, the trail leaves the prairie and enters an oak savanna where the landscape begins to rise and fall in various directions. At 0.4 miles, take in a great view of the prairie, marshland, and creek to the west.

After the overlook, the path runs beneath a canopy of gnarled oak limbs as it descends from the hilltop. Following a hairpin turn to the right, the path rises toward the Camelback Kame. Stay to the right at the next two trail junctions, and then head down the hill, saving the hike up the kame for the return trip. Turn right again at 0.8 miles into the hike after passing through the metal gate. From here, it's a straight walk to a small glacial kame alongside Valley Road.

While hiking along this trail, keep watch over the prairie for the northern harrier, a medium-sized hawk that is fun to watch as it hunts for its prey by cruising close to the ground above grasslands and marshes (another way to identify this frequent visitor to the park is by a clearly visible white spot on its rump). Once you reach the small kame, you'll have a better view of two more kames on the other side of the road. Follow Valley Road left as it crosses Nippersink Creek, and then turn left again on the horse-and-snowmobile trail that heads back on the other side of the creek.

At the junction near the footbridge, keep straight ahead as the path comes alongside this twisting section of the creek. At 2.2 miles into the hike, you'll pass another footbridge on the left. Before crossing this bridge, continue ahead on this pleasant streamside path until reaching the Keystone Road Landing, where you'll find an observation platform at the edge of the creek, as well as a picnic area, a canoe launch, and restrooms. After visiting the landing, return to the footbridge. Crossing the bridge, you'll notice a cattail marsh on the right that empties under the trail and into Nippersink Creek. The presence of many little feeder streams such as this one accounts for the Nippersink's name, which means "place of small waters" in the Algonquian language. As the trail leaves the edge of the creek, you'll enter a large mowed area at the base of Camelback Kame.

Each year in mid-October, the park hosts a large event in this spot called the Trail of History. Through exhibits, demonstrations, and people dressed in traditional costumes, visitors get a glimpse of life for early European settlers in the area. The wigwam frames on the eastern shore of the creek and the cabin that you'll pass on the way back to the metal gate serve as exhibits for this event.

At 3.3 miles, pass through the gate again, head up the hill, and turn right to ascend the spine of the Camelback Kame, named for its gentle double hump. Kames can be cone-shaped, like the ones by Valley Road, or they can be ridge-like, such as the Camelback. These glacial deposits are somewhat rare in the region, largely because many of them have been carted away for their sand and gravel.

As you descend the kame, continue straight ahead at the next two trail junctions. Soon the trail leaves the prairie and enters a savanna. On the left, you'll see the park's research field station. At 4.3 miles into the hike, just before reaching the main parking lot, follow the trail left as it runs through a picnic area. After crossing Harts Road, proceed straight ahead alongside a large marsh. First, however, you may want to take a short detour to an observation deck on the right.

When you cross the Deerpath Trail at 4.6 miles into the hike, continue ahead, following the sign for a bog boardwalk. The bog is dominated by leatherleaf, a shrub that keeps its leaves all year round. Finishing the short boardwalk, follow the loop that brings you back up to the Deerpath Trail, where you'll turn left. After the trail takes a steep drop, keep straight ahead at the next junction, and then turn left at another junction, heading up the hill and back to the Wiedrich Education Center parking lot.

▶ NEARBY ACTIVITIES

After entering the park on Harts Road, look for a parking lot for the Prairie Trail, a 25.9-mile multiuse path that stretches from the Wisconsin border south to Kane County. Once in Kane County, the Prairie Trail connects with a couple of other long trails: the Fox River Trail and the Illinois Prairie Path.

GOODENOW GROVE HIKE

UTM Trailhead Coordinates for Goodenow Grove Hike

UTM Zone (NAD27) 16T

Easting 449319

Northing 4583301

IN BRIEF

If you arrive early, you'll likely have these rolling hills, open grasslands, wooded ravines, and winding creek all to yourself. This delightful forest preserve remains undiscovered by people outside of the immediate area.

DESCRIPTION

For a 700-acre nature preserve, Goodenow Grove has a lot to offer. Along with hiking and picnicking, there is primitive camping and a nature center with a number of exhibits to engage kids. In the winter, the forest preserve clears a pond for ice skating and provides inner tubes for a sledding hill in the center of the preserve.

You might start this hike with a quick trip up the sledding hill for a view of the surrounding area. On the way down the hill, take the paved path to the right leading into the next parking area. Keep going past the main trailhead on the right and look for the second trailhead. This is where you'll head into the dense oak woods. After passing a side trail on the right, the trail pulls alongside a 40-foot-deep wooded ravine carved out by Plum Creek. Just beyond the old concrete foundation, turn left on the gravel trail. From this junction, the trail winds through groves of shrubs that soon give way to open space and savanna. At the picnic table (0.65 miles into the hike), take a left on the dirt trail leading into a dense and lush woodland beside Plum Creek. Stay to the right at the fork; the trail

DIRECTIONS

From Chicago, take I-90/I-94 south. Stay on I-90 for 15.1 miles after I-94 splits off. When I-94 reaches I-80, continue straight ahead on IL 394. Follow IL 394 for 14 miles. Turn left (east) on West Goodenow Road and proceed for 1.2 miles. Turn left (north) on Dutton Road and follow signs to the Plum Creek Nature Center.

Michigan City

394

Plum Creek

Bemis Rd.

Balmoral Woods Dr.

GOODENOW GROVE
FOREST PRESERVE

sledding
hill

Plum
Creek
Nature
Center

20

Snapper
Pond

Dutton Rd.

N

GOODENOW
GROVE HIKE

0.25 MILE

20

Goodenow Rd.   Goodenow Rd.

Park
Ave.

Kanka

INDIANA   ILLINOIS

1030
970
910
850
790
730
670
610
550

FEET

0.72   1.45   2.17   2.9
MILES

85

gains elevation and passes a few large oaks and scattered deadfall. A ravine containing bottomland forest and another section of Plum Creek opens on the right. As the trail takes a sharp turn left, it roughly follows the edge of this picturesque wooded ravine.

Returning to the gravel trail, head left as the trail rises up. Getting into the camping areas, several spur trails lead toward the sledding hill. A small cattail marsh appears on the right before reaching the parking lot for campers. Take the road heading left from the parking lot, and then turn left again at the sign for Foxfire Group I Camping.

This 1-mile loop section of the hike starts 20 yards to the right through the camping area. As you climb a wooded hillside, the trail turns into a wide, mowed path, and then passes a few buildings on the right. After the buildings, the trail curves left, drops into a short but steep ravine, and then enters an open space sprinkled with pines, oaks, apple trees, and shrubs.

Climbing a gradual hill, you'll have a nice view of the landscape of shrubs, thickets, and woods. From the hill, the trail swings left and then drops down next to goldenrod plants and sumac trees, and then runs through a wooded stretch before returning to the group camping area. In the camping area, continue straight past the restrooms and the water fountain back to the gravel trail, where you'll turn left. After crossing a small creek and passing Snapper Pond on the left, cross the park road and follow the path up the hill to the back side of the nature center. At the nature center, stay to the left, passing by some picnic tables and through the rows of lilies, black-eyed susans, and mint in the herb-and-flower garden.

The final section of this hike—called the Trail of Thoughts—starts across the park road in the Nodding Oaks picnic area. From the picnic area, stay to the right as you follow the paved path over a boardwalk, past a few benches and a wet prairie. You'll see that the trail gets its name from the nature quotations posted on signs along the way. The scenery gets wetter as the trail continues past a small pond and past viewing platforms at the edge of a cattail marsh and Snapper Pond. Complete the loop and follow the trail back up the hill to the parking lot.

▶ NEARBY ACTIVITIES

Not far away are a couple of nice outdoor-recreation areas owned by the Will County Forest Preserve District. The Monee Reservoir—a popular spot with fishermen, boaters, and picnickers—offers 2.5 miles of mowed turf trails near the 46-acre reservoir and through adjoining wetlands. Visitors can rent rowboats, canoes, and pedal boats, as well as other recreation items such as horseshoes and stakes, and snowshoes in the winter. The reservoir is open 6 a.m. to 8 p.m. during summer, and 8 a.m. to 5 p.m. during winter. Call (708) 534-8499 for more information.

Just east of the reservoir on the other side of the Illinois Central Gulf Railroad tracks and Governors Highway is the 210-acre Raccoon Grove Forest Preserve. Raccoon Grove has a half-mile trail that leads through gently rolling woodland and along the shore of Rock Creek. Hours are April to October, 8 a.m. to 8 p.m. and November to March, 8 a.m. to 5 p.m. From Goodenow, take Dutton Road south to Goodenow Road. Take Goodenow Road to the right and drive 8 miles (Goodenow Road becomes West Pauling Road halfway along this stretch). Shortly after passing Raccoon Grove Forest Preserve on the left, take South Ridgeland Road left to reach the reservoir.

GOOSE LAKE PRAIRIE STATE NATURAL AREA: PRAIRIE VIEW TRAIL

▶ IN BRIEF

Goose Lake Prairie State Natural Area provides visitors with a rare glimpse of what the Prairie State was like before farming became king. Be sure to climb the hill that rises up at the hike's halfway point for a panoramic view of the marshes and ponds surrounded by the state's largest stand of tallgrass prairie.

▶ DESCRIPTION

Goose Lake Prairie is one of the few places in Illinois where you can get a sense of the expansive grassland that was so common in the Prairie State 150 years ago. This prairie was spared from the plow not as a result of lack of interest on the part of local farmers, but because of the stubbornness of the land. As far back as 1890 farmers tried to make this land conducive for farming by draining 1,000-acre Goose Lake. Then, 35 years later, they dug drainage ditches to drain the water that remained in the marshes and ponds. Still, natural springs kept the ground too wet for farming.

With no chance for growing crops, farmers instead brought in livestock and allowed occasional mining. The two hills you'll encounter halfway through the hike resulted from coal mining carried out in the southern portion of the park in the 1920s. Along with coal, clay was pulled out of the former location of Goose Lake. The clay deposits—and the proximity of efficient transportation along the I&M Canal—brought in what

▶ DIRECTIONS

From Chicago, take I-90/I-94 south to I-55. Follow I-55 south for 51 miles until reaching Exit 240. Take Pine Bluff–Lorenzo Road to the right (west) for 2.9 miles. Turn right at the sign for Goose Lake Prairie State Natural Area (North Jugtown Road). Proceed ahead for 1 mile and then turn right at the sign for the visitor center.

ⓘ KEY AT-A-GLANCE INFORMATION

LENGTH: 2.9 miles

CONFIGURATION: Loop with a handle

DIFFICULTY: Easy

SCENERY: Tallgrass prairie, marshes, ponds, small hills

EXPOSURE: Completely exposed

SURFACE: Mowed grass. Depending on rainfall, you may encounter a few sections of the trail submerged under 1–3 inches of water. Waterproof shoes or hiking sandals are recommended. During the warmer months, some hikers may choose to strip off their shoes before hitting the wet spots. Call the visitor center for current trail conditions.

HIKING TIME: 1 hour

ACCESS: The park is open from sunrise to sunset; the visitor center is open 10 a.m.–4 p.m.

FACILITIES: Restrooms, picnic areas, a beverage vending machine, and a visitor center with exhibits

MAPS: Park map available at visitor center; USGS topo Coal City, IL

SPECIAL COMMENTS: Pets must be leashed. Contact the visitor center at (815) 942-2899. September and July are the best times for wildflowers. July offers the most color, while September is shimmering with goldenrod. Keep an eye out for ticks: on a visit in early summer, I picked off 5 ticks while on this hike. For more hiking in this area, see profile 22 (page 90).

UTM Trailhead Coordinates for Goose Lake Prairie State Natural Area: Prairie View Trail

UTM Zone (NAD27)   16T

Easting   389856

Northing   4579427

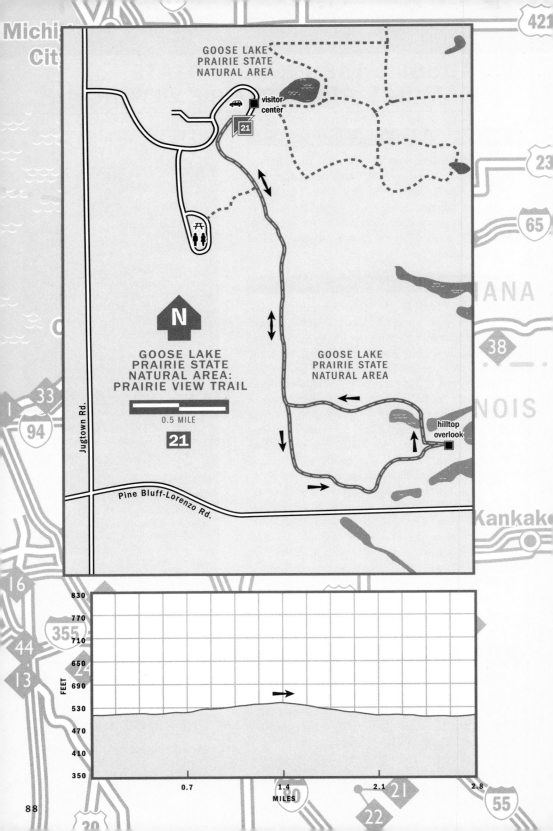

was likely the first mass producer of pottery in the state. Local history buffs will enjoy a recently added exhibit in the visitor center highlighting Jugtown Pottery Works, which started in 1856 and lasted for about 10 years in what is now the southwest corner of the park.

Another recently added exhibit in the visitor center features the plant and animal fossils from 300 million years ago that have been dug up at a mining operation at Mazon Creek, south of the park. One specimen—which happens to be the state fossil of Illinois—shows the imprint of a creature known as the Tully monster, which was about five-inches-long and worm-like, with unusual eyestalks and a long snout that ended in a claw with eight sharp teeth. Tully-monster fossils have only been found in Illinois, primarily around Mazon Creek.

Start the hike on the south side of the visitor-center parking lot. If the gate for the trail is closed, hikers are still invited to venture forth, as long as they understand that several sections could be flooded with a few inches of water. At 0.3 miles into the hike, a short trail branches on the right to the Prairie Grove Picnic Area. Beyond the trail to the picnic area, the terrain begins to roll very gently. During the warmer months, you'll see red-wing blackbirds perched on the tallgrasses and swallows swooping overhead. With the absence of trees, it doesn't appear that deer have many places to hide on the prairie. Keep alert, however, and you'll see how quickly they can disappear into the stands of bushes and taller grasses.

At 0.8 miles, stay right at the fork to begin a 1.2-mile loop. The trail swings left alongside Pine Bluff–Lorenzo Road, and then curves left again before arriving at a spur trail on the right heading up a 40-foot hill. While it seems like an insignificant mound on the prairie, the view from the top is striking. Along with several ponds at the base of the hill, you can see the visitor center 1 mile north, as well as a scattering of ponds and marshes east of the visitor center. Also, the Dresden Nuclear Power Plant is visible 3.4 miles to the northeast, and another power plant, the Midwest Collins Generating Station, is visible 2.1 miles to the west.

Coming down from the hill, the path continues between two ponds, and then passes a sign describing the park's efforts at restoring the area from coal mining by lowering the soil's acidity. After the sign, stay to the left. If the weather has been wet, expect to see a couple inches of water on the trail for about 15 yards or so. As the trail moves to drier ground, you'll pass a big cattail marsh on the right. Stay to the right at the fork, and then follow the trail for 0.8 miles back to the parking lot.

▶ NEARBY ACTIVITIES

Adjacent to Goose Lake Prairie is Heidicke State Fish and Wildlife Area, a 2,000-acre cooling pond for Midwest Collins Generating Station. During fishing season, you can walk along the dikes accessible on the east side of the lake. Heidicke Lake hosts a variety of water birds, and is a reliable spot for seeing bald eagles, particularly during winter. The boat ramp north of the entrance to Goose Lake Prairie has a concession stand that sells bait and food and rents boats and motors. To get to the east side of the lake, take Jugtown Road to Pine Bluff–Lorenzo Road and turn left (east). Turn left (north) on Dresden Road and follow signs for the lake.

GOOSE LAKE PRAIRIE STATE NATURAL AREA: TALLGRASS TRAIL

KEY AT-A-GLANCE INFORMATION

LENGTH: 2.4 miles

CONFIGURATION: Loop

DIFFICULTY: Easy

SCENERY: Tallgrass prairie, marshes, ponds, historic cabin, observation deck

EXPOSURE: Completely exposed

SURFACE: Mowed grass

HIKING TIME: 1.25 hours

ACCESS: The park is open from sunrise to sunset; the visitor center is open 10 a.m.–4 p.m.

FACILITIES: Restrooms, picnic areas, a beverage vending machine, and a visitor center with exhibits

MAPS: Park map usually available outside visitor center; USGS topo Coal City, IL

SPECIAL COMMENTS: Pets must be leashed; contact the visitor center at (815) 942-2899. For more hiking in this area, see profile 21 (page 87).

UTM Trailhead Coordinates for Goose Lake Prairie State Natural Area: Tallgrass Trail

UTM Zone (NAD27) 16T

Easting 389856

Northing 4579427

IN BRIEF

While making your way through this hypnotic tallgrass prairie, you'll skirt the edges of several marshes and ponds active with birds. For those interested in improving their prairie-plant identification skills, this hike offers a nice variety of grasses and flowers, as well as some interpretive signs to get you started. Near the end of the hike, the trail passes a reconstructed version of one of the earliest log homes in the county.

DESCRIPTION

There's a good reason why Illinois holds the position as the nation's top producer of soybeans and the second largest producer of corn—it's the sea of grass that once dominated the state. It wasn't just any grass that made the soil so fertile, but big, hearty, tallgrasses like big bluestem, Indian grass, and prairie cordgrass. Thousands of years of these grasses rotting on the ground created rich, dark soil more fertile than other grasslands farther west. Along with being more fertile, many people find tallgrass prairies the most dramatic type of grassland. This is especially true during mid- to late summer, when 10-foot-high grasses and an abundance of flowers decorate these vast spaces.

Unfortunately, Illinois's agricultural dominance has come at a cost. With only 0.5 percent of the state's surface area remaining as tallgrass prairie, it seems the Prairie State nickname is now a misnomer.

DIRECTIONS

From Chicago, take I-90/I-94 south to I-55. Follow I-55 south for 51 miles until reaching Exit 240. Take Pine Bluff–Lorenzo Road to the right (west) for 2.9 miles. Turn right (north) at the sign for Goose Lake Prairie State Natural Area (North Jugtown Road). Proceed ahead for 1 mile and then turn right (east) at the sign for the visitor center.

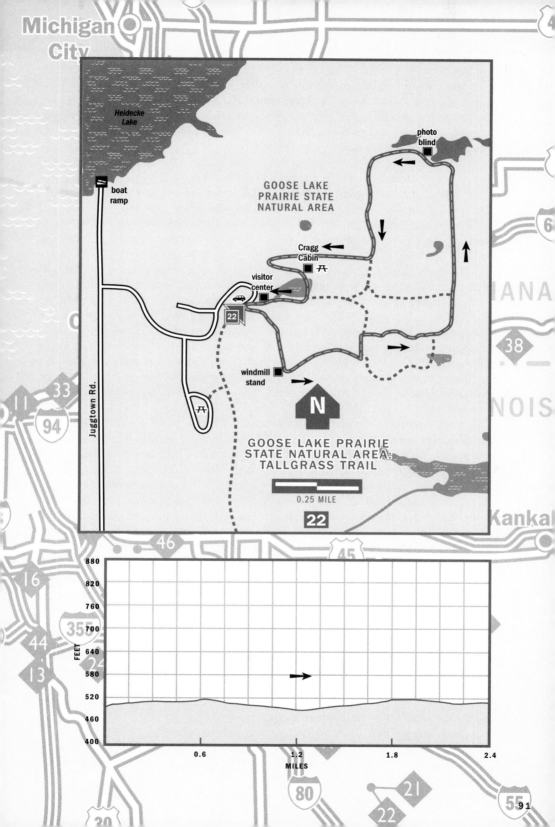

Michigan City

Heidecke Lake

boat ramp

GOOSE LAKE PRAIRIE STATE NATURAL AREA

photo blind

Cragg Cabin

visitor center

Juggtown Rd.

22

windmill stand

N

GOOSE LAKE PRAIRIE STATE NATURAL AREA: TALLGRASS TRAIL

0.25 MILE

22

IANA

NOIS

Kankak

FEET

880
820
760
700
640
580
520
460
400

0.6   1.2   1.8   2.4

MILES

One of the best places to experience the dramatic beauty of these big open grasslands and gain a better understanding of how they function is within the Chicago region. As the largest tract of tallgrass prairie in the state, Goose Lake Prairie State Natural Area gives visitors a taste of what it looked like when grassland covered two-thirds of the Prairie State.

Before starting the hike behind the visitor center, take in the view from the observation platform attached to the back of the building. If it's July, the prairie will be exploding with wildflowers of all shades; if it's September, goldenrod and compass plants will form a yellow carpet over the landscape. A few miles to the northeast, you'll see the Dresden Nuclear Power Plant (as you're hiking, you'll also notice another power plant, the Midwest Collins Generating Station, a couple miles to the west).

From the mapboard at the bottom of the platform's ramp, take the mowed trail on the right winding through the prairie. In the wet areas, you'll see Indian grass, prairie cordgrass, and sedge grasses. Big bluestem grass—perhaps the most common of tallgrass prairie plants—lines the trail. Sometimes called "turkey foot" for the arrangement of its seed heads, big bluestem grows most attractively in the late summer, when it reaches heights up to 10 feet and takes on various colors, from steely gray to wine red to muted lavender. In earlier times, livestock happily munched on big bluestem. At 0.2 miles into the hike, you'll see evidence of the grazing that once took place here in the old windmill stand that pumped water out of the ground for the livestock.

After passing a couple of smaller, cattail-fringed marshes—one with open water—a sign indicates that the trail heading to the right is closed. You can still proceed ahead, but must turn back once you reach the marsh because a bridge is in need of repair. Taking the next right brings you to the other side of the marsh, where a rebuilt covered wagon with a bench inside is situated on a slight rise above the open water. Given the scarcity of trees near the pond, the wagon's canopy provides a welcome shady spot when the sun is hot overhead. In the vicinity of this marsh, I've seen great blue herons, a kingfisher, and a foot-long snapping turtle that became utterly peeved when I attempted to touch its shell.

From the pond, stay to the right as you start the large rectangular loop. During the summer, tall compass plants grow on this section of trail, as well as small crab apple trees, and an attractive grass called Canada wild rye, which has a large, bushy, nodding seed head. Also, black-willow shrubs grow near the patches of open water on the left side of the trail. As the path curves left, a cattail marsh with open water appears on the right. The enclosed photo blind provides benches and small viewing doors that allow you to discreetly observe action in the marsh. After passing another marsh on the right, look for obedient plants during late summer (lavender, tubular flowers lined up on the stalk). This northern section of the park is dominated by Indian grass, which is often hard to identify until August, when the reddish-brown tassels and small yellow stamens come into bloom.

Finishing up the rectangular loop, turn right on the gravel trail, which leads along the backside of the Cragg Cabin, a replica of one of the first homes in Grundy County. The next left takes you to the cabin. Originally built by the Cragg family in

1830, south of the park along the Mazon River, the cabin became a stopover for travelers and for cowboys who herded cattle from St. Louis to the stockyards of Chicago. The cabin, which sits at the edge of this pleasant pond bordered by a quaking aspen and willows, has been reconstructed a couple of times, most recently in 1980 by the Youth Conservation Corps. The small interior of the cabin is laid out much like it would have been 175 years ago, with a bed frame, a fireplace, and a ladder leading up to a second-floor loft. Stay to the right after the cabin, and you'll hike along the edge of the pond back to the visitor center.

▶ NEARBY ACTIVITIES

Not far from Goose Lake Prairie, the town of Morris hosts Gebhard Woods State Park, a small but pleasant park that adjoins a stretch of the Illinois and Michigan Canal Trail. Inside the park, the 0.8-mile Nettle Creek Nature Trail runs along the winding creek and through stands of maple, cottonwoods, and sycamores. On the east side of the park, toward downtown Morris, is an old stone aqueduct where the I&M Canal flows over Nettle Creek. Morris, the Grundy county seat situated on the north bank of the Illinois River, was one of many towns that grew up alongside the I&M Canal. To reach Gebhard Woods from Goose Lake Prairie, take Pine Bluff Road to the right (west) for 5 miles to IL 47. Turn right (north) on IL 47 and continue over the river and into Morris, turning left (west) on County Road 2 (West Jefferson Street). Proceed for 0.9 miles and turn left (south) on Ottawa Street. The park is just ahead on the left.

GRAND KANKAKEE MARSH COUNTY PARK HIKE

KEY AT-A-GLANCE INFORMATION

LENGTH: 7.3 miles

CONFIGURATION: Loop with another attached loop

DIFFICULTY: Moderate to difficult for the length

SCENERY: Kankakee River, an enormous marsh, a maze of drainage ditches, bottomland forest, and an abundance of birds

EXPOSURE: Primarily shaded

SURFACE: Sandy two-track road, mowed grass

HIKING TIME: 3 hours

ACCESS: September–January, 7 a.m.–dusk

FACILITIES: Pit toilet, mapboard, drinking water, boat launch

MAPS: USGS topos Shelby, IN, and Demott, IN; map posted on board near restrooms

SPECIAL COMMENTS: The two-track roads that this hike follows are for authorized vehicles only. Once you get away from the fishing spots and boat launch, expect to have this park all to yourself. For more information, call (219) 552-9614. For another great hike through the Kankakee Marshes, see the LaSalle Fish and Wildlife Loop on page 150.

UTM Trailhead Coordinates for Grand Kankakee Marsh County Park Hike

UTM Zone (NAD27)   16T

Easting   476892

Northing   4562935

▶ IN BRIEF

Little known outside of its immediate area, Grand Kankakee Marsh County Park is huge, quiet, and persistently charming. The first part of this hike runs alongside the Kankakee River and through a vast marshland. The return trip takes you through a prairie and along the extensive network of drainage ditches dug when the park was all farmed.

▶ DESCRIPTION

At one time, the Kankakee River made 2,000 bends as it traveled from its source near South Bend, Indiana, to the Illinois state line. The river slowly meandered through an area roughly 75-miles long and 30-miles wide known as the Grand Kankakee Marsh. After farming interests straightened and channelized the Kankakee, the river's length dropped from 240 miles to 85 miles. The next step in making the land suitable for farming involved draining the enormous marshland through an elaborate system of ditches. After all the work of draining the marshes, farmers discovered that swaths of the former marsh were still terrible for farming. Crops drowned in wet years and burned out in dry years. Some of these tracts of marginal farmland were then set aside as nature refuges.

▶ DIRECTIONS

Driving from Chicago, take I-90/I-94 south until reaching the Chicago Skyway (I-90), Exit 59A. After traveling 23.7 miles southeast on the Skyway, take Exit 17 to I-65. Proceed south on I-65 for 21 miles until reaching Exit 240. Follow Route 2 for 1.2 miles to the left (east), and then follow Clay Street (Range Line Road) to the right (south) for 6 miles. The parking area is on the right, just before the old iron bridge over the Kankakee River.

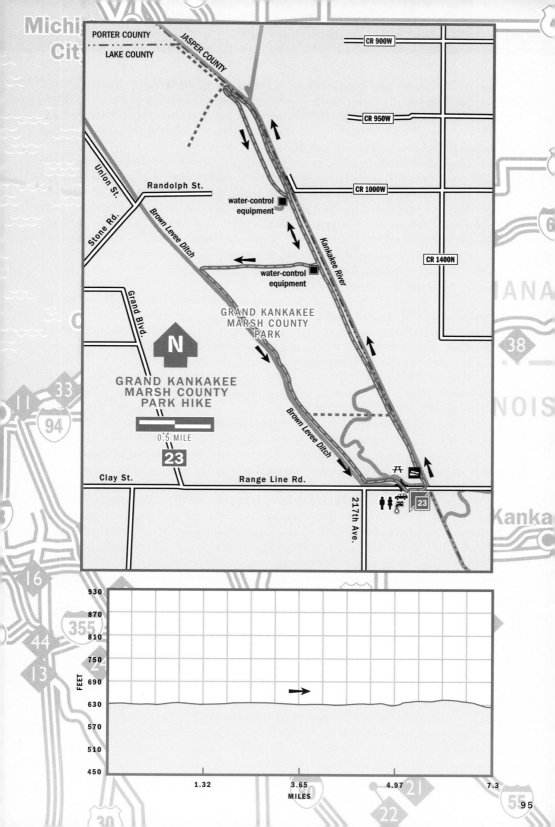

PORTER COUNTY
LAKE COUNTY

JASPER COUNTY

CR 900W

CR 950W

Randolph St.

CR 1000W

water-control
equipment

Union St.

Stone Rd.

Brown Levee Ditch

CR 1400N

Kankakee River

water-control
equipment

Grand Blvd.

**GRAND KANKAKEE
MARSH COUNTY
PARK**

N

**GRAND KANKAKEE
MARSH COUNTY
PARK HIKE**

0.5 MILE

23

Brown Levee Ditch

Clay St.

Range Line Rd.

217th Ave.

23

Kanka

Michigan City

On this hike, you'll get a chance to tour some of the wetlands that have been restored along the Kankakee River, as well as an extensive system of ditches and levees. Since two-track roads accompany many of these ditches, the 1,900-acre park offers plenty of opportunities for exploration along established routes—just bring your map and compass or GPS device.

Start the hike by heading to the right from the parking lot along Range Line Road toward the one-lane iron bridge over the Kankakee River. Just before the bridge, turn left on the dirt road that runs alongside the river toward the boat launch. The boat launch's gravel parking lot can be a busy place on summer afternoons, with fishermen showing off stringers of smallmouth and largemouth bass, walleye, bluegill, and pickerel. On the other side of the parking lot, pass through the gate and follow the sandy two-track road running along the levee. On the left, the bottomland forest contains patches of dense shrubs, occasional marshy spots, and thick stands of maple, cottonwood, and quaking aspen.

At 0.4 miles into the hike, a small pipeline is suspended with cables across the river between the wooded banks. Plenty of openings along the bank provide good views of the river and the opposite shore. You may notice that the two sides of the river look similar, each with a trail running on top of a levee. In spots on the other side of the river, small rocks reinforce the riverbank to prevent erosion. At the river's edge—about 15 feet below the level of the trail—look for painted and softshell turtles basking on logs (painted turtles have dark, smooth, rounded shells; softshells are flatter and larger with lighter coloring).

Keep straight ahead when you encounter a two-track road on the left at 0.6 miles into the hike. Farther ahead, also on the left, you'll see occasional patches of agricultural land alternating with more bottomland forest and marshy areas. At 1.7 miles, the trail passes some water-control devices that pump water back and forth between two drainage ditches and the river. Remember this spot: after taking a loop through a marsh ahead, you'll return here and head away from the river.

At 2.3 miles into the hike, you'll see more pumps and pipes, as well as the beginning of a restored portion of the Grand Kankakee Marsh. Keeping straight ahead on the levee for now, you'll begin to see small houses, some with homemade river docks, sprouting up on the opposite bank of the river. At 3.1 miles into the hike, take a sharp turn at the two-track road on the left for a hike through an expansive marsh. Bring your field glasses to see herons, ducks, and geese among fields of lush marsh grass and the scattered stands of cattails. Also, look for hawks perched in the cottonwoods and sand willows to the left. Far in the distance across the marsh, a farm serves as a reminder of this land's agricultural history.

Once you return to the river levee, follow the trail for 0.6 miles back to the first set of water-control devices you passed earlier. Here, take the middle trail away from the river. On this section of the hike, there's a ditch on each side of the two-track for the first half mile. After the ditch on the left cuts away, a picturesque tallgrass prairie develops on the left, and an agricultural field is visible on the right through the trees—again with the farm in the distance. Sections of this trail are bordered by thick stands of shrubs; watch out for stinging nettles hanging in your path (the two- to four-foot plants have heart-shaped, coarsely toothed leaves).

Reaching the Brown Levee Ditch at 5.2 miles into the hike, turn left and continue along another levee. Look for water birds hanging out in the lily pads and perched on occasional logs on the edge of the bank. While the prairie continues on the left, another levee appears on the other side of the ditch, as well as thick stands of cottonwood trees. Nearly a mile after the last turn, there's a hedgerow and the end of a ditch on the left, followed by a bridge over the ditch on the right. Across the bridge are short grain silos and a windmill with the blades removed. As you pass several side trails on the left, you'll also pass more ditches and hedgerows.

At 7 miles into the hike, you'll know you're getting close to the end when the trail becomes mowed turf. With open water on both sides of you, the trail curves back toward the Kankakee River. Pass a few picnic tables and possibly a few fishermen on your way to the bridge that leads toward the parking lot.

GREENE VALLEY FOREST PRESERVE LOOP

KEY AT-A-GLANCE INFORMATION

LENGTH: 4 miles

CONFIGURATION: Loop

DIFFICULTY: Easy

SCENERY: Woodland, oak savannas, grassland, stream crossings, and forested floodplain

EXPOSURE: Mostly exposed

SURFACE: Crushed limestone

HIKING TIME: 1.5–2 hours

ACCESS: 1 hour after sunrise to 1 hour after sunset

FACILITIES: Restrooms, benches, water

MAPS: Maps available at trailhead; USGS topo Romeoville, IL

TRAFFIC: Except at peak times on the weekends, Greene Valley is rarely busy. Consider hiking one of the spurs if you're looking for more solitude.

SPECIAL COMMENTS: This is a multiuse trail. Watch for cyclists and give equestrians right-of-way. Use caution when crossing the roads.

UTM Trailhead Coordinates for
Greene Valley Forest Preserve Loop

UTM Zone (NAD27)   16T

Easting   409499

Northing   4620801

IN BRIEF

At Greene Valley Forest Preserve, you'll find groves of stately oaks, quiet twisting streams, and wide-open swaths of grassland—very likely with a red-tailed hawk or two nearby, waiting for their prey.

DESCRIPTION

In 1835, two years before Chicago was incorporated as a city, the first members of the Greene family settled on land that's now part of the Greene Valley Forest Preserve. Like many other early residents of DuPage County, wheat fields and dairy cows were the Greene's bread and butter. In 1969, the county bought a portion of the Greenes's land, added it to existing holdings, and transformed it into a forest preserve named after the family. Some of the family's original structures, including a house built in 1841, remain on the corner of Greene and Hobson roads.

Though knowing the human history gives you a better sense of this place, it's not the star attraction here. Instead, what grabs you are spacious prairies, sprawling floodplains, and dappled savannas. These attractions may seem especially precious because they're surrounded by houses and streets humming with activity.

From the parking lot, start the hike by taking the trail on the left that cuts through open

DIRECTIONS

From Chicago, take I-290 west to I-88. Follow I-88 for 10.5 miles until reaching IL 53. Take IL 53 south for 0.2 miles, turning right (west) on 75th Street (County Road 33). Proceed along 75th Street for a half mile, and then turn left (south) on Greene Road, following it for another half mile. Turn right (west) on 79th Street and follow it for 0.4 miles until reaching Thunderbird Road on the left. The parking lot is 0.6 miles ahead, at the end of Thunderbird Road.

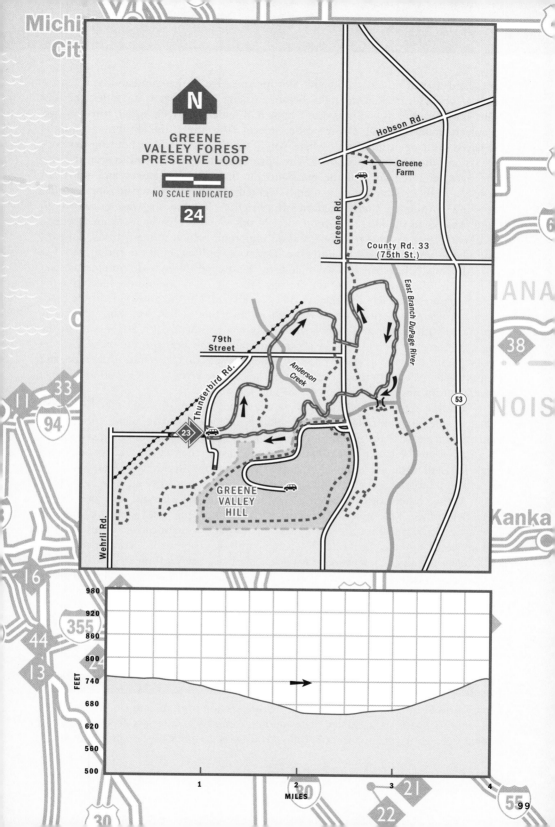

N

GREENE
VALLEY FOREST
PRESERVE LOOP

NO SCALE INDICATED

24

Michigan City

Greene Farm

Hobson Rd.

Greene Rd.

County Rd. 33
(75th St.)

East Branch DuPage River

79th Street

Anderson Creek

Thunderbird Rd.

23

53

Wehrli Rd.

GREENE VALLEY HILL

Kanka

FEET

980
920
860
800
740
680
620
560
500

1   2   3   4
MILES

grassland toward an oak woodland. Skirting the edge of the woodland, you'll soon pass a connector trail on the right. Before crossing 79th Street at 0.7 miles, the trail dips and then rises as you pass over a branch of Anderson Creek, which runs through a culvert under the trail. On the other side of 79th Street, the shrubby savanna is replaced with open grassland, where you'll see the encroaching housing developments and the nearby power lines. The open space also allows you to scan the sky, the trees, and the edge of the grassland for the red-tailed hawks and American kestrels, both of which are frequently sighted within the preserve. After another crossing of Anderson Creek, the trail swings right as it brushes against an oak woodland. Thanks to the long-term protection of this wooded area by its former owners, local naturalists say this tract serves as an important habitat to many birds, animals, and plants, and provides an impressive display of wildflowers in the spring.

Leaving behind the oak woodland, the landscape starts to slump more noticeably toward the East Branch of the DuPage River. At 1.4 miles into the hike, take the trail junction to the left and then cross Greene Road. On the other side of the road, turn left again, and head north through an area that is flat, wet, and generously sprinkled with poplar and sumac shrubs. As you approach 75th Street, stay to the right, passing a spur path that heads toward the Greene farm and the picnic shelters at the north end of the forest preserve. After the junction, the trail turns right and starts to run parallel to the East Branch of the Dupage River, which is 100 to 150 feet to the left through the stands of shrubs and the woods.

On the right side of this trail, you'll notice plenty of spots that have been cleared through controlled burnings, which removes invasive plant species and encourages native plant growth. As the trail moves farther away from the river, there's a junction on the left (if you'd like to see the East Branch of the DuPage, take this trail left and turn left again after crossing Anderson Creek). Continuing straight ahead, you'll pass another trail junction on the right before crossing Greene Road.

On the other side of Greene Road, you'll see a parking lot and restrooms on the left. Beyond the parking lot, stay to the left at the junction and follow the trail as it squiggles its way over Anderson Creek and through a mature oak woodland. Just south, you can't miss the former 200-acre landfill that is now the second-highest spot in DuPage County, 980 feet above sea level. Used as a landfill from 1974 to 1996, the hill is now planted with native grasses and shrubs, and offers some limited recreation. On weekends, spring through fall, visitors can drive to the top and hike a trail around the base of the hill (hours are 11 a.m.–6 p.m.).

As the landscape becomes more rolling, you'll pass a small ravine on the right, and cross over a few drainage culverts. Soon you'll pass a connector trail on the right, and then arrive back at the parking lot.

▶ NEARBY ACTIVITIES

Just south of the forest preserve, near the intersection of IL 53 and County Route 67 (Boughton Road), is a cluster of restaurants—mostly of the fast food variety. For some Chicago flavor, stop in at Portillo's Hot Dogs at 148 West Boughton Road.

ILLINOIS BEACH STATE PARK:
DEAD RIVER LOOP

IN BRIEF

After a ramble along the shore of the Dead River, this trail brings you through some of the only sand dunes left in the state of Illinois. Halfway through the hike, take a break on a surprisingly quiet stretch of Lake Michigan beach.

DESCRIPTION

While it's true that Illinois Beach State Park is one of the most popular beaches in the region, it's also true that visitors rarely seem to step away from the main beach and picnic area, leaving the trails and the out-of-the-way beach on this hike surprisingly quiet. The park consists of two separate areas, referred to as the northern unit and southern unit. The southern unit, where this hike takes place, is the larger section, with more amenities, such as a campground, a store, and even a resort and conference center.

After stopping at the nature center for a park map, catch the beginning of Dead River Trail near the far end of the parking lot, on the same side of the lot as the nature center. After hiking 0.2 miles through oak savanna, the trail meets up with the marshy waterway known as the Dead River. If you have the impression that this looks more like a long pond than a river, you're right; this river only flows during certain times of the year when the water levels rise. Most of the year a sandbar blocks the mouth at Lake Michigan, thus

KEY AT-A-GLANCE INFORMATION

LENGTH: 2.1 miles

CONFIGURATION: Loop, with a spur leading to the beach

DIFFICULTY: Easy

SCENERY: River, marshes, savanna, beach, dunes, Lake Michigan

EXPOSURE: Mostly exposed

SURFACE: Dirt, sand

HIKING TIME: 1 hour

ACCESS: Sunrise–8 p.m.

FACILITIES: Restrooms, water

MAPS: Maps available at the nature center; USGS topo Zion, IL

SPECIAL COMMENTS: Pets must be leashed. Large crowds descend upon the park in May for an annual RV show and in late July/early August for the National Jet Ski Championships. Call the park at (847) 662-4811 for exact dates.

If you're looking for a picnic area and a lively—sometimes crowded—stretch of beach, head back out on the main park road from the visitor center, take a right, and continue past the hotel on the right. North of the picnic area is the park's campground, offering 244 sites, many of which are fairly close to the beach.

DIRECTIONS

Follow I-90/I-94 northwest from Chicago. Stay on I-94 as it breaks off, and follow it north for 35 miles. Exit at Grand Avenue (IL 132) and go east for 3.5 miles. Then turn left (north) on Green Bay Road (IL 131). Proceed north 4 miles before turning right (east) on Wadsworth Road. Follow Wadsworth Road for 3 miles into the park. Turn right at the sign for the nature center.

UTM Trailhead Coordinates for Illinois Beach State Park: Dead River Loop

UTM Zone (NAD27) 16T

Easting 433571

Northing 4696835

to picnic
areas

BIKE TRL.

Illinois Beach
Resort and
Conference
Center

park road

nature
center

25

viewing
platform

DEAD RIVER TRL.

DUNE TRL.

DEAD RIVER TRL.

DUNE TRL.

Dead River

N

ILLINOIS BEACH
STATE PARK:
DEAD RIVER LOOP

0.25 MILE

25

Dead
Lake

spur to
the
beach

Dead River
sandbar

880
820
760
700
640
580
520
460
400

FEET

0.52   1.05   1.57   2.1

MILES

keeping the water contained. Another 0.2 miles ahead is a platform overlooking the river and the expansive wetland. Some geologists have said the once-sluggish Chicago River looked much like the Dead River in presettlement times.

While the water here may be at a standstill, the environment certainly is not. During the spring, summer, and into fall, the trail hosts a variety of wildflowers, including milkweeds, shooting stars, and genetians. You're likely to see some water birds in the water; and, if visiting during the winter after snow has fallen, you're likely to see a network of animal tracks on the ice.

Shortly after passing a kitchen stove–sized boulder in the middle of the stream, the trail turns toward Lake Michigan and the scenery starts to change. At 0.7 miles, turn right at the junction. Leaving the wooded stream bank and oak savanna, you'll enter a washboard landscape made of sand. Since the prevailing winds blow the sand out to the lake, these are low dunes with gentle slopes. Each line of dunes was a previous shoreline for Lake Michigan during the past few thousand years. Here and there the dunes are topped with scrawny oak trees that struggle to gather nutrients from the sandy ground. In all, an impressive 650 species of plants have been identified in the south unit of the park. Some of the low creeping plants to look for among the dunes are the bearberry, with small paddle-shaped leaves and little egg-shaped white flowers, and the Waukegan juniper, an evergreen with whitish berries that turn purple in the winter.

The lake will come into view near the junction at 1.2 miles into the hike. Continue straight ahead to a stretch of beach where you're likely to encounter few people, even on hot summer days. For a short beach stroll, walk 0.2 miles to the right to see the sandbar at the mouth of the Dead River. One-and-a-half miles to the south you'll see the Commonwealth Edison coal-fired generating plant, and 2.5 miles to the north is the Zion nuclear power plant, which provides electricity for much of the Chicago area. Dedicated beach ramblers can follow the beach north for 0.7 miles to catch the trail back to the parking lot.

To continue on the hiking route, head back up to the main trail and take a right. While walking parallel to the lake, one will see water between the swells of sand. At the base of the mounds, look for miniature blowouts where the wind has scoured away the plants and created hollow spots. As the trail bends inland, the oak trees grow larger and the landscape becomes blanketed in grasses typical of savannas and prairies. At 1.9 miles into the hike, turn left at the junction, and then pass a large marsh on the right before following a boardwalk for 30 yards over a shallow dune pond. From the boardwalk, the parking lot is a short distance straight ahead.

▶ NEARBY ACTIVITIES

Several more miles of hiking trails can be found in the northern unit of Illinois Beach State Park. To reach the northern unit, leave the park the way you entered via Wadsworth Road. After the train tracks, turn right (north) on Sheridan Road. Turn right (east) on 17th Street and stay to the left. Pick up the trail near the circle turnaround at the end of the road.

INDIANA DUNES NATIONAL LAKESHORE: BAILLY/CHELLBERG HIKE

KEY AT-A-GLANCE INFORMATION

LENGTH: 3.3 miles

CONFIGURATION: Combo

DIFFICULTY: Easy

SCENERY: Bottomland forest, marshland, oak woodland, Little Calumet River, a nineteenth-century working farm, and an early trader's homestead

EXPOSURE: All shaded, unless you take the alternate route through the prairie

SURFACE: Dirt

HIKING TIME: 2 hours

ACCESS: 8 a.m.–sunset

FACILITIES: Picnic tables and shelters, visitor center, restrooms

MAPS: Maps available at the mapboard and in the visitor center; USGS topo Chesterton, IN

SPECIAL COMMENTS: The Bailly/Chellberg Visitor Center is open Memorial Day–Labor Day, 11 a.m.–4:30 p.m. It's also open on weekends March–Memorial Day and Labor Day until the end of October, 11 a.m.–4:30 p.m. The Chellberg Farmhouse and the Bailly Homestead are open May–October on Sundays.

UTM Trailhead Coordinates for Indiana Dunes National Lakeshore: Bailly/Chellberg Hike

UTM Zone (NAD27)   16T

Easting   492570

Northing   4607900

▶ IN BRIEF

Get a glimpse of early settlement life in northwestern Indiana by touring the homesteads of two frontier families. You'll also see wooded ravines, rich bottomland forest that grows beside the Little Calumet River, and a curious old cemetery.

▶ DESCRIPTION

In 1874, ten years after immigrating from Sweden, Anders and Johanna Chellberg were farming 80 acres within a growing Swedish community in northwest Indiana. Over the years, three generations of Chellbergs made their living on the farm growing wheat, oats, corn, rye, and keeping farm animals. The Chellbergs farmed the land until 1972, when the National Park Service bought the property. To preserve the past, the park service continues operating this typical northwest Indiana farm in the same manner that the Chellbergs operated it in the late 1800s.

The hike starts 100 yards south of the farm, at the backside of the visitor center, where you'll follow the trail to the right as it runs along the top of a 40-foot wooded ravine. The first farm building you'll pass is the maple-sugar house, followed by a windmill with a pump house, a harness shop, a corncrib, a chicken house, the restored brick farmhouse built in 1885, and the large 100-year-old barn. Kids will enjoy the roaming chickens, the horses in the barn, and the hogs in the pen beyond the barn. Inside the farmhouse, visitors

▶ DIRECTIONS

From Chicago, take I-90/I-94 south until reaching the Chicago Skyway (I-90), Exit 59A. After traveling 29 miles southeast on the Skyway and the toll road, take Exit 21 to I-94. Follow I-94 east for 7 miles until reaching Exit 22B. Follow US 20 (Melton Road) for 4.1 miles. The entrance to the visitor center parking lot is on the left.

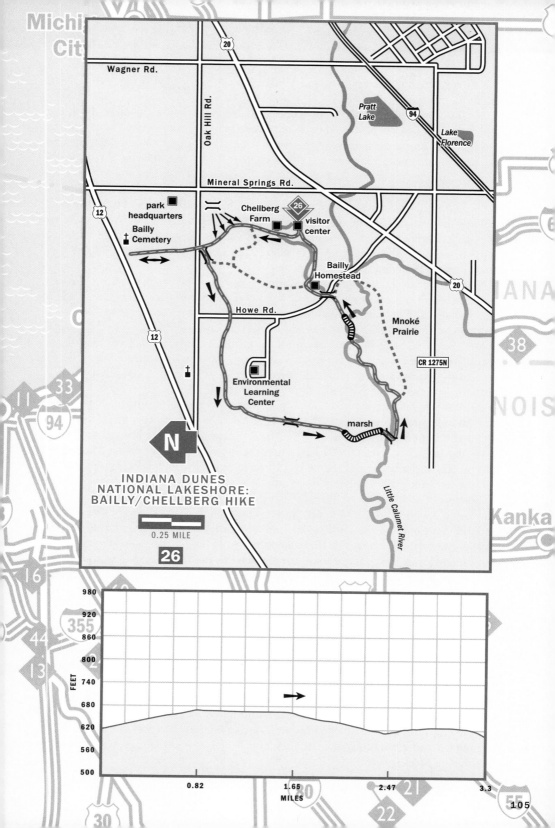

Wagner Rd.

Michi...
Cit...

Oak Hill Rd.

20

94

Pratt Lake

Lake Florence

Mineral Springs Rd.

12

park headquarters

Bailly Cemetery

Chellberg Farm

26

visitor center

Bailly Homestead

20

INANA

Howe Rd.

Mnoké Prairie

CR 1275N

38

Environmental Learning Center

N

INDIANA DUNES NATIONAL LAKESHORE: BAILLY/CHELLBERG HIKE

0.25 MILE

26

marsh

Little Calumet River

NOIS

Kanka

33

94

16

44

13

105

980
920
860
800
740
680
620
560
500

FEET

0.82   1.65   2.47   3.3
MILES

355

42

30

can tour the parlor, the kitchen, and a bedroom as they looked in the early days of the farm.

Continuing on the trail, cross a bridge and then follow a set of steps down into a pleasant wooded ravine carved by a running stream. Crossing several more bridges, the trail runs along the bottom of the ravine for a short stretch until a flight of stairs brings you back up to flat ground. Cross another bridge and then turn right at the junction for the out-and-back trail to the Bailly Cemetery. On the way to the cemetery, cross Oak Hill Road and a crushed-gravel trail, and then hike for 0.3 miles through bottomland forest. The cemetery—a walled-in earthen area built on a small hilltop—has a tomb-like quality to it. The wall was built in 1885 on what archeologists have surmised to be an existing cemetery: bones thought to predate European settlement have been uncovered at this site. After circling the cemetery, retrace your steps back to the main trail.

Back on the main trail, cross a bridge and then stay to the right at the next junction. Soon the trail crosses Howe Road and a crushed-gravel trail that leads to the Indiana Dunes Environmental Learning Center—a frequent stop for school groups visiting the dunes. After passing a spur trail on the left leading to the learning center, you'll see the building on the left through stands of hickory, maple, and locust trees. After passing between a few big white oaks on both sides of the trail, the trail turns left toward the Little Calumet River. From here, the woodland becomes shrubby savanna as the trail runs through a few small ravines.

At 1.9 miles into the hike, a 0.2-mile boardwalk carries you through a wet bottomland forest and a marshland, and ends at a scenic spot where a metal footbridge spans the Little Calumet. Stay to the left at a junction 0.2 miles beyond the bridge. After the trail curves left, you'll have sporadic views of the river, marshy areas, and the cattails at the bottom of the ravine. If the river level is high from rain or meltwater, the riverside path will likely be muddy or even flooded. In this case, you'll want to turn right at the sign for the 120-acre Mnoké Prairie. (The 0.6-mile trail winds through a delightful restored prairie and a short stretch of woodland before reaching a parking area. From the parking area, descend the hill, and then stay to the left, heading toward the bridge on Howe Road.) If you stay on the riverside trail, you'll have many lovely views above the Little Calumet as the trail zigs and zags at the top of the 30- to 40-foot ravines. In these riverside areas, groundcover plants are scarce due to the dense, leafy canopy above. When the trail drops down beside the river, you'll cross a couple of boardwalks over intermittent streams, and soon emerge on Howe Road, where you'll turn left and cross the bridge.

On the other side of the bridge, immediately turn right on the brick road that heads up the short hill to the Bailly Homestead. Montreal-born Honore Gratien Joseph Bailly de Messein was one of the first settlers in northwest Indiana when he arrived in 1822 to start a trading post. Well suited for trading due to the river and the intersection of two major Indian trails, Bailly exchanged blankets, guns, and cooking pots for skins of beaver, muskrat, and mink. As animals became scarce and the trading slowed, Bailly turned his attention to operating a local tavern and establishing a small community named after him, which was on land now occupied by Bethlehem Steel.

On the right is the restored wooden frame house built by the Bailly family in 1835. While Bailly died before construction of the house was finished, his family occupied the house until 1917. Over the years, the six-bedroom house has been a restaurant, an antique shop, and a retreat for an order of Catholic nuns. The ground floor of the house—unfurnished except for a beautiful fireplace mantle built by a local craftsperson—is open to the public on Sundays during the summer. Also on the property are a two-story cabin that served as employee's quarters, a small brick house, a chapel, and a reconstructed fur-trading cabin.

Beyond the house and the cabins, the path on the left, which leads to the Bailly Cemetery, is said to be part of an old Indian trail. The hike continues on the right, just beyond the wigwam frame and the National Historic Marker plaque. From the Bailly Homestead, it's a short woodland hike back to the visitor center.

▶ NEARBY ACTIVITIES

Just a few miles away, historic downtown Chesterton offers a couple of good dining options. Lucrezia Café at 428 South Calumet Road, (219) 926-5829, offers authentic Italian cuisine, and Popolano's Restaurant at 225 South Calumet Road, (219) 926-5552, has good family fare. To reach Chesterton from the visitor-center parking lot, turn right (south) on North Mineral Springs Road, turn left (east) on West Beam Street, and then turn right (south) on Sherman Avenue (Wagner Road), which quickly turns into North Jackson Boulevard. Turn left (east) on Broadway Avenue and then turn right (south) on South Calumet Road.

INDIANA DUNES NATIONAL LAKESHORE: COWLES BOG TRAIL

KEY AT-A-GLANCE INFORMATION

LENGTH: 4 miles

CONFIGURATION: Loop

DIFFICULTY: Moderate

SCENERY: Dunes, beach, marshes, woods, and savannas

EXPOSURE: Shady except for 0.2 miles along the beach

SURFACE: Dirt, sand

HIKING TIME: 1.5–2 hours

ACCESS: 6 a.m.–sunset

FACILITIES: Parking, restrooms

MAPS: Park maps available at trail board; USGS topo Dune Acres, IN

SPECIAL COMMENTS: If the weather is agreeable, consider a picnic at the beach. Learn more about the Indiana Dunes National Lakeshore by visiting www.nps.gov/indu.

UTM Trailhead Coordinates for Indiana Dunes National Lakeshore: Cowles Bog Trail

UTM Zone (NAD27)   16T

Easting   492818

Northing   4610591

IN BRIEF

The Cowles Bog Trail runs past wetlands, through oak forests, and over wooded dunes that increase in height as you approach the sandy beach.

DESCRIPTION

As one of the more famous spots at the Indiana Dunes National Lakeshore, Cowles Bog is well known for its beauty and its historical significance in the field of environmental science. Shortly after starting the hike from the Cowles Bog Trail parking lot, you'll pass a plaque on the right honoring Henry Cowles, the trail's namesake, whose work in the early twentieth century helped establish the science of ecology. Cowles, a professor at the University of Chicago, was drawn to the area partly for its impressive variety of plants. According to botanical surveys, there are more types of plants within the 12,000 acres of the Dunes National Lakeshore than there are in the half-million acres of the Great Smoky Mountains National Park.

DIRECTIONS

For rail service, take the South Shore Line from the Randolph Station in downtown Chicago to the Dune Park Station located at IL 49 and US 12.

By bike: On the north side of the railroad tracks, follow the Calumet Bike Trail west for 1 mile. Turn right at Mineral Springs Road and follow it for one-half mile north to the Cowles Bog trailhead.

Driving from Chicago: Take I-90/I-94 south until reaching the Chicago Skyway (I-90), Exit 59A. After traveling 29 miles southeast on the Skyway and the toll road, take Exit 21 to I-94. Follow I-94 east for 7 miles to Exit 22B. Follow US 20 (Melton Road) for 1.5 miles, then bear left (north) on North Mineral Springs Road. The parking lot for the Cowles Bog Trail is 1.5 miles ahead on the right, just before the Dune Acres guardhouse.

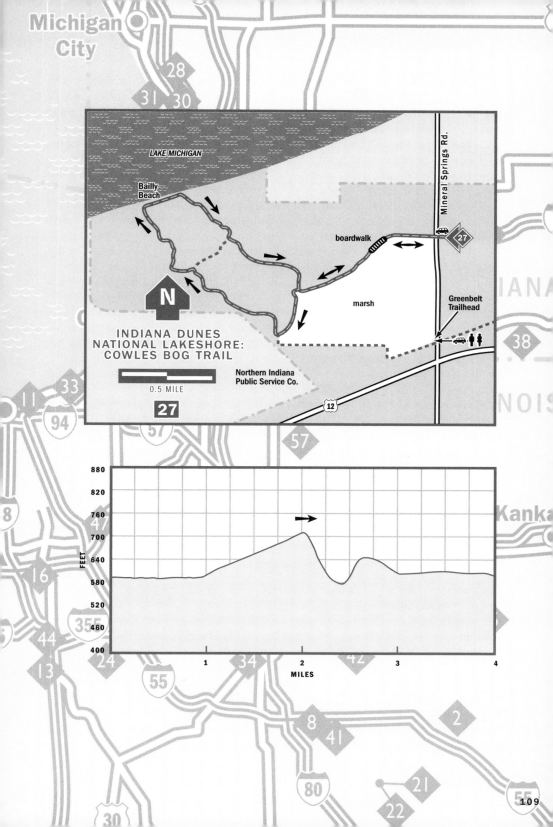

Michigan City

LAKE MICHIGAN

Bailly Beach

Mineral Springs Rd.

boardwalk

27

marsh

Greenbelt Trailhead

N

INDIANA DUNES
NATIONAL LAKESHORE:
COWLES BOG TRAIL

0.5 MILE

Northern Indiana
Public Service Co.

27

12

FEET

880
820
760
700
640
580
520
460
400

1   2   3   4
MILES

At 0.3 miles, a 200-foot-long boardwalk leads hikers through a lush marshy area. After the boardwalk, the trail runs close to the shore of more marshland. Although the interior of this wetland is called Cowles Bog, it's actually a fen. Fens have soil and water that are alkaline, whereas bogs are acidic; different plant communities inhabit each.

Turn left at the first trail junction, which appears at 0.8 miles. After skirting the west side of the large marsh for 0.3 miles, turn right at the next junction. Intermittent marshes with cattails and sedges appear on each side of this trail. Also on this stretch of the trail, you'll see some of the heavy industry that makes the existence of the National Lakeshore such an unlikely prospect. The behemoth on the left is Northern Indiana Public Service Co., a coal-fueled power plant that provides electricity to the local steel industry.

Keep straight ahead when reaching another connector trail on the right at 1.7 miles. As the oak forest becomes thicker, the dunes start to bulge upwards. The dunes come and go quickly, creating sudden dramatic shifts in the terrain, steeply sloping in one direction and then another. Getting closer to the shore, the dunes begin to soar—and so does your heart rate as you climb these steep, sandy slopes. If it's a hot summer day, keep in mind there's a cool, wet reward at the bottom of the last dune.

At 2.2 miles, the trail drops down to Bailly Beach, where, on a clear day, the skyscrapers of downtown Chicago are visible to the northwest. This beach is a popular spot for boaters on summer weekends; during the rest of the year and on weekdays, however, this beach is seldom used because it can't be reached by car. If a picnic or sunbathing is on the agenda, and boats are anchored offshore shoulder to shoulder, look for a quieter stretch of beach a half mile or so to the right. Try walking just beyond the fenced-in area that serves as a nesting site for the federally endangered piping plover (a pale-whitish sparrow-sized bird sporting a black breast band).

The trail continues up a dune 0.2 miles to the right of where you arrived on the beach. Back on the trail, take note of how quickly the vegetation changes from hearty dune grass toward the beach to oak woods at the top of the first dune. This swift transition fascinated Henry Cowles, and prompted him to investigate why oak trees didn't grow closer to the lake. In the course of his research here, he observed that oak trees and other plants need decomposed plant material in which to grow. As dune grasses die and add organic material to the sand, groundwork is laid for oak trees to sprout. In time, oak trees and other plants replace the dune grass. Through such observations, Cowles pieced together one of the major concepts in the field of ecology: as plants grow on a site, they change it.

Dropping down on the back side of the first dune, the sound of wind and water is hushed by the mounds of sand. Amid the stands of black oak and jack pine, look for flora rarely seen in the Chicago region, including the prickly pear cactus (it blooms yellow flowers in midsummer), blueberries, and, closer to the marshes, birch trees and large ferns. Continue straight ahead as you pass the first connector trail on the right, at 0.4 miles beyond the beach. Except for a few open spaces littered with large fallen branches, the trail in the summer is shaded under a canopy of oak leaves. Passing the second connector trail at 0.9 miles beyond the beach, the terrain flattens and leads you along the marsh and back to the parking lot.

INDIANA DUNES NATIONAL LAKESHORE: LY-CO-KI-WE HIKE

This sandy trail allows you to explore miles of deep woods, gentle dune ridges, and marshy thickets. Given the ample mileage and the sand-covered surface, you'll likely find yourself at the end of this hike with a type of blissful exhaustion that comes from scaling a mountain—or running laps in a sandbox. If you'd prefer a shorter walk, trim some mileage by heading back at one of the many trail junctions.

> ## DESCRIPTION

The name "Ly-co-ki-we"—which means "sandy ground" in the Miami Indian language—offers an inkling of what you'll encounter on this trail. Although you won't be climbing over monstrous sand dunes, you will follow a couple of gentle dune ridges as they gradually rise and fall. Like other sandy ridges in the area, these mild slopes mark the shores of a once larger version of Lake Michigan. In between the pleasant, tree-covered ridges are dense woods, shrubby wetlands, and open areas sprinkled with oaks and patches of exposed sand.

A quick look at a map of the Ly-co-ki-we Trail reveals multiple trail junctions throughout the hike—often, less than a half mile apart. With so many junctions, I suggest keeping the navigation simple by staying to the right. This will also keep you with the flow of equestrians and cross-country skiers, who are required to stay right throughout these multiple loops.

> ## DIRECTIONS

Take I-90/I-94 south until reaching the Chicago Skyway (I-90), Exit 59A. After traveling 29 miles southeast on the Skyway and the toll road, take Exit 21 to I-94. Follow I-94 east for 7 miles until reaching Exit 22. Go northeast on US 20 (Melton Road). Proceed ahead for 5.8 miles until reaching the Li-co-ki-we Trail parking lot on the left.

KEY AT-A-GLANCE INFORMATION

LENGTH: 12.2 miles

CONFIGURATION: A series of connected loops with 2 out-and-back segments

DIFFICULTY: Difficult for its length and sandy trail surface

SCENERY: Savannas, hardwood forests, wooded dunes, creeks, and marshes

EXPOSURE: Mostly shaded

SURFACE: Sand, both loose and firm, and a short, paved section.

HIKING TIME: 4–5 hours

ACCESS: Sunrise to sunset

FACILITIES: Restrooms, water, shelter, mapboard, and visitor center

MAPS: Maps available at trailhead and at visitor center; USGS topos Dune Acres, IN and Michigan City West, IN

SPECIAL COMMENTS: The majority of this hike is open to horses—be sure to give them the right-of-way. The Dorothy Buell Visitor Center can be reached at (219) 926-7561. The gentle terrain and the many straight-aways allow for good cross-country skiing.

UTM Trailhead Coordinates for Indiana Dunes National Lakeshore: Ly-co-ki-we Hike

UTM Zone (NAD27)   16T

Easting   498790

Northing   4610517

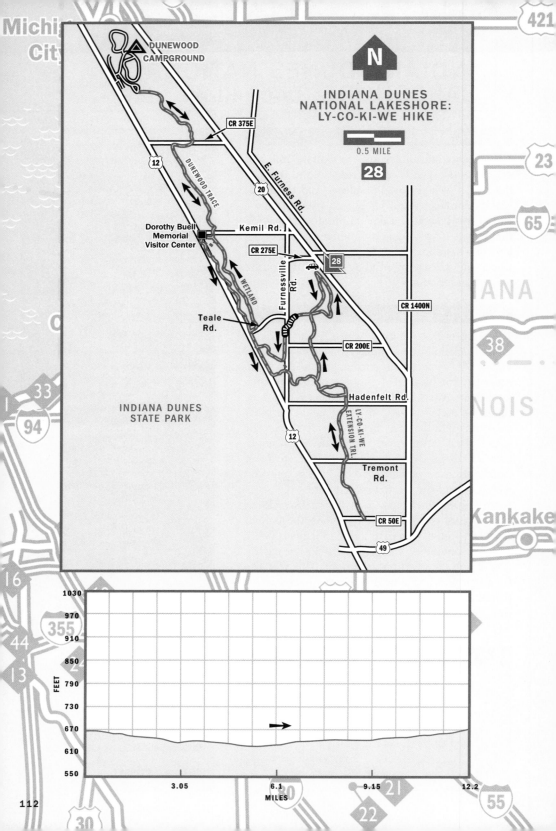

N

**INDIANA DUNES
NATIONAL LAKESHORE:
LY-CO-KI-WE HIKE**

0.5 MILE

28

DUNEWOOD
CAMPGROUND

CR 375E

Michigan
City

12

DUNEWOOD TRACE

E. Furness Rd.

20

Dorothy Buell
Memorial
Visitor Center

Kemil Rd.

CR 275E

28

WETLAND

Furnessville Rd.

CR 1400N

Teale
Rd.

CR 200E

INDIANA DUNES
STATE PARK

Hadenfelt Rd.

12

LY-CO-KI-WE
EXTENSION TRL.

Tremont
Rd.

CR 50E

49

This hike starts in a hardwood forest with scattered deadfall and stands of shrubs. After passing the first trail junction just beyond the trailhead and another junction at 0.5 miles, the flat terrain gives way to a lightly rolling landscape of low, wooded dunes. Before and after crossing Furnessville Road at 0.7 miles, you'll follow a couple of short boardwalks over marshy areas.

In this next section of the trail, look for small American holly trees, a conifer that rarely grows in this part of the Midwest. The green leaves of the American holly, often used for Christmas decorations, are broad, stiff, and leathery, with sharp spines on the edges; birds love the bright red berries that develop into flowers. Hollies are easiest to spot in fall, winter, and early spring, when it appears they are the only trees still bearing green leaves.

At 1 mile, stay right at a junction that appears in an open sandy area with small bare dunes on the left. After the next junction, the trail closely follows US 12 before crossing Teale Road and meeting another junction. Here, the path mounts a hill topped with a cluster of pine trees, and then passes several knolls and small ravines before dropping into a hardwood forest bordered on the right by a large marsh. This shrubby wetland will accompany the trail intermittently for the next few miles of hiking. At 2.3 miles into the hike, the trail meets with the 0.4-mile-long paved trail that loops in back of the visitor center. A short walk to the right along the paved trail brings you to the beginning of the 1.8-mile-long Dunewood Trace, an out-and-back trail that leads to the Indiana Dunes National Lakeshore's Dunewood Campground.

After crossing Kemil Road, the first half mile of the Dunewood Trace passes through a few open sandy areas bordered by hardwoods. In the open sand, look for a small brownish-tan fungi called the earthstar. When there's enough moisture in the air, the rays of this star-shaped fungus open several inches across; when the air is dry, it curls up into a ball. Much of the Duneland Trace runs next to wetland on the right; now and then, you'll also pass sections of a stream bed. After hiking for 0.9 miles on the Trace, the path reaches County Road 375 East. To catch the rest of the trail, turn right on the road and follow it for 0.1 miles, and look for the continuation of the trail on the left side of the road at the small brown sign for the Dunewood Campground. You'll soon cross a two-track, and then arrive in an open savanna. As the trail enters the savanna, look to the left for a bevy of prickly pear cactuses. After passing through a dense bottomland forest, the trail snakes by a series of irrigation ditches and a small pond. Just beyond the ditches, the trail ends at a campground road, where you'll turn around and retrace your steps back to the paved path near the visitor center.

Returning to the paved path at 6.1 miles into the hike, turn right for a stop at the Dorothy Buell Visitor Center, which offers books, brochures, and a few small exhibits. Visitors also can ask the park ranger to play a 15-minute video introduction to the National Lakeshore. Continue on the paved path on the north side of the visitor center near the restrooms, and then take the first right at the sign for the Ly-co-ki-we Extension Trail. Soon you'll cross a two-track and enter the familiar rolling terrain. Although much of this section of the hike runs closely to US 12, the road is not overly busy and takes little away from the tranquility of these woods. The trail continues along the wooded dune ridges and through gently sloping savannas with the occasional open sandy spots. As the trail moves away from US 12, watch for deer:

Sections of the Ly-co-ki-we Trail
are densely wooded.

if you're ambling close to dusk or dawn, you're virtually guaranteed to spot their bushy white tails as they scamper off into the woods.

At 8.2 miles into the hike, you'll arrive at the Ly-ko-ki-we Extension Trail, an out-and-back trail that is 1.2 miles each way. In the first half mile of the extension, you'll cross Hadenfelt Road and a stream called Munson Ditch, which winds through a beautiful wooded ravine. Beyond the stream, the trail straightens out on its way to Tremont Road. At Tremont Road, the trail continues 20 yards to the right with a short boardwalk. The final segment of the extension trail passes through flat terrain, with sections both open and wooded, before reaching County Road 50 East, which is where you'll turn around and retrace your steps.

Back at the beginning of the extension trail, stay to the right at the next three junctions before crossing County Road 200 East. While staying right at two more junctions, the trail passes over very lightly rolling terrain on your way back to the parking lot. During this deeply wooded section of the hike, look for black oak, white oak, tulip, sugar-maple trees, and the flowering dogwood tree, which is especially captivating in the spring.

▶ NEARBY ACTIVITIES

Dunewood Campground offers 25 walk-in sites and 54 drive-in sites. While the Dunewood sites aren't up against large dunes or the lakeshore, they do offer bigger sites and more privacy than Indiana Dunes State Park Campground. During summer months—particularly on weekends—reservations are likely needed at both campgrounds. For more information, call the national lakeshore at (219) 926-7561 and the state park at (866) 622-6746.

INDIANA DUNES NATIONAL LAKESHORE: WEST BEACH LOOP

▶ IN BRIEF

Take in great views on high dunes topped with marram grass, jack pine, and cottonwood trees. Coming off the dunes, the trail runs along a scenic lake, through a sandy savanna, and into dense woodland.

▶ DESCRIPTION

It's not just the high dunes and a long sandy beach that makes hiking at West Beach such a satisfying experience. What makes this hike so engaging is how the landscape and plants magically transform every half mile or so. Moving from the beach to the dunes to the wooded ridges to the savanna to a large lily-pad pond, it seems the landscape is always changing.

Starting the hike on the wide, paved path heading toward Lake Michigan, you'll pass a wind-scoured, bowl-shaped depression on the right. Known as a blowout, this depression contains a pond, because the wind has swept the sand away down to the water table. After passing through the center of the bathhouse and reaching the white, sandy beach, look for the boardwalk on the right leading over the small foredune. This part of the hike, called the Succession Trail, gives you a sense of how prevailing winds and plants change the bare beach into dense groves of oak,

▶ KEY AT-A-GLANCE INFORMATION

LENGTH: 3.15 miles

CONFIGURATION: Loop

DIFFICULTY: Moderate

SCENERY: High dunes, scenic lake, sand savanna, wooded ridges and ravines, and an unusual array of plants

EXPOSURE: Mostly exposed

SURFACE: Sand, wooden boardwalk, dirt

HIKING TIME: 1.5 hours

ACCESS: Sunrise to sunset

FACILITIES: Bathhouse, picnic areas, restrooms, telephone, snack shop

MAPS: Ask for a trail map at the guardhouse when you pay your entrance fee; USGS topo Portage, IN

SPECIAL COMMENTS: From Memorial Day to Labor Day an entrance fee of $6 per car is charged. Watch for cars while making 3 crossings of the main park road. Stay on the trail to prevent erosion of the dunes.

▶ DIRECTIONS

Driving from Chicago, take I-90/I-94 south until reaching the Chicago Skyway (I-90), Exit 59A. After traveling 23.2 miles southeast on the Skyway and the toll road, take Exit 17 to US 12 (US 20). Follow US 12 east for 4.5 miles until turning left (north) on North County Line Road. The entrance to West Beach is 0.2 miles ahead on the right. After stopping at the guardhouse to pick up a trail map and pay the entrance fee, follow the park road for 1 mile to the main parking lot.

UTM Trailhead Coordinates for Indiana Dunes National Lakeshore: West Beach Loop

UTM Zone (NAD27)   **16T**

Easting   **482602**

Northing   **4607624**

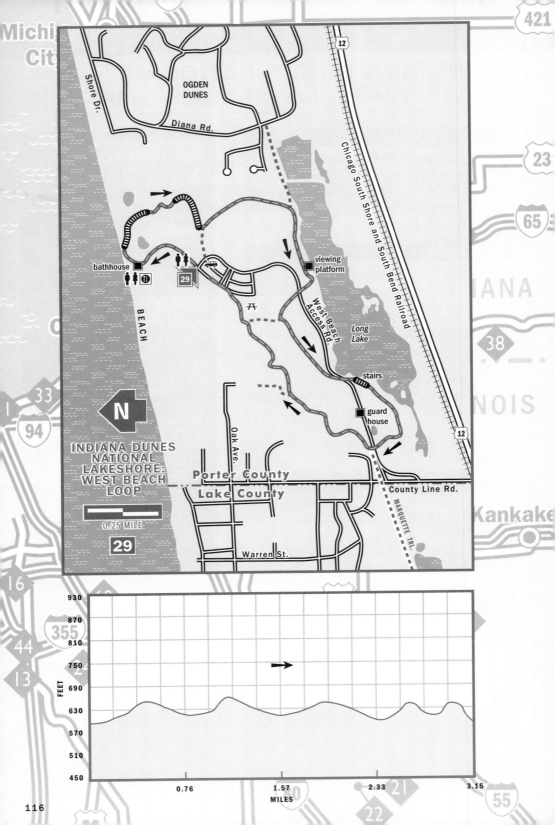

Michigan City

OGDEN DUNES

Shore Dr.

Diana Rd.

12

421

23

65

Chicago South Shore and South Bend Railroad

INDIANA

38

bathhouse

29

viewing platform

BEACH

Long Lake

stairs

West Beach Access Rd.

guard house

12

NOIS

N

INDIANA DUNES NATIONAL LAKESHORE: WEST BEACH LOOP

0.25 MILE

29

I 94

33

16

355

44

13

Oak Ave.

Porter County
Lake County

County Line Rd.

MARQUETTE TRL.

Kankake

Warren St.

FEET

930
870
810
750
690
630
570
510
450

0.76   1.57   2.33   3.15
MILES

21

22

55

hickory, and basswood in the span of a only few hundred yards. Where the trail drops between a couple of gentle dunes, you'll see clusters of jack pines, which typically grow farther north, but they also thrive in the harsh conditions at the dunes.

At 0.3 miles into the hike, another boardwalk takes you through the bottom of an old blowout. Stairs lead from the blowout to the dune wrapped in marram grass and topped with cottonwood trees. Cottonwood trees deal with the constantly shifting sand remarkably well: when their limbs are covered with blowing sand, the limbs sprout roots; likewise, when blowing sand exposes the roots, the roots grow stems and leaves. Some of the small cottonwoods at the tops of dunes may actually have 60 feet of trunk below the surface.

From the top of the dune, the trail drops and then quickly enters a woodland dense with oak, wild grape, basswood, and more cottonwood. Rising up again to the top of a dune, you'll have a fine view of the relatively flat area containing the parking lot and the lower dunes and wooded areas to the south. Before becoming parkland, the sand in this area as well as other spots along the Dunes Lakeshore was hauled away for making bricks, glass, and for filling in wetlands, as was done at Jackson Park in Chicago in preparation for the 1893 world's fair known as the World's Columbian Exposition.

At the bottom of the long flight of stairs, immediately turn left on a faint trail (you'd probably miss it unless you were looking for it). This wide, grassy trail runs through a savanna between a large dune rising on the left and a small ridge on the right. During the summer, goldfinches and king birds (dark gray on top, white below) dart among the poplar, white oak, and sumac trees. Closer to the ground, look for ferns, prickly pear cactuses, and a variety of wildflowers. At the junction, turn right so that you're walking alongside 60-acre Long Lake, blanketed by lily pads, fringed with cattails, and frequently visited by waterbirds. The trail to the left runs a quarter mile to the community of Ogden Dunes. Before crossing the park road, don't miss the observation deck overlooking the pond.

In the sand prairie across the park road, prickly pear cactuses line the sides of the trail; closer to the woods, plenty of milkweed plants and small sassafras trees push up through the sandy soil. Turn left at the junction and continue between the steep, wooded dune on the right and a small sand ridge on the left. Crossing the park road again, the trail follows the spine of an oak-covered dune ridge that drops steeply 50 feet or so on each side. From the winding trail, you'll have a fine view of a section of Long Lake sprinkled with small, grassy islands. Coming down from the ridge through dense, shrubby woodland, cross the park road again. The trail turns right along the chain-link fence and passes a few park-service buildings and a parking area before crossing a paved service road.

From the service road, the trail climbs a dune ridge under a thick oak canopy. In many places, you can see marshland—probably former blowouts—at the bottom of the wooded ravine. At the junction, stay to the right. (The trail to the left continues for 0.2 miles through wooded dunes to Wabash Avenue.) From the junction, the trail drops down alongside a marsh, and then makes a steep, sandy climb to the top of a dune overlooking a group of picnic pavilions and the parking lot. From the top of the dune, you can descend straight down through the open sand or, for a more gradual descent, follow the trail down to the left.

▶ NEARBY ACTIVITIES

The Marquette Trail is a linear hiking and bicycling path—3.2-miles long—that runs along an old rail bed from West Beach to Grand Avenue in Gary, Indiana. The crushed-gravel trail passes oak-wooded dunes and a cattail marsh with sections of open water. The western end is located not far from the 1.1-mile-long Miller Woods Trail and the nearby Paul H. Douglas Center for Environmental Education. Miller Woods, the western gateway to the National Lakeshore, hosts rolling oak savanna with interspersed ponds. The Marquette Trail starts on the park road between the West Beach guardhouse and the West Beach entrance.

INDIANA DUNES STATE PARK:
DUNE RIDGE LOOP

Indiana Dunes is one of the most beautiful and dramatic settings in the Chicago region. This hike is notable for its variety: after hiking through forest, wetland, and wooded dunes, you'll pass over spectacular sand dunes bordering the shoreline.

▶ **DESCRIPTION**

For more than a century, the Indiana Dunes State Park has captured the interest of local people looking for a spot close to home where they can experience breathtaking beauty. One person drawn to the dunes was the poet Carl Sandburg, who once wrote, "The dunes are to the Midwest what the Grand Canyon is to Arizona. . . . They constitute a signature of time and eternity." This hike could have been in the back of Sandburg's mind when he made that statement; few other places in the dunes display with such drama the unrelenting effects of wind and water. The main attraction on this hike is a stunning dune ridge that runs between large areas hollowed out by lake wind.

▶ **DIRECTIONS**

Driving from Chicago, take I-90/I-94 south until reaching the Chicago Skyway (I-90), Exit 59A. After traveling 29 miles southeast on the Skyway and the toll road, take Exit 21, which takes you back onto I-94. Follow I-94 east for 7 miles until reaching Exit 22B. Follow US 20 (Melton Road) for 3.1 miles, then bear left on IL 49 (north). Follow signs through the campground leading to the nature-center parking lot.

For rail service, take the South Shore Line from the Randolph Station in downtown Chicago to the Dune Park Station located at IL 49 and US 12. Follow IL 49 north into the park for 0.8 miles until turning right, just beyond the park office. Turn left 0.7 miles ahead, after the campground.

ℹ KEY AT-A-GLANCE INFORMATION

LENGTH: 4.5 miles

CONFIGURATION: Loop

DIFFICULTY: Moderate: the hike includes a few short climbs on loose sand

SCENERY: Bottomland forest, marshland, Lake Michigan shoreline, dunes, ravines, and blowouts—large depressions created by blowing sand

EXPOSURE: Mostly shaded

SURFACE: Hard-packed dirt and loose sand

HIKING TIME: 2–2.5 hours

ACCESS: All year, 7 a.m.–11 p.m.; a small fee is required for entry into the park

FACILITIES: Camping, picnic shelters, beach, and restrooms available all year; swimming, water, and concession stand available in summer

MAPS: Maps available at guardhouse or at park office; USGS topo Dune Acres, IN

SPECIAL COMMENTS: Part of this hike leads through a very damp forest; bring waterproof footwear, especially in the spring. Call the park office at (219) 926-1952 for information on camping. Also, see the Shoreline Loop in the Indiana Dunes State Park on page 123.

UTM Trailhead Coordinates for Indiana Dunes State Park: Dune Ridge Loop

UTM Zone (NAD27)   16T

Easting   495805

Northing   4611750

INDIANA DUNES STATE PARK: DUNE RIDGE LOOP

N

0.5 MILE

30

marsh

Furnessville Blowout

TRAIL 10

BOARDWALK

marsh

TRAIL 9

TRAIL 2

Beach House Blowout

Dune Creek

TRAIL 10

TRAIL 9

Wilson Shelter

Lake Michigan

30

nature center

TRAIL 8

Dune Creek

Beach House

park gate house

880							
820							
760							
700							
640							
580							
520							
460							
400							

FEET

1.12 2.25 3.37 4.5
MILES

The dunes were sculpted by the strong winds coming off the lake.

You'll encounter several quick turns shortly after starting the hike on Trail 9, to the right of the nature center building. After 0.1 miles, turn right on Trail 8. Immediately, you'll pass the junction with Trail 10 on the left before crossing the bridge spanning the east branch of Dune Creek. After the bridge, the trail reaches the Wilson Shelter, and continues in the far left corner of the parking lot on the other side of the restrooms. Turn left at the Trail 2 intersection, 0.2 miles after the shelter parking lot.

Trail 2 runs for nearly 2 miles through an exceedingly flat and sometimes very wet bottomland forest. During summer, you'll be hiking under a thick canopy of oak and beech trees; occasionally, these large trees are sprawled on the ground with root systems jutting up 15 feet. As these trees fall, the canopy opens, allowing shrubs to take hold on the forest floor.

At 1.4 miles into the hike, the trail curves left before reaching a bench at the beginning of a half-mile-long boardwalk spanning a section of what is called the Great Marsh, a long, thin wetland that once ran parallel to nearly the entire shoreline of the Indiana Dunes. Now much of the marsh has been filled in. Through this section of the marsh, patches of open water and marsh grasses are interrupted now and then by stretches of dry land and the occasional small pond. Completing the boardwalk, turn right on Trail 10, and then quickly turn left at the connecter path for Trail 9. When you finish the connector trail, turn right on Trail 9 proper.

Trail 9 passes over gradual ups and downs, and between small dunes rising on each side of the trail. After these minor dunes, Lake Michigan comes into view as the trail reaches the Furnessville Blowout. A blowout forms when winds blow sand inland, carving out what looks like a large amphitheatre of sand. From the Furnessville Blowout, Trail 9 curves left, beginning the best part of the hike—traversing a dune ridge for 0.7 miles on the way to the next blowout.

The section between these two blowouts offers some of the most striking natural scenery in the Chicago area. Left of the trail are tall white pines and black oaks rising out of a plunging ravine. On the right, the dune drops to the shore of Lake Michigan. Views along this squiggly ridge path are best when the leaves have left the branches: on a clear day, the Chicago skyline is clearly visible 30 miles to the northwest.

The trail reaches the edge of the Beach House Blowout at 3.4 miles into the hike. The bowl of the blowout, nearly 200 yards across, is mostly covered with marram grass. Also evident are the dead tree trunks—both standing and fallen—that are remnants of a forest that was swallowed and is now being uncovered by moving mounds of sand. You'll likely notice the illegal trails that zigzag this fragile sand canyon. To prevent further damage, the park requires hikers to stay on the marked trails. Continuing left along the rim of the blowout, be sure to avoid the steep and straight illegal trail on the left and continue on the trail toward the high point that affords a great view of the bowl, as well as the surrounding woods.

Dropping slightly from the high point, look for the post that marks a path meandering down the slope of the dune to the left. While hiking through these foredunes, as they're called, keep watch for the six-lined racerunner lizard, which has yellow and brown stripes on a body about nine inches long, including the tail. At 3.7 miles into the hike, after descending from the edge of the Beach House Blowout, take Trail 9 to the right and follow it until the second junction with Trail 10 at the nature-center sign. Once you turn right on Trail 10, the nature-center parking lot is just ahead.

INDIANA DUNES STATE PARK:
SHORELINE LOOP

▶ **IN BRIEF**

After hiking several miles on the beach and a couple of miles between forested dunes and a large marsh, you'll c limb the highest dunes on the southern shore of Lake Michigan. The views from the top are extraordinary.

▶ **DESCRIPTION**

Even though Indiana Dunes State Park is a fraction of the size of the Indiana Dunes National Lakeshore, the state park has long been one of the preferred destinations along the dunes shoreline. Part of the state park's appeal is its startling beauty, and part of the appeal is its distance (or apparent distance) from much of the human development in the area. Established in 1923 before much of the dunes landscape was gobbled up by either industry or housing developments, the state park remains the largest continuous tract of undeveloped dunes land along the Indiana shoreline.

Starting from the beach house, head to the right for a 2.7-mile walk along this wide, beautiful beach. On the slopes of the dunes closest to the beach, marram grass is mixed with patches of

▶ **DIRECTIONS**

Take I-90/I-94 south until reaching the Chicago Skyway (I-90), Exit 59A. After traveling 29 miles southeast on the Skyway and the toll road, take Exit 21 to I-94. Follow I-94 east for 7 miles until reaching Exit 22B. Follow US 20 (Melton Road) for 3.1 miles, then bear left (north) on IL 49. Park at the beach house, 1.7 miles ahead, just past the park guardhouse.

For rail service, take the South Shore Line from the Randolph Station in downtown Chicago to the Dune Park Station, located at IL 49 and US 12. Follow IL 49 north through the park for 1 mile until reaching the beach house.

ⓘ **KEY AT-A-GLANCE INFORMATION**

LENGTH: 7 miles

CONFIGURATION: Loop

DIFFICULTY: The first 5.75 miles of this hike are easy; the final 1.25 miles, however, are difficult, as they lead up and down very steep dunes.

SCENERY: Lake Michigan shoreline, dunes, oak and pine forest, a large marsh, and excellent views from the highest points on the Indiana shoreline of Lake Michigan

EXPOSURE: The first section of the hike— 2.7 miles along the lakeshore—is totally exposed. The rest of the hike is mostly shaded.

SURFACE: Loose and hard-packed sand, dirt

HIKING TIME: 3-3.5 hours

ACCESS: All year 7 a.m.–11 p.m. A small fee is required for entry.

FACILITIES: Camping, beach, and restrooms. Swimming, picnic areas, shelters, water, and concession stand available in summer.

MAPS: Maps available at the guardhouse or at the park office; USGS topo Dune Acres, IN

SPECIAL COMMENTS: Consider pitching a tent for a night; it will allow a day on this trail and a day on one of the other great trails within the Indiana Dunes. Call the state park at (219) 926-1952 for camping information. This is the busiest state park in Indiana; crowds thin out on weekdays and during non-summer months.

UTM Trailhead Coordinates for Indiana Dunes State Park: Shoreline Loop

UTM Zone (NAD27)   16T

Easting   494752

Northing   4612120

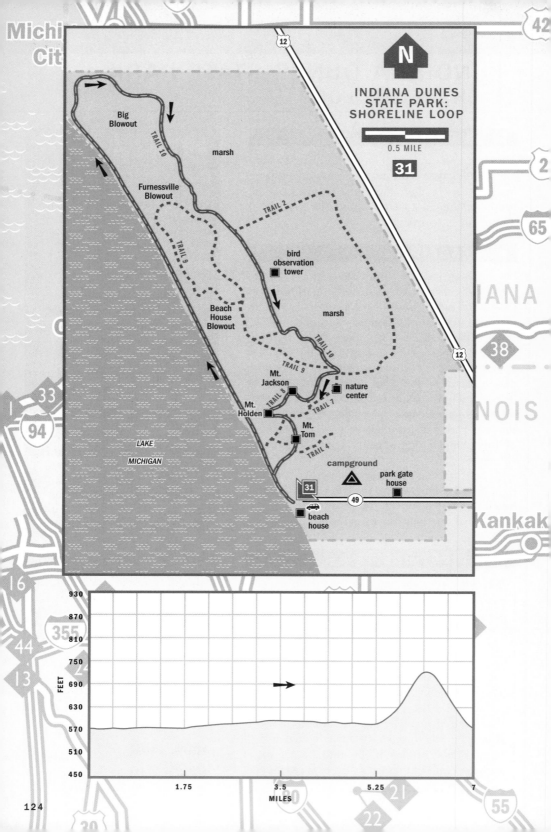

open sand and the occasional cottonwood tree. More cottonwood trees, as well as oaks, junipers, and white pines, rise from the tops of the dune ridge, farther back from the beach. At 0.4 miles, pass a marker on the right for Trails 4 and 7, going up the dune.

If hiking in the loose sand becomes tiresome, consider walking close to water on the packed wet sand. Near the water look for deer, raccoon, and skunk tracks. You'll likely see zebra-mussel shells, which are one- to two-inches long with black-and-white stripes. Zebra mussels have multiplied at alarming rates in the Great Lakes since they arrived in the late 1980s from their native waters in the Black and Caspian Seas—presumably making the voyage in the water ballasts of freighter ships.

While walking the shoreline, keep on eye on the dunes for blowouts, which are spots where wind has carved out an amphitheater of sand. You'll pass a couple of smaller blowouts before reaching the Beach House Blowout at 1 mile, and then the Furnessville Blowout at 2 miles, followed by the Big Blowout at 2.3 miles. Each has a unique shape and set of contours, and different patterns of grass and tree growth. If you're itching for a closer view of the blowouts, resist the temptation for now—you'll have a bird's eye view of a couple of the larger ones on the Dune Ridge Hike described on pages 119–122. Also, keep in mind that off-trail hiking is strictly forbidden. As you'll see in many spots where snow fencing has been erected, illegal trails seriously damage the dunes.

Nearly reaching the park's eastern boundary after walking 2.75 miles along the shoreline, head inland at the Trail 10 marker. Immediately the trail rises into a forest of oak and pine. On the left is a steep 60-foot ravine sprinkled with deadfall. From here, the trail skirts the edge of a large dune on the right, and then proceeds under a tunnel of trees growing at an angle on the sides of dunes rising at each side of the trail. The trail flattens considerably, shortly before it brushes against East State Park Road.

As the trail bends to the right, it follows the backside of the Big Blowout and smaller forested dunes. At 3.3 miles into the hike, you'll pass over a short boardwalk and then hike alongside what is called the Great Marsh for the next 1.8 miles. At the edge of this marsh, surface water is occasionally visible, but more often you'll see wet ground covered by thick stands of shrubs. As forested dunes come and go on the right, watch for towering white pines, as well as the mature black oaks, some with trunks a yard in diameter. This is also prime territory for seeing the park's resident species of woodpeckers. Most likely, you'll see red-headed woodpeckers, and if you're fortunate, you'll come upon the shy and less common pileated woodpecker, an elegant, crow-sized bird with a prominent red tuft on its head.

At 4.3 miles into the hike, keep straight ahead as you pass a connecter path to Trail 9 on the right, soon followed by a junction with Trail 2 on the left. A quarter mile beyond the junction with Trail 2, a 20-foot-high platform overlooks the Great Marsh. At 5.25 miles is the first of two successive junctions with Trail 9. Just after the second junction, at 5.6 miles, you'll reach a large sign for the nature center. Take the trail on the right side of the nature-center sign and quickly turn right at the marker for Trail 8.

While scaling the first dune on Trail 8, you'll see the nature center down on the left and a steep 80-foot drop on the right. After a short walk along a ridge, the trail drops down a bit, then starts a steep climb to Mt. Jackson, which has an elevation of

A crayfish on patrol at the beach.

176 feet. The trail takes a short dip before climbing again, this time up to Mt. Holden, eight feet higher than Mt. Jackson. After taking in a great southern view at Mt. Holden, you'll cross Trail 7 and then traverse another ridge that drops sharply on each side.

Starting up the stairs on the final stretch to Mt. Tom, a junction with Trail 4 shows up on the right. At 6.5 miles into the hike, Mt. Tom—elevation 192 feet—provides a stunning view of the shoreline west of the park. Stay on Trail 8, leading to the right, to descend the dune. As you get closer to the beach, stay to the left as the trail proceeds over the last dune. At the beach, turn left and hike for 0.2 miles back to the parking lot.

▶ NEARBY ACTIVITIES

If you're looking for a restaurant, or just a stroll through a charming small town, consider stopping in nearby Chesterton. To reach downtown Chesterton, drive 3.5 miles south of the state park on IL 49, and then turn right (west) on Porter Avenue.

IROQUOIS COUNTY STATE WILDLIFE AREA HIKE

IN BRIEF

Gloriously remote, the Iroquois County State Wildlife Area offers a serene place to stretch your legs. During the summer, wildflowers decorate the sides of the trail, while bluebirds and woodpeckers dart among the stately oak trees in the savanna.

DESCRIPTION

The state of Illinois first started acquiring land at the Iroquois County State Wildlife Area in the 1940s in an effort to prevent the further decline of prairie chickens. Widespread in the area during the nineteenth century, the prairie chicken is known for its striking courtship displays: it inflates orange air sacs around its neck and performs elaborate dances. Despite both Indiana and Illinois setting aside tracts of prairie that this chicken-like bird needs in order to breed, the bird disappeared from the Chicago region by 1974.

While the prairie chicken didn't survive, the Iroquois Wildlife Area did, largely as a hunting preserve. Surrounded by fields of corn and soybeans, most of the southern half of this 2,480-acre wildlife area is wetland and prairie, while the northern and eastern sections are mostly woodland with patches of former cropland. No hunting is allowed on nearly 500 acres of sandy savanna

DIRECTIONS

Take I-90/I-94 south from Chicago. Continue on I-94 until you reach I-57 south. Follow I-57 south for 46 miles. Take Exit 312 east on IL 17 (East Court Street). Continue on IL 17 for 5.7 miles until you reach IL 1. Take a right (south) on IL 1 and proceed for 9.1 miles through the community of St. Anne. At County Road 3300, turn left (east). The wildlife area's headquarters is 6.9 miles ahead on the right, and the trailhead is 9.8 miles ahead at the edge of parking area 8 on the right.

KEY AT-A-GLANCE INFORMATION

LENGTH: 2.15 miles

CONFIGURATION: Barbell

DIFFICULTY: Easy

SCENERY: Oak savanna, prairie, wet prairie, marshland, woodland

EXPOSURE: Mostly exposed

SURFACE: Grass

HIKING TIME: 1 hour

ACCESS: Sunrise to sunset. The Hooper Branch Savanna Nature Preserve is open all year. Hiking is allowed on a restricted basis in the rest of the wildlife area October through December, due to deer and pheasant hunting. Call the wildlife area at (815) 435-2218 for specifics.

FACILITIES: The parking area offers a picnic table, a grill, and a pit toilet.

MAPS: Maps are available outside the wildlife area's headquarters at the corner of county roads 3300 and 2800; USGS topos Donavan, IL, IN; Leesville, IL, IN. *Note:* These topo maps both straddle the border between the two states

SPECIAL COMMENTS: Keep dogs on leashes. Along with the 2 adjacent trails described here, another established trail is accessible from parking area 2 near the headquarters. This 1.2-mile trail includes a 0.3-mile paved section that is wheelchair accessible. The easiest way to hike this trail is to take the first left off the concrete trail and then stay to the right.

UTM Trailhead Coordinates for Iroquois County State Wildlife Area Hike

UTM Zone (NAD27)   16T

Easting   452725

Northing   4538163

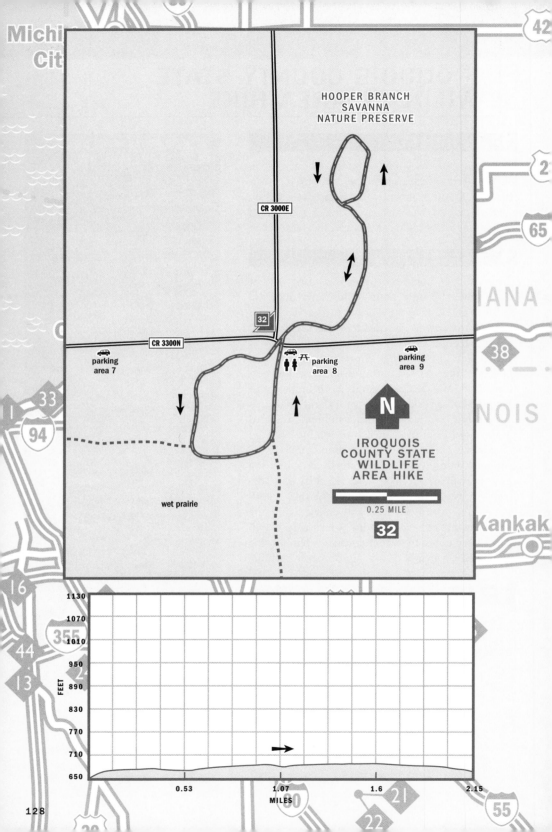

Michigan City

HOOPER BRANCH
SAVANNA
NATURE PRESERVE

CR 3000E

32

CR 3300N

parking
area 7

parking
area 8

parking
area 9

N

IROQUOIS
COUNTY STATE
WILDLIFE
AREA HIKE

0.25 MILE

32

wet prairie

Kankak

NOIS

IANA

FEET

1130
1070
1010
950
890
830
770
710
650

0.53   1.07   1.6   2.15
MILES

that serves as a state nature preserve. The preserve—known as the Hooper Branch Savanna Nature Preserve—is where this hike starts.

Look for the wide grassy trail heading into the nature preserve directly across the road from parking area 8. Entering the preserve, you'll notice right away the sandy soil that was left here by a glacial lake that receded some 14,000 years ago. Near the beginning of the trail, you'll see a small mound rising on the right. Farther into the savanna, a dense layer of 5- to 6-foot-tall oak shrubs and smaller sumac shrubs blanket the sides of the trail. Rising above the shrubs are 40- to 60-foot-tall black and pin oak trees, many of which are shaped like funnels: wide at the top and narrowing quickly. A number of still-standing dead oak trees seem appealing to bluebirds, red-headed woodpeckers, and flickers.

Indian, porcupine, and big bluestem grasses grow in the open spaces on the sides of the trail. Mixed in with the prairie grasses are flowers such as partridge pea, thistle, goldenrod, and round-headed bush clover. Before turning right at the beginning of the loop, look for a large marsh 100 feet off to the right. Once you've started the loop, the oak canopy thickens and the savanna briefly looks like a woodland landscape. After passing an open grassland on the right, the shrubs become thick on the sides of the trail. Once you've completed the loop, retrace your steps back to the parking lot.

Continue the hike on the other side of the road in back of the picnic area. Taking the trail to the right brings you into a shrubby savanna and through stands of pine. At 0.4 miles into this section of the hike, you'll pass a trail junction on the right and see an enormous wet prairie through stands of shrubs. If you feel like doing a bit of bushwhacking, it's well worth a short walk out into this prairie, which is dominated by bluejoint grass, cord grass, and sedges.

According to the Illinois Department of Natural Resources, the Iroquois State Wildlife Area contains one of the largest networks of wet prairie, sedge meadow, and marshes in Illinois (on the continuum of wetness, wet prairies are the driest, while marshes are the wettest). During the summer, the edges of this prairie are thick with yellow-flowered compass plants. Back on the trail, stay to the left as you pass through groves of quaking aspen, and then stay left again at the next junction. On the way back to the parking lot, the trail passes a dense oak woodland speckled with ferns.

Note: As you hike the established trails mentioned here, you'll encounter a number of other wide grassy trails along the way. While none of the trails in this wildlife area are marked, curious hikers with a GPS device can find a lot of pathways to keep them busy.

▶ NEARBY ACTIVITIES

Just across the state line from the Iroquois County State Wildlife Area is the enormous Willow Slough Fish and Wildlife Area. While Willow Slough does not have any established trails, there are plenty of two-track roads that can be explored on foot. A pleasant 4.3-mile walk starts in parking area 6A, about 2 miles west—as the crow flies—of the hike described above. From parking area 6, follow the two-track road heading into the oak woodland. Take the first left, which comes at a third of a mile. After hiking through a hilly savanna area with white and black oak, take a right to cross a levee that divides the enormous J. C. Murphy Lake on the right from Rookery Lake on the left.

After the levee, the road heads through a woodland and then mounts a grassy hill, which provides a great view of J. C. Murphy Lake and the Pogue Marsh to the east. Staying to the left brings you past a half-mile-long stand of river birch on the right, and then through a shrubby savanna before reaching a levee that divides Salisbury Marsh on the right and Rookery Lake on the left. At the parking lot, take the road to the left, leading to the first levee you crossed. From the levee, follow the road back to parking lot 6A. This area is closed during deer-hunting season.

To reach parking lot 6A at Willow Slough from parking lot 8 at Iroquois, head north on County Road 3000, and then turn right on Oak Avenue (CR 7500). Take another right on CR 17000, and turn left on CR 800 (Delaware Road). Turn right on State Line Road, and then look for parking lot 6 on the left. Parking lot 6A, which is unmarked, is the next lot on the left.

Pick up a map of the 10,000-acre Willow Slough Fish and Wildlife Area at the office (follow signs just south of parking lot 6A on State Line Road). Call the office at (219) 285-2704 before visiting to find out about restricted access due to hunting. Camping is available. In future years, keep an eye out for possible hiking opportunities just north of Willow Slough at Kankakee Sands, a recent 7,200-acre acquisition by the Nature Conservancy.

JACKSON PARK LOOP

At the heart of Jackson Park is a wooded island, a serene Japanese garden, and placid lagoons lined with cattails. Much of this quiet refuge is a remnant of one of the most important events in Chicago history: the World's Columbian Exposition of 1893.

▶ DESCRIPTION

In preparation for Chicago's 1893 World's Columbian Exposition, a team of the nation's most significant architects and sculptors came to the grounds of Jackson Park to create the "White City," made largely of plaster buildings designed in a classical style. The city included sculptures, fountains, and some 200 buildings exhibiting art, machinery, animals, plants, food, and many other items. The exposition was an absolute success: over 27 million people attended this event, held to celebrate 400 years of post-Columbus civilization. After the exposition, the city converted the ground's 700 acres—from East 56th Street south to East 67th Street, and from the shoreline west to South Stony Island Drive—back to a city park.

While the exhibition was not meant to be permanent, one notable exception was the sprawling Palace of Fine Art, which was eventually

▶ DIRECTIONS

Take Lakeshore Drive south to the Science Drive exit (just after the 57th Street exit). Stay left as you enter the parking lot, located next to the lagoon at the backside of the Museum of Science and Industry.

For rail service, take the South Shore Line from the Randolph Street station downtown to the 59th Street station. On East 59th Street, head east (toward the lake), crossing South Stony Island Avenue and South Cornell Avenue, for 0.3 miles to the Clarence Darrow Bridge.

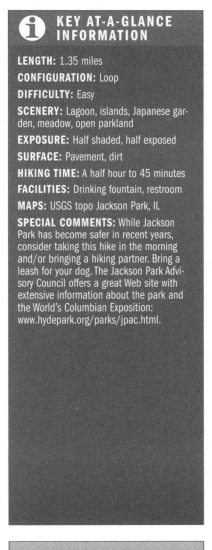

ⓘ KEY AT-A-GLANCE INFORMATION

LENGTH: 1.35 miles

CONFIGURATION: Loop

DIFFICULTY: Easy

SCENERY: Lagoon, islands, Japanese garden, meadow, open parkland

EXPOSURE: Half shaded, half exposed

SURFACE: Pavement, dirt

HIKING TIME: A half hour to 45 minutes

FACILITIES: Drinking fountain, restroom

MAPS: USGS topo Jackson Park, IL

SPECIAL COMMENTS: While Jackson Park has become safer in recent years, consider taking this hike in the morning and/or bringing a hiking partner. Bring a leash for your dog. The Jackson Park Advisory Council offers a great Web site with extensive information about the park and the World's Columbian Exposition: www.hydepark.org/parks/jpac.html.

UTM Trailhead Coordinates for Jackson Park Loop

UTM Zone (NAD27) 16T

Easting 451644

Northing 4626230

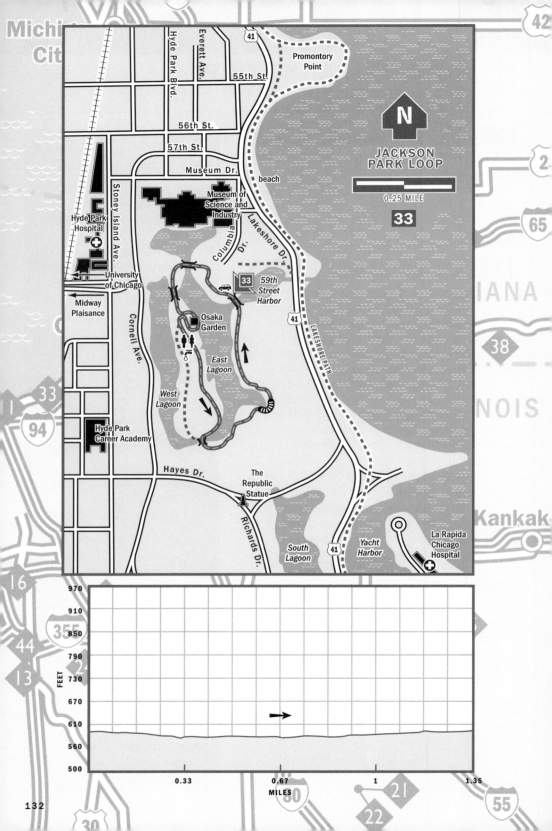

converted into the Museum of Science of Industry. Another attraction leftover from the exposition is a lovely Japanese garden, one of the first stops on this ramble through Jackson Park.

The hike starts on the west side of the parking lot, on the bridge overlooking a pool lapping at the back steps of the museum. This bridge is named after Clarence Darrow, a famous Chicago defense lawyer who was one of the many speakers at the 1893 Exposition. On the other side of the bridge, looking south, is the East Lagoon, along with a wooded island, and a sprinkling of tiny islands. After crossing the Clarence Darrow Bridge, take a quick left to cross North Bridge.

Over the bridge, pass through the wooden gates on the left to enter a storybook Japanese garden on the shore of the lagoon. Built for the Columbian Exposition in 1893, the garden was virtually abandoned after World War II, and then was rebuilt in 1981. In 1993, the garden was renamed the Osaka Garden in honor of Chicago's sister city in Japan. While walking along the 0.15-mile winding gravel path lined with red granite blocks taken from Chicago's old streetcar tracks, you'll enjoy a pleasant waterfall, stone lanterns, and a little bridge arching over a rock-lined lily pad pond. The teahouse, added to the garden in 1981, is one of many places where you can have a seat and enjoy the view.

Continuing south on the island, you'll pass drinking fountains and a portable restroom just beyond the garden entrance. Take either route at the fork: both trails lead through a densely wooded area and offer spur trails to the shore of the lagoon. Formally known as the Paul H. Douglas Nature Sanctuary, this small island is a hot spot for birders: 250 bird species have been sighted here, while 55 species make nests here. One bird species dwelling in Jackson Park and the surrounding neighborhoods, but rarely seen elsewhere around Chicago, is the monk parakeet—a green, loudly chattering, medium-sized bird native to South America. Since the parakeets mysteriously appeared a few decades back, their origin remains a matter of speculation: some say they were pets set free; others say they escaped from a crate at the airport.

At the southern tip of the island, cross the bridge and then cut left along the shoreline. First, however, you may want to take a short detour straight ahead to Hayes Drive and then left to South Richardson Drive to visit an impressive shining bronze statue called The Republic, a replica of the much larger statue that was built for the Columbian Exposition.

Continuing along the shore of the lagoon, you'll pass groves of weeping willows and a lagoon featuring prairie plants. After 0.2 miles hiking along the shore of the lagoon, and past the soccer fields on the right, follow the boardwalk that starts at the limestone fishing platform. Stay left through the small parking lot to the beginning of the trail through Bobolink Meadow.

Largely ignored by human visitors, this meadow is alive with animals and plants: rabbits scurry across the trail and songbirds serenade each other while perched on big bluestem, Indian grass, goldenrod, and other prairie plants. On your left, several side trails lead toward the trees drooping lazily over the water. Prior to the Columbian Exposition, this was a swampy marshland. Later it was used for athletic fields, and, surprisingly, from 1956 to 1971, it hosted an Army missile base. Since 1982, this plot has served as a nature preserve. Stay left as you pass through the gate, and head toward the bridge overlooking 100 or so boats moored in 59th Street Harbor. Continue along the shore of the lagoon, straight ahead to the parking lot.

▶ NEARBY ACTIVITIES

While visiting Jackson Park, consider taking a short walk to Promontory Point, perhaps the best slice of open parkland in the city. From the parking lot where the hike starts, head toward the lake on the paved path that runs on the north side of the harbor. After passing a lawn-bowling green on the left, the path enters a tunnel under Lakeshore Drive. Emerging from the tunnel, turn left and continue past the beach, arriving at Promontory Point 0.4 miles north of the tunnel. Known simply as "The Point," the park occupies a small piece of land jutting into the lake, and offers plenty of benches and big rocks from which to enjoy a great view of the downtown skyline.

Heading out of the Jackson Park parking lot, you'll encounter the southern edge of the University Of Chicago campus and the Midway Plaisance, a mile-long strip of green space running east–west. During the Columbian Exposition, the Midway Plaisance hosted amusement rides and a collection of re-created villages from around the world; now, it's open parkland with statuary and an ice rink operating in the winter. Starting at the east end of the Plaisance—closest to Jackson Park—you'll pass the large round Perennial Flower Garden, a statue of St. Wenceslas, the Rockefeller Memorial Chapel (with dozens of outdoor statues of religious figures), another garden, and several university residence halls.

Architecture fans will enjoy the English Gothic style that characterizes many of the University of Chicago's buildings. To see more of the campus, turn right on South Woodlawn Avenue, just east of the Rockefeller Chapel. One block ahead, turn left on East 58th Street toward the center of campus. At the northeast corner of Woodlawn and 58th, don't miss Frank Lloyd Wright's Robie House—considered to be the most complete expression of the architect's Prairie School style (call (773) 834-1847 for tours).

The Museum of Science and Industry is open 9:30 a.m. to 4 p.m. Monday through Friday, and 9:30 a.m. to 5:30 p.m. Saturday and Sunday (free admission on Thursday). Visit www.msichicago.org or call (773) 684-1414 for more information.

JOLIET IRON WORKS HIKE

▶ **IN BRIEF**

The Joliet Iron Works Historic Site provides a snapshot of how a large-scale iron-making operation worked in the late nineteenth century. Through reading the interpretive signs and wandering among the crumbling remains of buildings, you can trace the practice of iron-making, from raw materials to the casting bed.

▶ **DESCRIPTION**

In the nineteenth century, Joliet was known as the City of Steel and Stone. The stone was quarried from the nearby banks of the Des Plaines River, while the steel was produced at the Iron Works. Constructed in the 1870s, the Joliet Iron Works employed some 2,000 workers when production reached its peak at the turn of the century. Much of the steel made in Joliet went toward barbed wire and train-rail production.

For decades after the factory's closing in the 1930s, the Iron Works lay forgotten. In the early 1990s, the Will County Forest Preserve bought the property, and then opened the 51-acre site to the public in 1998. While much of the immediate

▶ **DIRECTIONS**

From Chicago take I-90/I-94 south. Continue on I-94 until reaching I-57. Take I-57 south for 13.5 miles to I-80 west. After 18.5 miles on I-80, take Exit 132 and follow US 53 north for 1.7 miles. Follow IL 53 through downtown Joliet, and then look for the Joliet Iron Works Historic Site sign as IL 53 follows East Columbia Street to the left.

For rail service from Chicago, take either the Rock Island District Metra Train from the LaSalle Street Station or the Heritage Corridor Metra Train from Union Station. Both lines end in downtown Joliet. From the Joliet station, follow West Jefferson Street west for half a block, and then proceed north on North Scott Street for 0.7 miles.

ⓘ KEY AT-A-GLANCE INFORMATION

LENGTH: 1.3 miles

CONFIGURATION: Loop

DIFFICULTY: Easy

SCENERY: Concrete and brick remnants of the historic Joliet Iron Works, wooded surroundings

EXPOSURE: Nearly all exposed

SURFACE: Paved

HIKING TIME: 1 hour

ACCESS: Summer, 8 a.m.–8 p.m.; winter, 8 a.m.–5 p.m.

FACILITIES: Bike racks, mapboard, benches, interpretive signs

MAPS: Mapboards are posted at the south and north ends of the site. Download a map from www.fpdwc.org/ironworks.cfm; USGS topo Joliet, IL

SPECIAL COMMENTS: Beware of crumbling walls and foundations. Adults should keep a close eye on children during this hike.

At the hikes's halfway point you have the option of following the Joliet Iron Works Heritage Trail to the left. This segment of the 11.4-mile Heritage Trail takes you to a lock in the historic I&M Canal.

For a thorough introduction to the Joliet area, visit the recently opened Joliet Area Historical Museum downtown at 204 North Ottawa Street. The museum's main gallery covers 7 distinct thematic areas: River City, the Canal, City of Steel and Stone, Metropolitan City, World War II, and the All-American City. Call (815) 723-5201 or visit www.jolietmuseum.org.

UTM Trailhead Coordinates for Joliet Iron Works Hike

UTM Zone (NAD27)   16T

Easting   409860

Northing   4598737

area around the Iron Works is wooded, you'll see the general location has maintained its industrial character; the railroad tracks on the right that once served the steel mill are still used today.

About 50 yards north of the parking lot, the first stop on the tour is the stockhouse, where the raw materials—iron ore, limestone, and coke—were stored. A sign along the path explains that the raw materials were transported via elevator nearly 100 feet up to be dropped in the top of the furnace. Next stop is the site of the blast furnace where the iron was made by heating raw materials to 3,500 degrees Fahrenheit for eight hours. After passing the casting bed where the iron was molded for transporting, you'll see foundations of four more blast stoves.

Many of the explanatory signs along the path describe the often dangerous jobs laborers performed at the mill. There are also plenty of photos of men who served in jobs such as stove tenders, claybusters, ladle liners, and cinder snappers. A few of the signs describe the laborers' lives outside of work. One sign offers a map of where the different ethnic groups lived in relation to the mill, and explains that the western Europeans often lived farther away from the grime and noise of the mill, while the eastern and southern Europeans lived closer to the mill and tended to have the lower-paying jobs.

Continuing ahead, a series of octagonal and rectangular foundations are remnants of the gas-washing plant, where gases were cleaned before they were burned in the gas engines. Next are four pass stoves that heated the air for furnace 4. After passing the doghouse, which is where workers monitored the stoves and the iron flow, the path heads up a set of stairs to blast furnace 3, a big bowl-shaped depression on the left. After blast furnace 4, follow the ramp down as you pass a large tunnel that penetrates layers of brick and concrete.

Across the railroad tracks, you won't miss the Illinois State Penitentiary, built with locally quarried limestone in 1858, and codesigned by the same architect who designed the famous Water Tower in Chicago. The 25-foot walls of the penitentiary are five-feet thick at the base. The next stop on the Iron Works tour looks more like the ruins of a lost city than part of a former factory. The large concrete footings at this site served as mounts for the enormous gas engines that powered the plant.

At 0.7 miles into the hike, turn right and follow the gravel-surfaced Joliet Iron Works Heritage Trail back to the parking lot. You can also add some extra mileage to your hike by taking the Heritage Trail to the left. This multiuse, crushed-limestone trail runs north along the I&M Canal for 11 miles to the town of Lockport. A half mile north of the Iron Works, the Herigate Trail crosses a couple of bridges that span two former locks, which were used to raise and lower boats in the canal. Also, along this section of trail you'll see another one of the state penitentiary's imposing guard towers.

Following the Heritage Trail to the right toward the parking lot leads you across a gravel road and close to the train tracks until it reaches the skull house. The skull house is where workers known as ladle liners would remove molten iron residue from the ladle cars. After removing the hardened residue, the ladle liner would re-line ladle cars with fire bricks and clay, so that these cars could be used again for transporting molten iron around the plant for processing. From the skull house, the parking lot is 0.3 miles ahead.

KANKAKEE RIVER STATE PARK HIKE

 KEY AT-A-GLANCE INFORMATION

LENGTH: 4.8 miles

CONFIGURATION: Out-and-back

DIFFICULTY: Easy

SCENERY: Kankakee River, bluffs, limestone canyon along Rock Creek

EXPOSURE: About half exposed and half shaded

SURFACE: Paved path, dirt

HIKING TIME: 2.5–3 hours

ACCESS: April 1–October 31, 6 a.m.–10 p.m.; November 1–March 31, 6 a.m.–6 p.m.

FACILITIES: Picnic areas, concession stand, bike and canoe rental, restrooms, park office, water fountains

MAPS: Maps available at the park office; USGS topo Bourbannais, IL

SPECIAL COMMENTS: Exercise caution while looking out from the ledges along Rock Creek—especially if kids are along. The seasonal concession stand offers ice, vending machines for drinks, bait, and canoes and bicycles for rent. Dogs must be kept on leashes.

UTM Trailhead Coordinates for Kankakee River State Park Hike

UTM Zone (NAD27)   16T

Easting   415088

Northing   4562406

IN BRIEF

The first section of this river hike takes you along the wooded bluffs above wide sections of the Kankakee River. After crossing a pedestrian suspension bridge, you'll follow Rock Creek along a dramatic canyon to a frothy waterfall.

DESCRIPTION

The focal points of Kankakee River State Park are the craggy cliffs and vertical walls of Rock Creek Canyon as it gently curves toward the Kankakee River.

This beautiful and dramatic rock formation has been captivating visitors for many generations. At the time of the first European contact, the Miami Indians were numerous along this part of the Kankakee River; by 1770, Indians from the Potawatomi, Chippewa, and Ottawa tribes—known as the "three fires"—dominated the area. The last Indian settlement at the confluence of Rock Creek and the Kankakee River was a sizable Potawatomi village. Most of the Potawatomi had been removed by the end of the decade, except for Chief Shawanasee, who lived the rest of his life here, and whose grave is commemorated with a boulder along a trail in the northern section of the

DIRECTIONS

Take I-90/I-94 south from Chicago. Continue on I-94 to I-57 south. Follow I-57 south for 42.7 miles. At Exit 315, head south on IL 50 for 0.3 miles to Armour Road. Turn right (west) on Armour Road and proceed for 2 miles to IL 102. Turn right (northwest) on IL 102 and continue for 5.8 miles to the park's visitor center, where you can pick up a park map. From the visitor center, continue heading northwest on IL 102 for 1.7 miles to Warner Bridge Road. Turn left on Warner Bridge Road. The parking lot is on the right, just before the bridge.

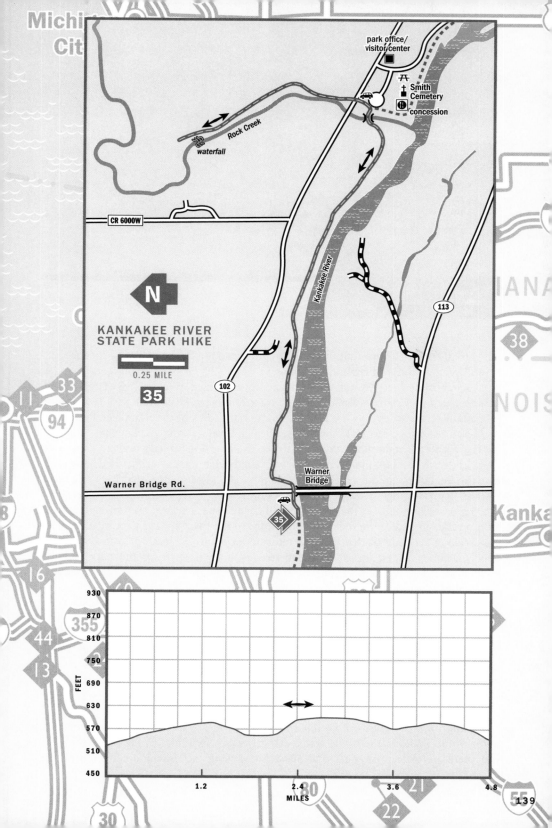

Michigan
City

park office/
visitor center

Smith
Cemetery

concession

Rock Creek

waterfall

CR 6000W

N

KANKAKEE RIVER
STATE PARK HIKE

0.25 MILE

35

113

Kankakee River

102

Warner Bridge Rd.

Warner
Bridge

35

Kanka

INDIANA

ILLINOIS

38

33

94

16

355

44

13

FEET

930
870
810
750
690
630
570
510
450

1.2   2.4   3.6   4.8
           MILES

30

22

139

A view of Rock Creek from the pedestrian suspension bridge.

park. (Unfortunately, the trail that runs by this boulder has been closed for the past several years because of erosion problems.)

Established in 1948, the park was greatly expanded over the years largely from land donated by Commonwealth Edison. Now Kankakee River State Park is 11-miles long and encompasses 3,932 acres, straddling both sides of the Kankakee River.

Before starting out from the Warner Bridge Road parking lot, I suggest taking a short walk to the right along the river to see the limestone pillars built to support a train bridge in the late nineteenth century. The bridge was never finished, however, because financiers ran out of money before the railroad was completed. Heading back toward Warner Bridge Road, the trail runs under the bridge before turning left and making a steep climb. At the top of the hill, you'll pass a farm and an agricultural field on the left before the trail turns right toward the river. For the next mile the trail glides along the side of this wooded bluff about 40 to 50 feet up from the river's edge. In some places, the drop to the river is steep enough for the park to have erected steel fencing along the trail. The season that you're hiking will determine how well you can see the river; if the leaf cover is heavy, look for the occasional openings in the shrubs that will allow you to see shorelines in the distance and the low islands. Shortly after passing a picnic table with a shelter overlooking the river, the trail curves left up a hill toward the suspension footbridge spanning Rock Creek.

The bridge offers a great vantage point from which to enjoy the beginning of this dolomite rock canyon. The stone walls—sometimes vertical and sometimes slanted or step-like—become even more pronounced as you head upstream. On the other side of the bridge, at 1.6 miles into the hike, turn left to cross IL 102. On the other side of the highway, continue ahead, ignoring the old emergency-access sign.

Approach the cliffs on the left with care: there are no guardrails between you and a 50- to 70-foot drop to the water. Oak trees are often thick at the top of the cliff, but there are dozens of spots that allow for viewing the dramatic canyon and the river. At 0.3 miles after crossing the highway is a sign indicating that the waterfall is a half mile ahead. Just beyond the sign, the dilapidated pavement ends and the wide dirt path begins. To the right, a line of pine trees starts to run parallel to the trail. In a few places, you'll see horse trails heading off to the right into the shrubby woodland. While these trails are on park-owned land, hiking on them is not encouraged.

At the next picnic table, look upstream for a view of the waterfall, which makes a sloping descent for about eight feet. Enjoy the view while you can: according to the Illinois State Geological Survey, the waterfall is moving upstream at a rate of three inches per year. If you continue ahead, there's another perch where you can look out directly above the falls. This is also where you'll see the chain-link fence signaling that it's time to turnaround and head back toward the highway.

Crossing back over IL 102, the park visitor center is 0.15 miles to the left. Along with a few mounted animal and bird specimens, the visitor center hosts an impressive collection of fossils and arrowheads—nearly all of which were found in the park.

Heading toward the Kankakee River from the visitor center, you'll come upon a paved path that runs next to the river. To the left, the path runs 1.8 miles through riverside picnic areas, near the community of Altorf, and next to the site of an old mill and distillery. From there, the path surface turns to crushed limestone and runs for 3.7 miles near the park's Potawatomi Campground, and through a secluded wooded area with a few scattered marshes, streams, and savannas. The trail, which is a great route for biking or hiking, ends at the Davis Creek Group Camping Area.

Heading to the right along the Kankakee River and back toward the beginning of the hike brings you past a couple of lookout platforms above the river. Near the covered pedestrian bridge is a knoll with a fenced-off cemetery at the top. Most of the gravesites contain infants and children from the Smith family, who died from yellow fever at the turn of the century. Heading back towards the suspension bridge brings you past the log-cabin concession stand and the restrooms. From the bridge, retrace your steps 1.6 miles back to the parking lot on the other side of Warner Bridge Road.

▶ NEARBY ACTIVITIES

Kankakee River State Park is full of enjoyable activities. The park's riding stable offers guided half-hour to day-long rides, pony rides, lessons, and cookouts all year around. Groups range from 8 to 12 riders; private rides are an additional fee. To get to the stable, head north for 0.75 miles on the first road east of the park's visitor center. The stable is at 6500 North 5000 W. Road. Reservations are required and can be made by calling (815) 939-0309.

If canoeing is more your style, you can rent canoes to paddle near the park, or park staff can drop you off in the town of Kankakee for a 10-mile paddle back to the park. Call (815) 932-6555 for reservations.

In addition to the trails described here, there's a long equestrian loop trail that can be hiked on the other side of the river, and there's hiking in Area A in the western tip of the park. Check in at the visitor center to find out if hunting season is underway at either of these spots. In the visitor center, you can also find out about camping at the park's two campgrounds. The park office phone number is (815) 933-1383.

LAKE KATHERINE TRAIL

KEY AT-A-GLANCE INFORMATION

LENGTH: 3.2 miles

CONFIGURATION: Combo

DIFFICULTY: Moderate

SCENERY: Lake, canal, woodland, specialty gardens, man-made waterfalls

EXPOSURE: Mostly shaded

SURFACE: Woodchip, dirt, gravel

HIKING TIME: 1.5 hours

ACCESS: Sunrise–10 p.m.

FACILITIES: Benches, restrooms, an environmental learning center with exhibits, and an ice-skating rink in winter

MAPS: Maps available from the learning center; USGS topo Palos Park, IL

SPECIAL COMMENTS: Dogs must be leashed and picked up after. The environmental learning center is open Monday–Friday, 9 a.m.–5 p.m., and weekends, 10 a.m.–4 p.m. Closed Sundays during winter months. Call (708) 361-1873 for more information.

UTM Trailhead Coordinates for
Lake Katherine Trail

UTM Zone (NAD27)   16T

Easting   433317

Northing   4613961

▶ IN BRIEF

As an urban nature walk, this is one of the best in the area. Nestled alongside the Calumet-Sag Channel, 136-acre Lake Katherine Preserve features an attractive lake, an arboretum, a waterfall garden, an herb and a conifer garden, and expansive views from atop a ridge in the eastern section of the preserve.

▶ DESCRIPTION

In the 1980s, this patch of land was an eyesore. People had left mounds of debris and junk car parts amid piles of boulders and overgrown bushes. Then the city of Palos Heights decided to transform this dumping ground on the banks of the Calumet-Sag Channel into parkland. The result is a charming urban park, half of which is carefully landscaped and the other half fairly wild. In 1992, First Lady Barbara Bush presented the preserve with a National Landscape Award, sponsored by the American Association of Nurserymen.

Much of this hike runs alongside the Cal-Sag Channel, a 16-mile waterway between the Little Calumet River and the Sanitary and Ship Canal. Slow-moving barges frequently use this channel to

▶ DIRECTIONS

From Chicago, take I-55 southwest to Exit 283. Follow IL 43 (South Harlem Avenue) 8.4 miles to the left (south) to IL 83 (West College Drive). Turn right on IL 83 and proceed to the entrance of Lake Katherine Preserve, 0.3 miles ahead on the right.

Alternate directions from the northwest: Heading southeast on I-294, take the US 12/US 20 exit, heading east. Immediately turn right on IL 43, heading south for 3 miles to IL 83 (West College Drive). After turning right on IL 83, the entrance to the preserve is just ahead on the right.

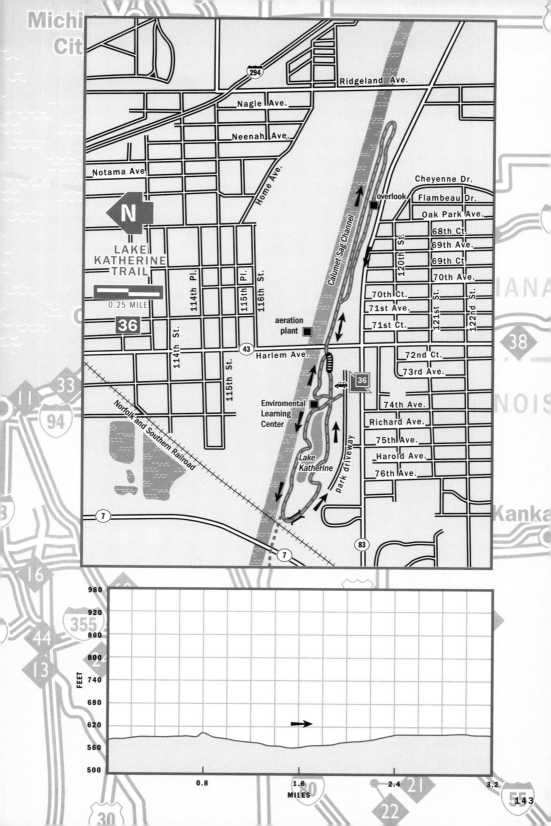

Michi
City

294
Ridgeland Ave.

Nagle Ave.

Neenah Ave.

Notama Ave.

Home Ave.

Cheyenne Dr.

overlook
Flambeau Dr.

Oak Park Ave.

68th Ct.

69th Ave.

69th Ct.

70th Ave.

N

LAKE
KATHERINE
TRAIL

0.25 MILE

36

114th Pl.

115th Pl.

116th St.

Calumet-Sag Channel

120th St.

70th Ct.

71st Ave.

71st Ct.

121st St.

122nd St.

ANA

38

aeration
plant

43   Harlem Ave.

114th St.

115th St.

Norfolk and Southern Railroad

72nd Ct.

73rd Ave.

36

74th Ave.

Richard Ave.

75th Ave.

Harold Ave.

76th Ave.

NOIS

Enviromental
Learning
Center

Lake
Katherine

park driveway

7

83

7

Kanka

980
920
860
800
740
680
620
560
500

FEET

0.8   1.6   2.4   3.2
MILES

355

44

13

16

30

80

21

22

51

143

transport cargo such as fuel oils, coke, and gasoline between the Mississippi River and Calumet Harbor, the largest harbor on the Great Lakes. The digging of the channel started in 1911 for the purpose of creating a feeder channel for the Illinois and Michigan Canal. It also brought polluted water away from Lake Michigan, keeping Chicago's drinking water safe and clean. In coming years, after the channel was widened and dredged, it proved to be an important shipping route.

From the parking lot, head toward the buildings on the edge of the lake. The first building on the right is the E. G. Simpson Clubhouse—a remnant of a former gun club that is now used for banquets. After passing the small pier and the environmental learning center, which caters largely to school groups, you'll see a small herb garden with dozens of plants growing in raised beds. If you've ever wondered what curry, horseradish, lavender, oregano, or basil plants look like, here's your chance. Next is a bird-and-butterfly garden hosting a variety of shrubs, flowers, grasses, and vines meant to attract the winged creatures.

Continuing on the woodchip trail brings you past a cluster of conifer trees and a bench overlooking the canal. Farther along is an observation platform at the edge of the lake. At the sign for the children's forest, continue straight ahead, and then, before the bridge, take the trail on the left, leading you into an area dense with cottonwood and shrubs. If you continue ahead, you can hike for another third of a mile under two bridges—one that serves the Norfolk and Southern Railroad and one that serves IL 7. The children's forest on the left had its beginnings on Arbor Day in 1990, when some 500 children and their families planted trees and bushes on this several-acre plot.

As you walk parallel to the train tracks up on the embankment, stay left and cross a wooden bridge over an intermittent stream. Keep straight ahead through the children's forest until you're back at the woodchip trail near an arch from the front doorway of a former Palos Heights elementary school. Continuing around Lake Katherine to the right, the shoreline opens up, providing a view of the cattails, sedge grasses, and lily pads out in the water.

While conifers and cottonwood grow fairly thickly on the north side of the lake, the south side hosts about 70 different tree species, many of them identified with plaques. Along with more than a dozen crab apple trees, there are silver maple, burr oak, gingko, locust, green ash, American filbert, and swamp white oak. As the trail winds around the lake, multiple benches are situated on the little pieces of land jutting into the lake. On the wooded island across from one of the promontories, look for the heron rookery made from two-by-fours.

At the clubhouse, cross over the trail that you started on and then continue straight ahead to the waterfall garden, featuring a maze of rocks and trees built up on a little hill. At the top of the hill, lake water is pumped out among the stands of Norway spruce, quaking aspen, and staghorn sumac, before tumbling over four short waterfalls and through several shallow intermediate pools. From the base of the falls, the water runs along a brook back to the lake. On the backside of the waterfall, dozens of shrubs, trees, and groundcover plants grow in the small conifer garden (look for the identification tags on individual plants). From the conifer garden, look for the paved road that runs next to the canal, and follow it away from the environmental learning center.

After passing under the Harlem Avenue Bridge, you'll see a series of waterfalls flowing over concrete embankments on the opposite side of the canal. This is one of five SEPA (sidestream elevated pool aeration) stations along the canal and the Little Calumet River. The SEPA stations clean the water by cooling it and increasing its oxygen content, while also providing a pleasant recreation area for local residents. Beyond the bridge, look for the small side trail leading to a bench overlooking the SEPA station.

After the SEPA station, you'll pass a mountain of woodchips and a couple of junctions on the right. Soon a clearing provides a nice view of the wooded banks across the channel. As the trail turns right, a small side trail leads to a bench with a view of the Ridgeland Avenue Bridge. Continuing to the right, follow the arrow pointing to the trail heading into the woods. Although this less-used trail may be slightly overgrown in spots with shrubbery, it's still easy to follow. The trail occasionally becomes rugged and steep as it follows the rise and fall of a ridge running parallel to the canal on the right and IL 83 on the left.

Nearly halfway through the ridge hike, you'll encounter an overlook with a pavilion and benches. Among the trunks of cottonwood, elm, and hickory, you'll notice half-buried chunks of limestone. In 1955, when the Army Corp of Engineers widened the Cal-Sag Channel, they formed this ridge with the excavated earth and stone. At one point, the trail drops down sharply before crossing an intermittent stream on a line of boulders. Continuing on, the trail grows wider and the surface becomes fuzzy with moss. Once you reach the open gravelly area, head back down to the trail on the side of the canal.

Just after passing under the bridge on the way back to the parking lot, take a left on the wide woodchip trail. This trail leads to a boardwalk and a set of stairs and benches that winds through a wooded gully containing an intermittent stream. Following the stairs up the side of the gully brings you to the vegetable garden, complete with scarecrows and a variety of flowers and common vegetables. At the edge of the garden, a half-dozen pieces of old farm equipment are on display. From the vegetable garden, continue to the left through the small prairie and back to the parking lot.

LAKEWOOD FOREST PRESERVE LOOP

KEY AT-A-GLANCE INFORMATION

LENGTH: 2.6 miles

CONFIGURATION: Loop

DIFFICULTY: Easy

SCENERY: Oak forest, marshes, lakes, prairie, savanna

EXPOSURE: Mostly shaded

SURFACE: Wide dirt

HIKING TIME: 1–1.5 hours

ACCESS: 6:30–sunset

FACILITIES: Trailhead offers pit toilets and water. The larger preserve provides several picnicking areas, shelters, playgrounds, and lakes for fishing. The preserve also hosts the Lake County Discovery Museum, described in "Nearby Activities" section. In the winter, a skating rink and a sledding hill open at the Millennium Trail parking area.

MAPS: Use the mapboards on the trails; USGS topos Grayslake, Lake Zurich, IL

SPECIAL COMMENTS: Most users of this trail are equestrians. Always give them the right-of-way. No dogs allowed. On summer evenings as the sun goes down, check out the cluster of bat houses across Ivanhoe Road in the picnic area on the left. Across the park road from the bat houses, you can explore more than 3 miles of woodland trails.

UTM Trailhead Coordinates for Lakewood Forest Preserve Loop

UTM Zone (NAD27) 16T

Easting 408668

Northing 4678617

IN BRIEF

This quiet hike takes you through a gently rolling oak forest dotted with cattail marshes and attractive lakes. After finishing up this hike, visitors may want to explore one of the best county museums in the state, or go for a spin on a recently completed bicycle/pedestrian trail.

DESCRIPTION

During much of the 1800s, Lakewood Forest Preserve was little more than a source of lumber and firewood for local farmers. After the Civil War, however, trees were cleared and small farms were built in the area. In 1937, some of these small farms were absorbed by Malcom Boyle as he assembled a country estate that included livestock, orchards, gardens, and crops. Many of Boyle's efforts are still visible today, such as 16 major structures and the landscaping around the lakes. In 1961, Boyle's estate was transformed into a dairy farm that lasted only a few years. During the next 30 years, the county slowly acquired nearly 2,600 acres, making it the largest forest preserve in Lake County. Many of the former estate's buildings—including a couple of barns and a chicken coop—are still in use as offices, storage, and the museum.

DIRECTIONS

Follow I-90/I-94 northwest from Chicago. Continue on I-90 for 15.5 miles after I-94 breaks off. Exit on IL 53 and head north for 5.4 miles until reaching US 12 (North Rand Road). Turn left (northwest) on US 12 and proceed for 10.8 miles. Turn right (north) on South Main Street and then drive for 300 yards until turning right again on Ivanhoe Road. Stay on Ivanhoe Road for 1.3 miles, passing the equestrian parking area on the right. Just after the major forest preserve entrance on the left, turn into the parking area on the right, next to the service buildings.

Michigan City

176 Liberty St. 176

N

Lake County
Discovery
Museum

**LAKEWOOD FOREST
PRESERVE LOOP**

Davis
Lake

0.25 MILE

37

Schreiber
Lake

Forest Preserve Rd.

37

Heron
Pond

horse
facility

Ivanhoe Rd.

cropland

prairie

Fairfield Rd.

38

Acorn
Lake

Beaver
Lake

Milton Rd.

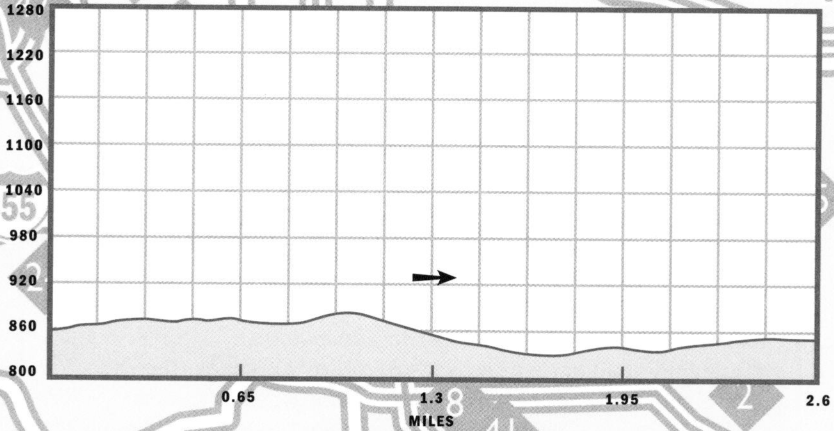

FEET

1280
1220
1160
1100
1040
980
920
860
800

0.65   1.3   1.95   2.6
MILES

From the parking lot, follow the wide trail on the right as it heads south alongside Heron Pond, named for the Great Blue Herons often seen along its shore. At the first junction, take the trail to the left and stay left as you pass a couple of junctions. While there are a handful of unmarked junctions throughout this hike, it's fairly easy to navigate. If you do get disoriented, trail boards showing your location are posted at most major junctions. Keep in mind, though, that the mapboards don't show all of the short connector trails.

After dropping down a small hill and walking along the pond's wooded shore again, the trail rises steeply under a thick canopy of oak. The path curves right before arriving at a T-junction. (To add a half mile to your hike, take a left at the T and pass through oak woodland as you make your way near a couple of houses and a large horse facility.) To continue the hike, hang a right at the T and then take an immediate left. This fairly flat stretch of trail runs through stands of quaking aspen and to the right of a spacious prairie dotted with black willows in the low spots.

Continue straight ahead at the junction, passing a cattail marsh on the right; the landscape here becomes more rolling. Burr oaks multiply and provide more shade for the trail. Just before the trail turns right, you'll pass a marsh on the left thick with grasses and cattails. Stay left as the trail dips and rises to the next junction and then descends a big hill and passes a series of intermittent streambeds on both sides of the trail. After entering a savanna, the trail runs through clusters of buckthorn on its way to the next junction. Staying left at the junction brings you through a short loop and close to the shore of a large marsh fringed with oak and cottonwood trees. While it's difficult to get much of a view of the marsh's open water through the thick cattails, you can do a little bushwhacking on the shoreline to seek out a better vantage point. This search may be rewarded by seeing a kingfisher, some waterfowl, or a hawk perched in a tree above the edge of the marsh. Stay to the left as you complete the short loop and swing around to the other side of the marsh.

Continuing through a savanna, take the next right on a short connector trail that leads to a couple of lovely little lakes. Beaver Lake offers grassy areas in which to sit down and enjoy the scene. The land around the lake is densely wooded, while the water's edge—stretching out of view to the left—is sprinkled with stumps and fallen trees. Heading left from the junction takes you through more savanna and past a junction on the left at Acorn Lake. This lake is smaller, largely covered with algae, and swampy in parts. Continuing straight ahead past a couple of junctions on the right brings you back to the parking lot.

▶ NEARBY ACTIVITIES

The Millennium Trail is a planned bicycling/pedestrian trail that will eventually curve through the mid-section of Lake County. The new Lakewood section of the Millennium Trail runs through woodland and savanna and next to a marsh and a few lovely lakes. While fairly popular with cyclists on warm weekends, the wide crushed-gravel trail offers plenty of room for hikers, too. Catch the trail from the parking lot at the corner of Ivanhoe and Fairfield roads, just a half mile east of the trailhead for the hike above. This 2.4-mile hike is a loop with out-and-back sections on each end. The turnaround point is a picturesque spot where a bridge runs over a small dam that divides Owens and Davis lakes.

From the parking lot, the trail leads down a hill and through groves of pine, quaking aspen, cottonwood, and oak. Taking a right at the junction leads down to a boardwalk spanning part of a large cattail marsh. From the boardwalk, the trail winds through an attractive rolling savanna that has grown alongside a marsh dotted with black willow. Skip the trail on the right that leads to Schwerman Road. Instead, take the next right, which runs near Schreiber Lake. Soon, you'll reach the turnaround point: a pleasant spot where a small bridge and dam separate Owens Lake on the right and Davis Lake on the left. Heading back to the last junction, take a right to complete the other side of the loop. After taking in a nice view of Schreiber Lake from a hilltop, take the two-track road on the right through a savanna to the shore of Davis Lake. Continuing ahead on the main trail, take the junction right, heading back to the parking lot. The parking area for the Millennium Trail offers restrooms, water, a skating rink, and a sledding hill.

The highlight of the Lake County Discovery Museum is an exhibit showcasing the largest public collection of postcards in the world. Kept in a nearby building at the forest preserve, the 2.5 million items in the collection were once owned by Lake County resident Curt Teich, the owner of what was one of the largest printers of post-cards in the world. The exhibit features rare and unusual postcards, and examines postcard artists and themes. Other exhibits at the museum are focused specifically on Lake County history, such as the founding of Zion and the abundance of lotus blos-soms that brought tourists to the Chain O' Lakes area. Outside the museum are sculptures of an American mastodon and what's called an Indian trail-marker tree.

The museum is open Monday to Saturday, 11 a.m. to 4:30 p.m. and Sunday, 1 p.m. to 4:30 p.m. Call (847) 968-3400 or visit www.co.lake.il.us/forest/educate.htm for more information.

LASALLE FISH AND WILDLIFE AREA LOOP

KEY AT-A-GLANCE INFORMATION

LENGTH: 5.2 miles

CONFIGURATION: Loop

DIFFICULTY: Moderate

SCENERY: Kankakee River, expansive marshland, large lake, prairie, savanna, woodland, numerous drainage ditches, and a stream

EXPOSURE: Mostly exposed

SURFACE: Sand/dirt two-track road

HIKING TIME: 3–3.5 hours

ACCESS: Much of the west half of this hike is closed for waterfowl hunting from October 1 to December 1. If you're visiting during that time, stick to the east half of the fish-and-wildlife area.

FACILITIES: Boat launch at parking area

MAPS: USGS topos straddle the state line between Illiana Heights, IL and Schneider, IN; map posted at park office

SPECIAL COMMENTS: Since this wildlife area is largely undeveloped, you're likely to be all alone once you get away from the prime fishing spots.

UTM Trailhead Coordinates for LaSalle Fish and Wildlife Area Loop

UTM Zone (NAD27) 16T

Easting 458293

Northing 4557326

IN BRIEF

If you like riverside hikes and sprawling marsh-lands busy with birds, you'll find this to be one of the great undiscovered hikes in Chicagoland. Nearly every inch of this hike accompanies either a river, a drainage ditch, a pond, or a marshland.

DESCRIPTION

About 150 years ago, the Grand Kankakee Marsh was the largest wetland in the Midwest, stretching for nearly a million acres through northwest Indiana. Then in the mid-1800s, the marshes were drained, and the Kankakee River was deepened and channelized in order to use the flat, moist landscape for farming. Drainage tiles were installed, ditches were dug, and pumps were instaled to push water away from the cropland. Also, an extensive levee system was built to reduce flooding near the waterways. According to the United States Geological Survey, only 13 percent of the Kankakee Marsh remain.

Grand Kankakee Marsh was named by the early French explorers who came through major waterways of the area looking for a water route to the Pacific Ocean. One of these explorers was Robert Cavalier, Sier de LaSalle, for whom the 3,797-acre fish-and-wildlife area is named. LaSalle Fish and Wildlife Area—one of the few

DIRECTIONS

From Chicago, take I-90/I-94 south. Stay on I-94 as I-90 splits off. When I-94 reaches I-80, continue straight ahead on IL 394 for 4.8 miles. Turn left (east) on US 30 (East Lincoln Highway) and proceed for 6.1 miles to US 41 (Wicker Avenue). Hang a right (south) on US 41 and continue for 23.8 miles until you reach IL 10 (County Road 1000). Turn right (west) on IL 10 and proceed for 2.4 miles until you see the sign for parking lot 3A.

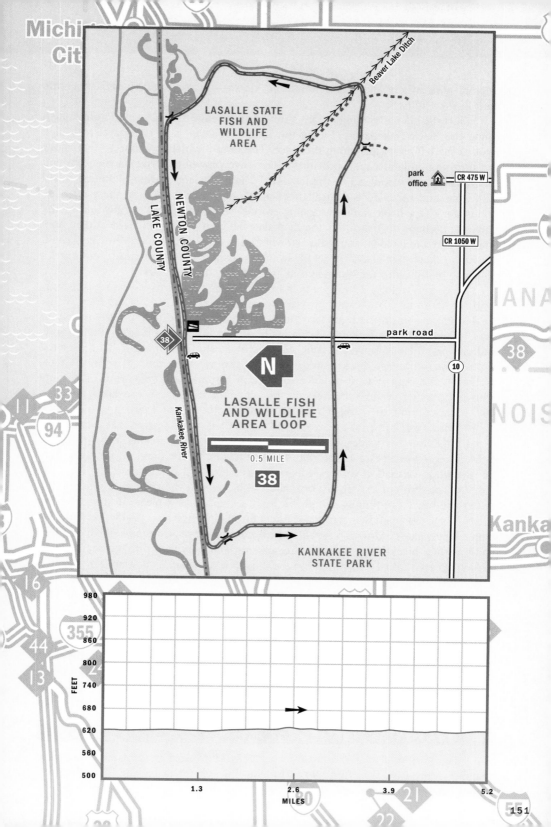

Michi
Cit

LASALLE STATE
FISH AND
WILDLIFE
AREA

Beaver Lake Ditch

LAKE COUNTY

NEWTON COUNTY

park office

CR 475 W

CR 1050 W

park road

Kankakee River

N

LASALLE FISH
AND WILDLIFE
AREA LOOP

0.5 MILE

38

10

38

NOIS

Kanka

KANKAKEE RIVER
STATE PARK

94

33

16

355

44

13

FEET

980
920
860
800
740
680
620
560
500

1.3

2.6
MILES

3.9

5.2

original remnants of the Grand Kankakee Marsh—was first established as a state park in the 1960s.

Start the hike in parking lot 3A, situated at the edge of a vast, open water marsh called the Black Oak Bayou. Facing the Kankakee River, take the gravel two-track road to the left as it runs along the levee. The levee—which is about 15 feet above the surrounding landscape—provides a bird's-eye view of the river on the right and the marshes and woodland to the left. At 0.2 miles, a large, swampy pond covered with algae and speckled with dead trees opens on the left. Many of these riverside ponds are shaped like short, wriggling worms—indicating their former life as the curves or perhaps the oxbows of the Kankakee before it was channelized. After a brief stretch of cottonwoods and oaks growing in a wet savanna on the left, you'll encounter more marshland alive with swallows soaring among the dead trees, turtles plopping off logs into the water, and lily pads tilting in the breeze.

Once you've logged nearly a mile of hiking, the trail turns left and passes over a bridge spanning a waterway between the marshes on each side of the trail. As the small open marsh on the right turns into an algae-covered ditch, and the marsh on the left fades into stands of cattails and willows, the trail turns left again. Prairie grass and compass plants fringe the trail, while willows and cottonwoods hang over the algae-covered drainage ditches on each side of the two-track road. Beyond the foot-bridge on the right that provides a connection to parking lot 4B, you'll see some cropland peeking through the trees on the left as the trail enters a savanna.

After crossing the road at 2.25 miles into the hike, you'll pass a wet, shrubby prairie with a backdrop of oak woodland on the left. At the point where two-track roads come from both sides, continue straight ahead as the trail angles slightly to the right. Soon, two successive footbridges cross the continuous ditch on the right. Stay on the two-track road as you cross a gravel road and then swing left.

As the trail curves left, Beaver Lake Ditch splits to the right and left, running under the road. Continuing ahead, the trail accompanies a pleasant stretch of the sandy-bottomed creek that gently meanders through wet savanna and woodland. The damp, shady sides of the trail are thick with horsetail grass, the stems of which come apart at their black-fringed joints. After passing a marshy area through the trees on the left, Beaver Lake Ditch flows into the Snag Boyou, which is bordered by quaking aspen and oak. Once you cross a bridge, the trail hits the Kankakee River.

Turning left, finish off the hike with a mile-long stroll between the straight, fast-moving Kankakee River, and the immense bayou with stands of dead trees jutting upwards and patches of green algae on the surface. Above the cattails and sedge grasses, listen for the loud chattering of belted kingfishers, and watch for them hovering over water as they scout out a meal. The view of the marsh is obscured now and then with berry bushes, small trees, and full-sized cottonwoods. In places where the bayou meets the edge of the trail, you'll see that the water level in the marsh is several feet higher that the water level in the river. Continue ahead on the levee until you reach the parking lot.

▶ NEARBY ACTIVITIES

Ten miles northwest of the LaSalle Fish and Wildlife Area is the Grand Kankakee Marsh County Park Hike (page 94). Thirteen miles south of LaSalle is the Iroquois County State Wildlife Area Hike (page 127).

MARENGO RIDGE HIKE

▶ IN BRIEF

If you enjoy hikes through hilly terrain criss-crossed with intermittent streams and blanketed with dense groves of oak, hickory, and conifers, you'll be charmed by this hike in southwestern McHenry County. Situated up on a ridge left by the last glacier, this wonderfully wooded landscape provides visitors with an unusually isolated atmosphere.

▶ DESCRIPTION

Rising 930 feet above the surrounding agricultural land, the 3-mile-wide Marengo Ridge runs north and south through western McHenry County to Kane County. A glacial moraine left by the last ice age, the ridge is largely sand, gravel, clay and boulders. Situated nearly at the top of the ridge is 400 acres of hilly woods known as the Marengo Ridge Conservation Area. One of the many attractive features of this conservation area is the abundance of conifers. A former landowner, Dr. Emerson Kunde, planted the pine trees in 1955 with the hope that they would survive in the harsh soil that had been damaged from overgrazing. Along with 15 species of conifers planted by Kunde—including Norway spruce, Douglas fir, red pine, and scotch pine—the woods are also thick with oak, hickory, poplar, sumac, and ash trees.

Starting from the trailhead located between the mapboard and the water pump, the gravel trail immediately climbs a hill through stands of oak, hickory, and conifer. At the top of the hill, keep

▶ KEY AT-A-GLANCE INFORMATION

LENGTH: 3.1 miles

CONFIGURATION: 3 connected loops

DIFFICULTY: Moderate

SCENERY: Hilly woodland, pine plantations, numerous intermittent streams

EXPOSURE: Shaded

SURFACE: Dirt, mowed grass

HIKING TIME: 2 hours

ACCESS: Sunrise to sunset

FACILITIES: Pit toilet, water, picnic tables, campground

MAPS: Available at mapboard; www.mccdistrict.org/Maps.htm; USGS topo Marengo North, IL

SPECIAL COMMENTS: Dogs must be leashed. The Marengo Ridge Campground offers 30 wooded campsites, 6 of which are walk-in sites. The campground is open May–October. Contact the McHenry County Conservation District at (815) 338-6223 for more information.

▶ DIRECTIONS

Take I-90/I-94 northwest. Continue on I-90 for 42 miles after I-94 splits off. Exit on US 20 and head north (left) toward Marengo. Follow US 20 for 9.1 miles until reaching IL 23. At IL 23, turn right (north). The entrance to Marengo Ridge is 2.5 miles ahead, on the right.

UTM Trailhead Coordinates for Marengo Ridge Hike

UTM Zone (NAD27) 16T

Easting 386917

Northing 4658026

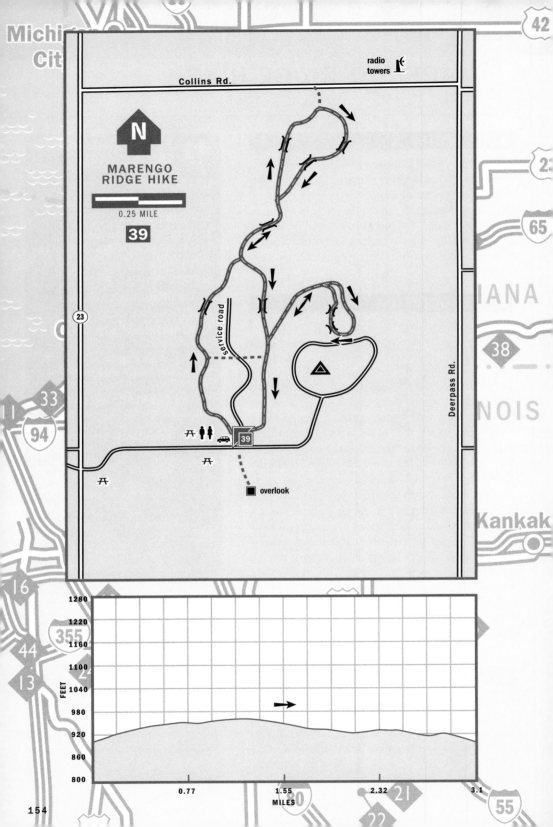

MARENGO
RIDGE HIKE

0.25 MILE

39

Collins Rd.

radio
towers

23

service road

39

overlook

Deerpass Rd.

straight as you pass the trail heading to the right (with a couple of exceptions on the campground loop, stay to the left throughout this hike). After descending a small hill through stands of elm, cross a bridge over an intermittent, rocky-bottomed stream.

In the streambeds and scattered on the sides of the trail are boulders ranging in size from softballs to soccer balls. Known as glacial erratics, these rocks were carried here by the Wisconsin Glacier as many as 24,000 years ago, and can be traced back to the bedrock around Lake Superior 350 miles to the north. Some of the boulders contain gneiss (pronounced "nice") or basalt, indicating they came from central or eastern Canada. Gneiss is coarsely textured with parallel streaks or bands, while basalt is dark and finely textured.

At 0.6 miles into the hike, stay left at the junction, and soon you'll pass stands of white and red pine, as well as quaking aspen and sumac. The trail takes a short dip before rising to a large prairie blanketed with goldenrod and dotted with thistle plants for much of the summer. Quickly entering the woods again, you'll pass a cluster of erratic boulders before crossing another intermittent stream. The many intermittent streambeds throughout the conservation area carry meltwater or water from heavy rains to the nearby Kishwaukee River. When the streams aren't running, there still may be puddles left in the streambeds (the edges of these puddles are good places to look for animal tracks). Some of the deeper streambeds provide a glimpse of the layers of sand, rock, gravel, and dirt deposited by the last glacier.

Stay to the left and start the next loop as the trail narrows and rises up a small hill. While the trail weaves through the trees on this less-used path, watch for boughs of thorny bushes hanging over the trail and occasional deadfall that must be stepped over. After crossing another bridge, a narrow side trail heads left to Collins Road. Growing near two bridges over intermittent streams are thick stands of elm and white oak. Nearby, you'll pass a pile of smaller boulders likely collected by an early farmer.

Keep to the left as you finish the upper loop, backtrack along the connector trail, and then return to the lower loop. Back on the lower loop, the trail passes through a savanna and then enters a fragrant stretch where the sides of the trail are lined with wild raspberry, rosehips, gooseberry, and honeysuckle bushes. After crossing a bridge, the trail rises to another pine plantation. Midway through the plantation, a marker indicates where you'll turn left to start the campground loop.

The narrow connector trail takes you through rolling landscape on its way to the campground loop. Turning left on the loop, the trail makes a long, winding descent before passing two successive trails on the left, leading to the campground (the first trail provides access to restrooms and a water spigot). After the wide, grassy trail takes a couple of banked turns, you'll cross two bridges and then climb a hill before returning to the connector trail.

Once you've returned to the pine plantation via the connector trail, continue left down the hill. Passing a few campsites through the trees on the left, the trail runs under a cluster of picturesque 60-foot Norway spruce trees with large drooping branches. On the ground, you'll see the big 6-inch pine cones this tree produces (among spruce trees, these are the largest pine cones). The trail passes through groves of white pine and walnut trees before dropping you off in the picnic area by the parking lot.

After enjoying Marengo Ridge's main course, there are a couple of short walks that can serve as the dessert. To visit the small fishing lake, walk along the main park road toward the campground. Just before the RV dump station, take the trail to the right for a short trip down to the small lake. Also, directly across the main park road from the trailhead parking lot is a short, paved path that leads to a pleasant overlook of the farmland and countryside south of the park.

▶ NEARBY ACTIVITIES

The nearby town of Union hosts several fun historical attractions. In downtown Union is a school built in 1870, now occupied by the McHenry County Historical Museum (6422 Main Street). On the property there's also a log home built in 1847 and a one-room schoolhouse from 1855. The museum is open May to October, Sunday and Tuesday through Friday, 1 p.m. to 4 p.m. Visit www.mchsonline.org. To reach the museum from Marengo Ridge, take IL 23 left and turn left again on IL 176. Turn right on North Union Road, heading toward downtown Union.

Just outside of Union, the Illinois Railway Museum has dozens of electric street cars, street trolleys, steam and diesel locomotives, passenger cars, freight cars, and cabooses on display. The museum has many artifacts, too, such as signals, signs, tools, uniforms, and even buildings. Visitors can ride a streetcar line around the main museum grounds and take a 40-minute round-trip to Kishwaukee Grove on a historic train. Several segments of major Hollywood films have been shot on the grounds in order to use the museum's extensive collection of historic trains. Follow the signs from downtown Union. Learn more by visiting www.irm.org.

Signs from downtown Union also point the way to Wild West Town, which includes a re-creation of a gold rush–era mining operation, a historic jail, saloon, and blacksmith shop. There are also pony rides, a train ride, and a "Wild West Show." Visit www.wildwesttown.com for more information.

MATTHIESSEN STATE PARK DELLS AREA HIKE

▶ IN BRIEF

Formerly a private retreat for a local industrialist, the highlight of Matthiessen State Park is a narrow, mile-long canyon carved in sandstone by a stream. Beginning at the dam and lake at one end of the canyon, you'll encounter a couple of dramatic waterfalls while exploring the moist and shady canyon floor and the wooded bluffs above.

▶ DESCRIPTION

Often overshadowed by the far more popular Starved Rock State Park 2 miles to the north, Matthiessen State Park is often unjustly ignored by the many visitors to the area. Although the 1,938 acres at Matthiessen State Park don't offer as many miles of trails nor as many canyons as Starved Rock, they still have plenty of geological charm—plus a much quieter atmosphere.

The area was first developed as a private park by a LaSalle businessman named Frederick William Matthiessen, who reportedly employed some 50 people to build the trails, bridges, stairways, and dams. Matthiessen also built a not-so-modest summer home with 16 bedrooms and 9 baths, and a smaller mansion for one of his children. While Matthiessen's structures no longer remain, visitors will see the handiwork of his grounds crew in the dams, stairs, and soaring concrete footbridges. By 1940, 22 years after Matthiessen's death, his heirs donated the property to the state.

Similar to Starved Rock, the beautiful sandstone walls at Matthiessen were carved out by

▶ KEY AT-A-GLANCE INFORMATION

LENGTH: 2.2 miles

CONFIGURATION: Loop with out-and-back segment

DIFFICULTY: Moderate to difficult

SCENERY: Sandstone canyons, waterfalls, wooded bluffs, lake, high footbridges over creek

EXPOSURE: All shaded

SURFACE: Gravel, dirt

HIKING TIME: 1.5–2 hours

ACCESS: 8 a.m.–sunset

FACILITIES: Picnic tables, pavilion, water, flush toilets

MAPS: Park maps are available at trailhead; USGS topo LaSalle, IL

SPECIAL COMMENTS: Cross-country ski rentals are available December–March when weather permits. Maps at horse-trailer parking areas show the routes for 13 miles of equestrian trails available at Matthiessen. Horse rentals are available on IL 71, a half mile west of IL 178.

▶ DIRECTIONS

From Chicago, take I-55 to I-80. After driving for 45 miles on I-80, take Exit 81 south to Utica. Proceed south along IL 178 for 5.1 miles, passing through Utica and over the Illinois River. The entrance to the Dells Area at Matthiessen State Park is on the right, just south of IL 178.

UTM Trailhead Coordinates for Matthiessen State Park Dells Area Hike

UTM Zone (NAD27) 16T

Easting 330367

Northing 4573386

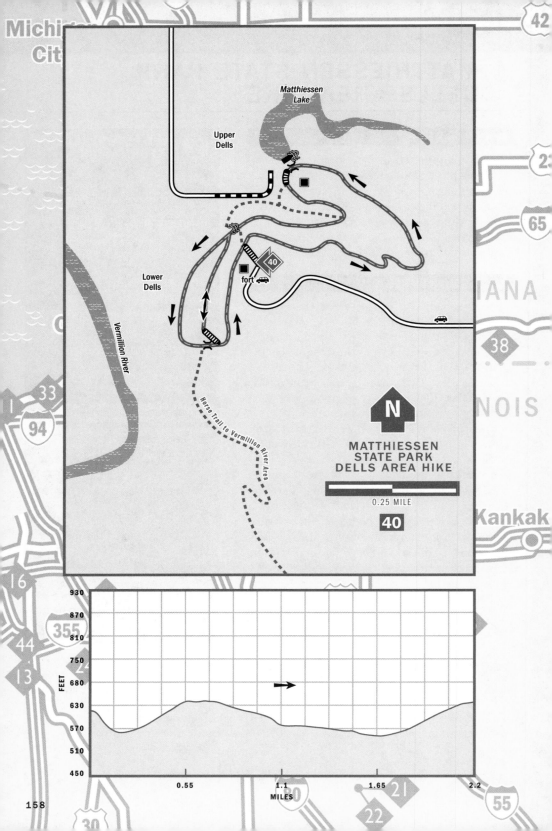

centuries of flowing water. The mile-long canyon at Matthiessen is nearly 100 feet deep in places and ranges from 50 to 140 feet wide. The section closest to the dam and Matthiessen Lake is called the Upper Dells, and the path of the canyon closest to the Vermillion River is called the Lower Dells (the canyons here were called "dells" during Matthiessen's time—since then the name has stuck). The two sections of the canyon are separated by a dazzling 40-foot waterfall.

From the parking lot, head toward the small log fort, which is a replica of forts the French built in the Midwest during the 1600s and early 1700s (the French constructed one of these forts on Starved Rock in 1683). Start the hike by heading down the stairs and taking the first trail to the right. This elm-lined, wide gravel trail follows the bluff above the creek deep within the sandstone canyon on the left. At 0.2 miles, as the path starts to curve, you'll begin to see rock on the other side of the canyon and you'll begin to hear a couple of waterfalls down below. Stay to the left as you pass over the creek flowing through a culvert under the trail (the trail to the right leads to the horse-trailer parking area).

Continuing on the other side of the canyon underneath a canopy of sugar-maple trees, the trail soon becomes paved. Before crossing the bridge over Lake Falls, pay a visit to the overlook on the left for your first view of the Lake Falls as it drops 40 feet from the top of a dam to the floor of the canyon. After crossing the bridge, which provides a nice view of the wooded banks of Matthiessen Lake and the falls underneath, the first trail on the left brings you down closer to the falls and then descends to the floor of the Upper Dells.

On the canyon floor, you can gingerly step through a mix of sandstone, rock, and mud to get a better view of the falls. Mosses, liverworts, and ferns grow on the damp, shady, 30- to 40-foot walls of the canyon. Farther along in the canyon, solid sandstone channels the stream over a small waterfall that empties into the pool called the Giant's Bathtub. Geologists say these pools develop and grow larger by the action of rocks and pebbles getting swirled around. Continuing ahead, several places require using boards and rocks to cross the stream. As the canyon curves to the right at a place called Cedar Point (due to the abundance of cedar trees), continue ahead past stairs leading up to the bluff.

Farther ahead, take the stairs out of the canyon and then follow the sign for the Lower Dells and proceed along the bluff, passing Cascade Falls on the left. After walking along the bluff, cross the bridge and follow the stairs to the Lower Dells. The short box canyon on the right is called the Devil's Paint Box, because the walls are decorated with swaths of yellow, orange, and brown, formed by minerals seeping out of sandstone. In the main canyon, look for spots where lichen has changed the rock to light green. Look for changes in the texture of the walls, too: some sections are smooth and flat, while others are rough, pitted, and almost grotesque. The cracks in the walls form much like the cracks in pavement during the winter, growing bigger and chipping apart when water freezes inside.

Similar to the Upper Dells, the trail here alternates between mud and rock and requires stream crossing via large rocks and concrete blocks. More trees grow in this canyon, particularly sugar maples, some of which are draped with vines. At the end of the canyon, listen for the soothing echo created by the 40-foot waterfall. Frederick Matthiessen named his private retreat Deer Park in honor of the Native American practice of using these canyons for confining deer. Heading back up the stairs, turn left at the sign for the fort and parking lot. Turning right at this junction leads to the Vermillion River Area within the park (see "Nearby Activities" section, below). Heading toward the parking lot, the trail rises and then curves left. Complete the hike by climbing the stairs back up to the parking lot.

▶ NEARBY ACTIVITIES

South of the Dells Area, the Vermillion River Area within the park offers 1.9 miles of hiking along the wooded bluffs above the river. While there are no canyons in this section of the park, there is exposed rock in places, and there is a striking view from a high bluff. Visitors can drive to the Vermillion River Area by heading south on IL 178 from the Dells Area entrance. A better way to make the trip, if you have the time and energy, is to take the mile-long horse trail, which starts on the right after emerging from the Lower Dells.

Shortly after starting on the horse trail, pass through a gate and take the trail to the right. From the gate, the trail takes a long switchback before rising to a prairie, where you'll follow the wide, grassy road lined with berry bushes and shrubs. When you reach the horse-trailer parking area, follow the gravel driveway to the paved park road. Continue straight ahead on the park road until reaching the first parking area on the right. From the parking area, proceed along the mowed trail as it runs between the woods on the left and the picnic area on the right. Before dropping down to the river at the first junction on the left, continue ahead on the mowed path another 0.2 miles for an expansive view of the river valley and the surrounding woodland. Taking the trail down to the river, stay to the right for the full loop. If you get confused on some of the side trails, look for the posts with colored dots: white dots lead to the fort or parking areas, and yellow dots lead away from the fort or parking areas.

MCKINLEY WOODS LOOP

▶ IN BRIEF

Half of this hike runs next to expansive ravines and along bluffs overlooking the historic Illinois & Michigan Canal and the Des Plaines River; the other half brings you down beside a scenic stretch of the long-abandoned canal. The unusually rugged landscape combined with the lack of crowds makes McKinley Woods an appealing hiking spot.

▶ DESCRIPTION

Southwest of Joliet, just before the confluence of the Des Plaines and the Kankakee rivers, the Des Plaines arcs around a series of steep bluffs and plunging ravines. The inside of the arc is tipped by McKinley Woods, where you'll find 473 acres of dramatic slopes, thick with oak and hickory, overlooking the Des Plaines and the I&M Canal. On the west side of the McKinley Woods, the canal grows wide, creating an attractive spot for ducks and other water birds.

Before starting the hike, I suggest a quick visit to the Des Plaines River by taking the footbridge located to the right of the picnic shelter. On the other side of the bridge, you'll cross the I&M Trail, which runs left to Joliet and right to Marseilles. The limestone viewing platform at the river's edge as well as the stone picnic shelters in McKinley Woods were built by the Civilian Conservation Corps, which had a camp at McKinley Woods in the 1930s. Later, during World War II, McKinley Woods was used as a prisoner-of-war camp.

▶ KEY AT-A-GLANCE INFORMATION

LENGTH: 1.8 miles

CONFIGURATION: Loop

DIFFICULTY: Steep sections may be difficult for some

SCENERY: Bluffs, ravines, and woods along the Des Plaines River and the I&M Canal

EXPOSURE: Shaded

SURFACE: Dirt

HIKING TIME: 1 hour

ACCESS: 8 a.m.–8 p.m., April–October; 8 a.m.–5 p.m., November–March. The steep road to Frederick's Grove parking lot may be closed if conditions are icy.

FACILITIES: Water pump, picnic tables, shelters, restrooms, grills, and a small campground. There's also camping nearby on the I&M Canal.

MAPS: Visit www.fpdwc.org or call (815) 727-8700 weekdays to receive a map; USGS topo Channahon, IL

SPECIAL COMMENTS: Consider combining this hike with the I&M Canal Trail. From the Frederick's Grove parking area, the I&M Canal Trail is located across the bridge spanning the canal. See Channahon State Park: I&M Canal Trail on page 36 for more information.

▶ DIRECTIONS

Take I-55 2 miles south of I-80 to Exit 248. From this exit, head southwest on US 6 (West Eames Street) for 3.5 miles. Turn left (south) on McKinley Woods Road and proceed for 2.5 miles. Park at the end of the road at the Frederick's Grove picnic area.

UTM Trailhead Coordinates for McKinley Woods Loop

UTM Zone (NAD27) 16T

Easting 396288

Northing 4582009

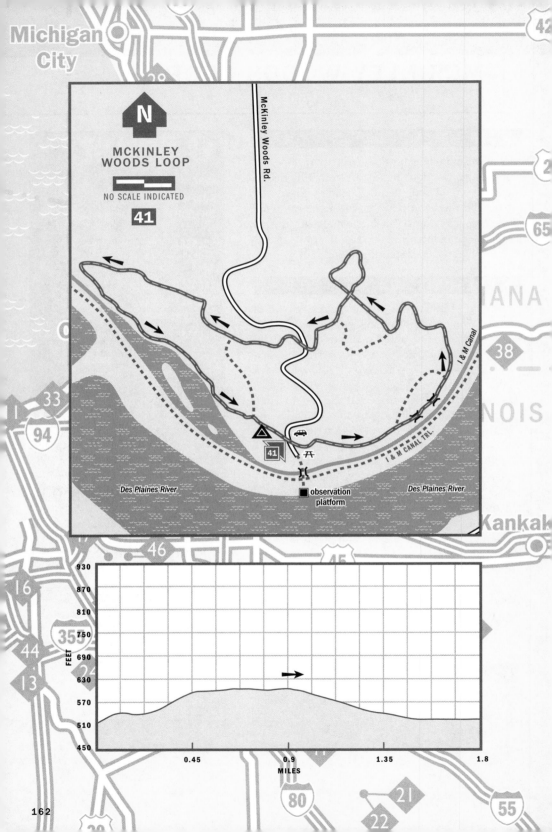

N

MCKINLEY WOODS LOOP

NO SCALE INDICATED

41

McKinley Woods Rd.

I & M Canal

I & M CANAL TRL.

41

Des Plaines River

observation
platform

Des Plaines River

Michigan City

Kankak

NOIS

ANA

FEET

930
870
810
750
690
630
570
510
450

0.45   0.9   1.35   1.8
MILES

Returning to the parking lot, start the hike by heading to the right past the picnic shelter and the sign for the Heritage Trail. The landscape rises quickly on the left and slopes steeply down to the canal on the right. Stay to the right when the trail forks (navigating this hike is easy: just stay right at all the trail junctions). A couple of small ravines appear quickly, each with footbridge crossings. After the second footbridge, the trail curves right, and then passes a trail ascending the bluff on the left. Watch your step as you drop down a short but steep section of the path into the bottom of a small ravine that is nearly at water level. From the bottom of the ravine, follow the trail up the bluff for a steep climb of 80 feet or so. Depending on how wet the ground is, a small stream may be flowing through this picturesque ravine strewn with deadfall. Reaching flat ground again, the path curves left, following the edge of the ravine.

After a short dip in the trail, you'll come to a trail junction and a bench situated at the edge of the ravine. Following the trail to the right, the landscape flattens out completely and becomes dense with shrubs and small trees. Stay right at three successive trail junctions before reaching the park road at 0.9 miles into the hike. At the park road, a limestone picnic pavilion sits on the left, not far from a viewing platform, which, unfortunately, doesn't offer much of a view because the surrounding trees have grown too dense. Continuing straight ahead on the Trail of the Old Oaks, you'll quickly reach the edge of the bluff, which slopes down 80 feet to the canal and the river. As the name of this trail suggests, there are plenty of large old oaks along this section of the trail. Shortly after crossing a small bridge over an intermittent stream, you'll come to a trail junction marked by an enormous hollow oak tree trunk laying on its side. Stay to the right and cross another bridge spanning an intermittent stream. Soon you'll see a dramatic ravine on the right.

Before heading down the bluff, take a look at the landscape—if leaf cover permits—immediately across the Des Plaines River. This was the location of a village of early Native Americans known as the Fisher Site. The 16.5-acre village contained 9 mounds and over 50 lodges marked by circular depressions in the ground. While exact dates are hard to come by, archeologists report that the village was occupied as early as 500 B.C. and as late as 1675 A.D. Even though the site had been repeatedly excavated since the 1920s, most of it remained unexcavated by the time it was destroyed by a gravel-quarrying operation.

As you're descending the bluff, look for the stream in the ravine on the right. After dropping about 60 feet, the path takes a sharp turn to the left and begins to run parallel with the canal. Across the canal, you'll see that the I&M Trail passes over a small dam; during spring, look for the bright pink flowers of Eastern redbud trees hanging over the water. According to the Will County Forest Preserve District, this is the only spot in the county where redbud trees grow wild. After rambling alongside the canal for 0.3 miles, you'll come upon a picnic table and a short dock extending into the canal. The dock provides a good view of this wide and sometimes marshy eddy in the canal, where birds such as herons, egrets, and kingfishers are often spotted. As the trail enters the Boatman's Landing Campground, instead of turning left, continue straight ahead through the grassy open area and up a small hill to return to the parking lot where the hike started.

MIDEWIN NATIONAL TALLGRASS PRAIRIE HIKE

KEY AT-A-GLANCE INFORMATION

LENGTH: 5.2 miles

CONFIGURATION: Large loop with small loop

DIFFICULTY: Moderate

SCENERY: Woodland, savanna, farmland, pond, prairie, and abandoned munitions bunkers

EXPOSURE: Mostly exposed

SURFACE: Gravel two-track, mowed grass, pavement

HIKING TIME: 2–2.5 hours

ACCESS: Sunrise to sunset

FACILITIES: Restroom and picnic tables are available near the parking lot and at Turtle Pond

MAPS: Download a map from www.fs.fed.us/mntp or get one at Midewin Welcome Center; USGS topo Elwood, IL

SPECIAL COMMENTS: While this route is called an "interim trail," the U.S. Forest Service expects to keep these trails open until approximately 2008 or 2009, at which time they hope to start opening an extensive new network of trails. Watch for signs restricting access to areas the Army is cleaning up. The forest service asks visitors not to disturb the soil, particularly along rail beds where arsenic was once used as an herbicide. Also, watch out for heavy farming equipment.

Dogs are allowed on leashes up to 8 feet long.

UTM Trailhead Coordinates for Midewin National Tallgrass Prairie Hike

UTM Zone (NAD27) 16T

Easting   409906

Northing   4582776

▶ IN BRIEF

Formerly the largest ammunition-production plant in the world, Midewin National Tallgrass Prairie is now the biggest—and perhaps the most tranquil—piece of protected land in northeastern Illinois. While much of this hike borders farmland that is slowly being converted to parkland, you'll also see remnants of the former arsenal, woodland, savanna, and an extremely pleasant pond with a picnic area on the last leg of the hike.

▶ DESCRIPTION

Established in 1996 as the first National Tallgrass Prairie in the United States, Midewin is an enormous work in progress. Converting the former Joliet Army Ammunition Plant into what will be the largest swath of tallgrass prairie in the country is a multi-decade project with a goal that is reflected in its name: in the Potawatomi language, "Midewin" means healing. Today, Midewin encompasses more that 15,000 acres; after the Army finishes its cleanup efforts, the park will add another 4,000 acres and eventually some 40 miles of trails. About 5,000 acres containing nearly 15 miles of trails are now open to the public.

At its peak, the Joliet arsenal employed some 14,000 people and produced 5.5 million tons of TNT a week. The arsenal—in operation from World War II through the Korean and Vietnam wars—was shut down in 1975, leaving 1,300

▶ DIRECTIONS

From Chicago, take I-55 south. Four-and-a-half miles south of I-80, take Exit 245. Follow Arsenal Road (County Road 17) east for 6.1 miles. Just after crossing IL 53, turn right (south) on South Chicago Road. Follow South Chicago Road south for 2.4 miles until it ends at the trailhead parking lot.

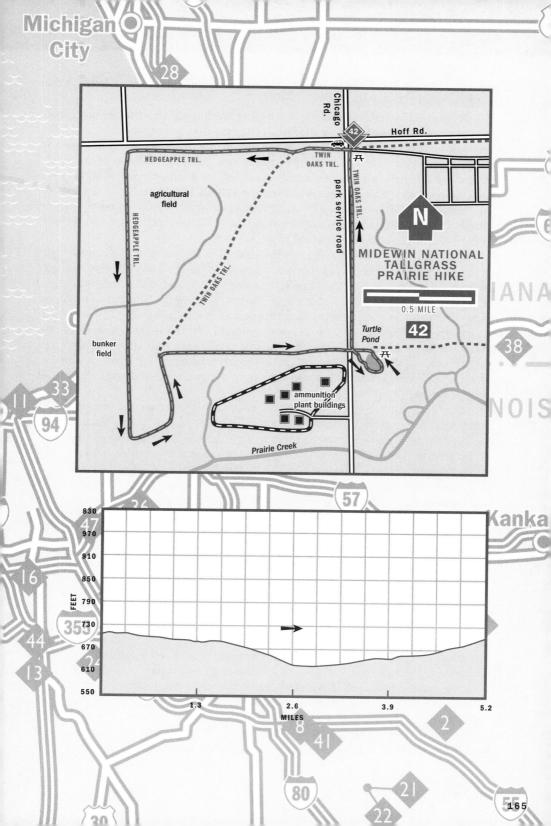

Michigan City

28

Chicago Rd.

42

Hoff Rd.

HEDGEAPPLE TRL.

TWIN OAKS TRL.

agricultural field

park service road

TWIN OAKS TRL.

HEDGEAPPLE TRL.

TWIN OAKS TRL.

N

MIDEWIN NATIONAL TALLGRASS PRAIRIE HIKE

0.5 MILE

42

Turtle Pond

bunker field

ammunition plant buildings

Prairie Creek

38

94

33

INDIANA

ILLINOIS

Kanka

830
970
910
850
790
730
670
610
550

FEET

1.3   2.6   3.9   5.2
MILES

57

355

47

16

44

13

26

2

80

41

22

21

55

30

structures, 200 miles of roads, 166 miles of rail bed, and 392 concrete bunkers that had been used to store the TNT.

While the arsenal was a busy place during much of its lifespan, the majority of its land was leased out for crops and livestock grazing. Wherever possible, this farmland will be converted eventually back to tallgrass prairie. In the eastern section of Midewin, however, the park will not restore the grassland, because that would require removing the underground drain tiles that are so ubiquitous in Midwestern farmland (by 1935, Illinois farmers had installed about 150,000 miles of drain tiles). Since removing the drain tiles will cause drainage trouble for the adjoining private farmland, much of this eastern section of the park will be transformed into various types of bird habitats as the farmland is phased out.

Start the hike by passing through the chain-link fence and heading to the right on the two-track road known as the Twin Oaks Trail. For the first mile, this trail cuts between farmland and the massive power lines on the left and Hoff Road to the right. At a quarter mile into the hike, after passing a small pond in the field and a farmhouse across Hoff Road, stay right on the Hedgeapple Trail as the Twin Oaks Trail curves left.

High-speed hikers will have to apply the brakes on this section of the trail: the ground surface is bumpy and uneven. Scattered poplars offer a bit of shade along the trail, and a small gully—a former rail bed—appears on the right. At 0.9 miles into the hike, the trail turns left and shoots straight as an arrow through a dense hedgerow of trees separating two fields.

The trail tunnels through a passageway lined with walnut, hickory, and hedgeapple trees, more commonly known as Osage orange. Before barbed wire, grassland farmers planted Osage oranges to serve as fences. These thorny trees kept the livestock in, while the fruit gave them something to eat. Now these trees are playing an important role in bringing back the loggerhead shrike, a robin-sized gray-and-white bird that preys on insects, but also eats small birds and rodents. Since shrikes lack talons to hold their prey while eating, they sometimes impale their prey on thorns in order to tear it apart. Midewin planners hope to boost the dwindling numbers of shrikes in the state as well as other grassland birds, such as bobolinks and the state-endangered upland sandpipers.

The trail gently descends and then emerges from the hedgerow before passing through a gate and then over a stream culvert into open space. Off to the right, the grass-covered bunkers look like wrinkles in a vast green carpet. Placing earth on top of the bunkers served the dual purpose of maintaining a stable temperature inside for the TNT while camouflaging the sites from aerial view. While these 70 or so bunkers are off limits to the public, there is one open to the public in the bunker field at the far eastern end of the Twin Oaks Trail. As you pass the six rows of bunkers stretching for a mile to the right, you'll also cross a series of access roads.

Beyond the bunker field is a cattle pasture on the right, followed by sections of open prairie. After curving left through savanna, and taking a right on the trail heading to Turtle Pond, you'll start seeing a series of buildings far off beyond the fencing on the right. In these buildings, workers packed TNT into various munitions and washed imperfect shell casings that were to be reused or discarded.

At 3.8 miles into the hike, across the paved road, raised beds of prairie plants provide native seeds for prairie restoration at Midewin. On the other side of the beds, look for the beginning of the mowed trail that circles Turtle Pond and cuts through an adjoining picnic area. Created for the recreation of the arsenal employees, Turtle Pond is pleasantly fringed with cattails, sedge grasses, and trees hanging over the water.

Unless you're hiking in July, in the midst of the winter wheat harvest, or in October when it's time for the soybean harvest, you may notice that Midewin is one of the quietest places in the Chicago region. After a few miles of hiking, this serene ambience provides unparalleled outdoor-napping opportunities. Following a short snooze on the edge of Turtle Pond, I watched a line of wild turkeys pecking their way across a recently harvested field of winter wheat. Finishing the short Turtle Pond loop, take a right on the paved road to head back to the parking lot. Far off to the right, in between the groves of trees that appear intermittently along the road, you'll see timber frames of warehouses that will be eventually demolished.

Note: Water and flush toilets are available at the Midewin Welcome Center, located on the east side of IL 53, 4 miles south of Hoff Road. The welcome center is open daily, 8 a.m. to 5 p.m., except in fall and winter. The welcome center can be contacted at (815) 423-6370. Learn more about Midewin by visiting www.fs.fed.us.mntp.

▶ NEARBY ACTIVITIES

More of Midewin's interim trails lie 4 miles southwest of the Hoff Road Trailhead. Henslow and Newton Trails, each 1.5 miles long, are mowed paths for hiking only, and accessible from the same trailhead. The Henslow Trail runs through open, gently rolling prairie, while the Newton Trail, flatter, with a mix of prairie and woodland, brushes up against Prairie Creek. To reach these trails, head east on Hoff Road for 2 miles and turn left (south) on IL 53 and proceed for 2 more miles. Turn right (west) on Explosives Road and drive for a half mile; the trailhead is where the road ends.

On summer weekends, the U.S. Forest Service offers a dozen different tours, walks, and bicycle rides to introduce Midewin visitors to everything from local butterflies to the history of the ammunitions plant. Contact the Midewin Welcome Center for more information.

MORAINE HILLS STATE PARK HIKE

KEY AT-A-GLANCE INFORMATION

LENGTH: 8 miles with several cutoff points for shorter hikes

CONFIGURATION: 2 loops

DIFFICULTY: Moderate to difficult

SCENERY: Woods, marshes, ponds, lakes, hills, prairies, and the Fox River

EXPOSURE: A mix of shaded and open

SURFACE: Crushed gravel; 5-feet wide with mowed sides

HIKING TIME: 2-3 hours

ACCESS: The park is open 6 a.m.–9 p.m.; the nature center is open 9 a.m.–4 p.m.

FACILITIES: Picnic areas, playgrounds, fishing, boat rental, water, restrooms, and concessions on first floor of visitor center and at the dam. Benches situated occasionally throughout the trail system.

MAPS: Maps are available at the park entrance and at the visitor center; USGS topo Wauconda, IL

SPECIAL COMMENTS: There are 800 acres of wetlands at Moraine Hills: be sure to bring mosquito repellent. Cross-country skiers and cyclists must follow the directional arrows; hikers may proceed in any direction. Pets must be on leashes. In summer, boat rentals are available at the visitor center; during winter, cross-country ski rentals are available. The park offers a number of programs, including a nature photography contest in May. In the nature center, pick up a brochure for the 0.5-mile-long self-guided interpretive trail along the boardwalk on the shore of Lake Defiance.

UTM Trailhead Coordinates for Moraine Hills State Park Hike

UTM Zone (NAD27) 16T

Easting 398518

Northing 4686253

IN BRIEF

It's a good thing this hike is 8 miles long: the entire distance is needed for you to get a complete picture of Moraine Hills' mosaic of marshes, lakes, prairies, bogs, wooded hills, and streams.

DESCRIPTION

When glaciers receded from the landscape at Moraine Hills State Park some 15,500 years ago, they left behind the hills, the wetlands, and the centerpiece of the park, Lake Defiance. Fed by a sprawling network of marshes, ponds, and old irrigation ditches within the park, Lake Defiance was initially formed when a chunk of ice from a retreating glacier left a watery depression in the ground. Lake Defiance is one of the few glacial lakes in Illinois that has remained undeveloped and in a near-natural state. Another highlight of the park, also the result of retreating glaciers, are the moraines, which develop when an ice sheet stops in its tracks, and the idling glacier acts as a sort of conveyor belt, depositing gravel and rock at its edges and sides. The wooded hills and ridges at Moraine Hills serve as records of where glaciers paused during their retreat.

While the park offers more than a half-dozen parking/picnic areas where this hike could begin, I recommend starting at Northern Woods. It offers a playground, flush toilets, water, and

DIRECTIONS

From Chicago, head north on I-90/I-94. Follow I-94 as it separates from I-90, and continue on I-94 until you reach West Belvidere Road (IL 120). Follow West Belvidere Road west for 17 miles until reaching North River Road. Turn left (south) on North River Road and travel for 3.2 miles. Turn left (east) at the sign for the park and proceed for 2 miles to the Northern Woods parking lot and picnic area.

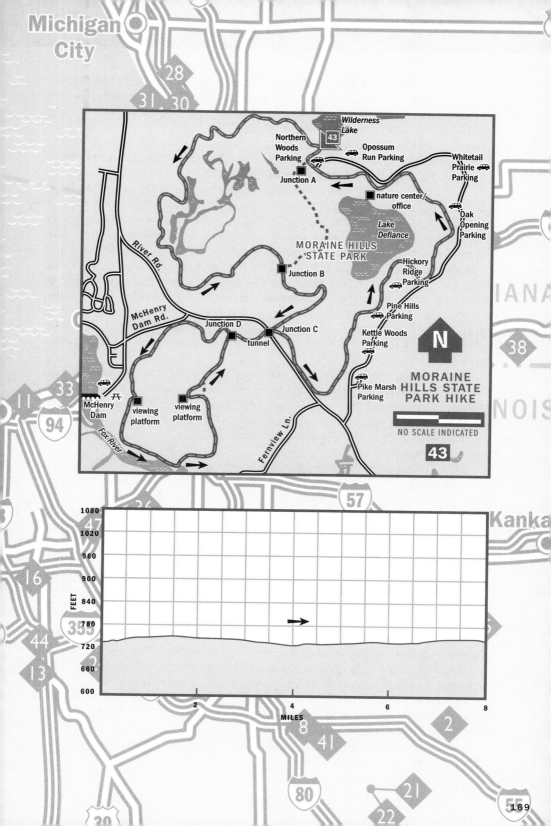

MORAINE HILLS STATE PARK

Michigan City

Wilderness Lake

Northern Woods Parking

Opossum Run Parking

Whitetail Prairie Parking

Junction A

nature center/office

Oak Opening Parking

Lake Defiance

MORAINE HILLS STATE PARK

River Rd.

Junction B

Hickory Ridge Parking

McHenry Dam Rd.

Junction D

Junction C

tunnel

Pine Hills Parking

Kettle Woods Parking

N

MORAINE HILLS STATE PARK HIKE

viewing platform

viewing platform

Pike Marsh Parking

Fernview Ln.

McHenry Dam

Fox River

NO SCALE INDICATED

43

Kanka

| | | | | | | | |

1080
1020
960
900
840
780
720
660
600

FEET

2   4   6   8

MILES

plenty of picnic tables. Also, it's fairly close to the nature center where you can stop to pick up a map and learn more about the park. At the Northern Woods picnic area, catch the access trail at the left of the restrooms. For now, follow the arrows by turning right on the main Leatherleaf Bog Trail, and then turn left when you reach the intersection for the Opossum Run picnic area. Right away the trail starts to climb a hill through dense stands of oak and hickory (two of the most common trees found in the park are shagbark hickory and white oak.)

At the bottom of the hill, a cattail marsh extends out to the left while Tomahawk Lake opens up on the right. Without delay, the trail rises, granting a better view of the enormous marsh on the left. As the landscape flattens, you'll pass one of the sheltered benches that are widely spaced throughout the length of the trail. After skirting the edge of more open water on the right, the trail begins a half-mile stretch of twisting and turning in and out of prairies, savannas, and brief wooded sections, while offering glimpses of Leatherleaf Bog and occasional patches of open water on the left. On this section, you may consider exploring the occasional narrow spur trails that will allow you a closer view of the marshes and the bog. Before reaching Junction B, the trail meanders through a wet prairie sprinkled with stands of cattails, and then passes a drainage channel that cuts through the marsh on the left. At Junction B, stay to the right.

Between Junctions B and C, the trail turns left sharply, and then runs through dense woods and rolling terrain. At 2.9 miles into the hike, turn right at Junction C, which takes you through the tunnel under River Road. After the tunnel, a large wetland appears on the left. Just ahead, at Junction D, continue straight ahead as the trail meanders alongside River Road and then runs by a viewing platform overlooking Black Tern Marsh.

At 4.1 miles into the hike, the trail meets up with the Fox River and the McHenry Dam picnic area. The dam, by far the busiest spot in the park, brings in a steady flow of anglers and picnickers on warm summer days. You can see the 4-foot-high dam by walking just 0.1 miles to the right along the edge of the parking lot. First built in 1907, the dam was reconstructed in 1934 by the Civilian Conservation Corps. In 1939, the state acquired the dam and some surrounding property—the kernel of what would eventually become this 1,690-acre state park.

Following the dam, the trail runs between the Fox River and open marshes before passing a levee and a drainage channel on the left. Next, the trail mounts a couple of small hills that afford a good view of the large wetland you saw earlier (while on a summer walk on this trail, I counted several sandhill cranes, and more than a dozen snowy egrets from these two hills). On the second hill, take the trail branching left, which leads to another viewing platform overlooking Black Tern Marsh.

Reaching Junction D again at 5.4 miles into the hike, turn right, pass through the tunnel, and turn right again at Junction C. For 0.35 miles after C, the trail runs next to River Road and alongside a recently installed, paved bicycle path that follows much of River Road through the park. For the remaining 2.1 miles of the hike, the trail runs by eight separate parking and picnicking areas. Some are right at the edge of the trail, while others are a short walk off the trail. Each is well marked and each offers drinking water and pit toilets.

Beyond the turnoff for Pike Marsh, the trail skirts the edge of a marsh on the left and soon starts to roller-coaster up and down a series of small wooded hills (many of the steep sections are paved to prevent erosion). After passing the trail to the Pine Hills picnic area, and a short spur on the left that provides access to Lake Defiance, the trail turns right and then accompanies the park road for a bit. Just beyond the spur leading to the Whitetail Prairie picnic area, the trail heads up a hill overlooking the 48-acre Lake Defiance. At the base of the hill, the trail again runs alongside the park road until you reach the nature center. From the nature center, proceed through the prairie for 0.3 miles to the Northern Woods parking lot.

MORTON ARBORETUM EAST HIKE

 KEY AT-A-GLANCE INFORMATION

LENGTH: 5 miles

CONFIGURATION: 2 connected loops

DIFFICULTY: Easy

SCENERY: Rolling hills, dense woods, oak savannas, and prairie

EXPOSURE: Mostly covered

SURFACE: Woodchips, dirt

HIKING TIME: 2.5 hours

ACCESS: April–October (when Daylight Savings Time is in effect), 7 a.m.–7 p.m.; November–March, 7 a.m.–5 p.m.

COST: $5 adults, $4 seniors, $2 children; on Wednesday, $3 adults, $2 seniors, $1 children; children under 2 and members, free.

FACILITIES: Restrooms, benches, picnic tables, water, visitor center, cafe, arboretum shop, public phone

MAPS: Maps available from the attendant at the gate; USGS topo Wheaton, IL

SPECIAL COMMENTS: Runners are asked to use the roads rather than the trails. Cross-country skiing is not allowed. For information about guided tours on an open-air tram, inquire at the visitor center.

At the visitor center, learn about scores of classes the arboretum offers in disciplines such as ecology, zoology, botany, botanical art, and nature photography. Plenty of kids' programs are available, too. For more information call the main office at (630) 968-0074, or visit the arboretum's website at www.mortonarb.org.

UTM Trailhead Coordinates for
Morton Arboretum East Hike

UTM Zone (NAD27) 16T

Easting 413056

Northing 4629958

IN BRIEF

Want to check out trees from places such as Korea or Appalachia? Or maybe you'd like to see a sampling of the 43 types of oak trees and 60 types of maple trees that grow here. Tree lovers could be kept busy for weeks exploring hundreds of types of trees grouped according to geographical origin, species, and habitat. Trees, however, are just part of the appeal of this place. The gently rolling terrain offers plenty of scenic beauty in the way of native woodlands, savannas, streams, marshes, and ponds.

DESCRIPTION

Occupying 1,700 acres of rolling wooded terrain, and bisected by the East Branch of the DuPage River, the Morton Arboretum will captivate anyone with even a slight interest in woody vegetation. Joy Morton, founder of the Morton Salt Company, established the arboretum on his country estate in 1922. Morton's arboreal interests were passed down to him from his father, Julias Sterling Morton, who served as Secretary of Agriculture under President Grover Cleveland, and founded Arbor Day (typically the last Friday in April, but the date varies from state to state).

Joy Morton's plan for the arboretum was to gather trees and shrubs from around the world that could live in the Northern Illinois climate. In the first year, the arboretum planted 138,000

DIRECTIONS

From Chicago, take I-290 west to I-88. Follow I-88 for 10.5 miles until reaching IL 53. The entrance to Morton Arboretum is just a quarter mile north on IL 53, on the right. After paying at the gate and receiving a map, follow Main Route East Side for 2.5 miles until reaching the Big Rock Visitor Station, which will appear on the right side of the road.

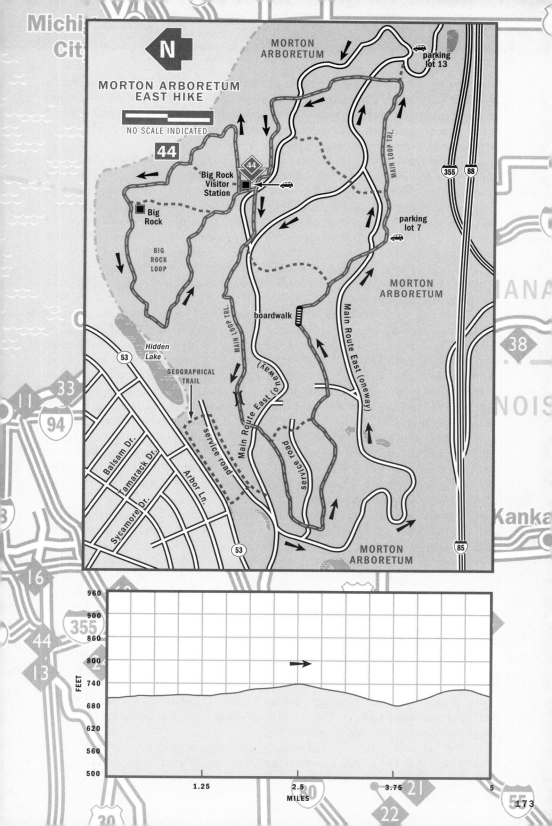

N

MORTON ARBORETUM
EAST HIKE

NO SCALE INDICATED

44

MORTON
ARBORETUM

parking
lot 13

Big Rock
Visitor
Station

Big Rock

BIG
ROCK
LOOP

MAIN LOOP TRL.

parking
lot 7

MORTON
ARBORETUM

boardwalk

Main Route East (oneway)

Hidden
Lake

GEOGRAPHICAL
TRAIL

MAIN LOOP TRL.

Main Route East (oneway)

service road

Balsam Dr.

Tamarack Dr.

Sycamore Dr.

Arbor Ln.

53

53

MORTON
ARBORETUM

85

355

88

38

Kank

NOIS

MANA

trees; now there are some 3,400 varieties of plants and trees, many of them organized according to botanical groups such as elm, maple, oak, willow, and spruce trees, and geographical origins such as Japan, China, Appalachia, and Northern Illinois. Mixed in with this extraordinary collection of trees and shrubs are a variety of gardens highlighting herbs, native plants, and hedges.

Most of this hike follows the outer edge of what's called the Main Trail, which is a series of four connected loops, numbered from west to east. Facing the Big Rock Visitor Station, look for Main Trail Loop 3 to the left, heading west across the park road from the shelter. Passing a picnic spot, the trail enters rolling open terrain with the occasional bluebird house attached to a post. At 0.2 miles, you'll see a connector trail that runs left into a bulb meadow and through collections of beech and maple trees. Continuing on the Main Trail, you'll cross a park road and soon enter flat, dense woodland with the occasional stand of spruce. At a half mile into the hike, where the woodland gives way to shrubby trees and more open space, you'll cross a wooden footbridge spanning a small ravine.

Up ahead, as the trail crosses the park road, a sign indicates that the plants of Appalachia have been planted in this area. After passing another connecter trail on the left, the path runs next to one striking Appalachian specimen—the northern catalpa tree, identified by its long, thin, bean-like fruit and large showy flowers that bloom in the spring. Gradually descending a gentle hill, the trail is accompanied by a small stream on the right. At 1 mile into the hike, a sign on the right announces the beginning of the Geographical Trail, a short loop showcasing the trees of China and Japan. Continuing on the Main Trail, you'll pass a collection of maples and then cross a service road that brings you into a collection of azaleas, rhododendrons, and other types of ornamental shrubbery. The trail quickly rises to a small stone platform with a couple of benches. Behind the bench on the right is an eastern-redbud tree, which produces masses of pink flowers in early spring; behind the other bench is another flowering tree, the wild black cherry.

From the benches, take the trail to the left past plantings of locust, honeysuckle, and viburnum trees. In the open space on the right are a small pond and the park road at the far edge of a clearing. As the trail enters an area with plants from Korea, look for trees common in Asia—such as mock orange and koyama spruce—that are marked on the side of the trail. After passing a grouping of large hedges, the Crowley Marsh appears on the right, soon followed by a connector trail on the left. Cross the park road and you'll enter an area planted with trees from the buckeye family. As the trail curls around Burr Reed Marsh, you'll mount a short boardwalk and viewing platform that offers an ideal spot from which to look for birds during migratory months.

Passing another small pond and another connector trail, keep straight ahead as you enter a savanna and woodland area containing 43 types of oaks from around the world. Among these you'll find six main types of oaks growing in the Chicago region: white, swamp white, bur, black, red, and northern pin. After leaving the oaks, cross the park road and then pass by parking lot 7. Keep straight ahead at the next junction that appears alongside a winding creek bed.

Here the trail straightens and starts to gradually rise as it cuts through a fairly dense woodland. The stands of shrubs and abundant deadfall seem to draw in the critters. On one of my visits to this corner of the arboretum a couple of days after a snow fall, the hiking trail was criss-crossed with countless animal trails, some apparently used by more than one type of animal. Raccoons, mice, squirrels, rabbits, chipmunks, and deer all left behind their imprints. Along this section of the trail in winter, I've also seen large patches of ground where deer had kicked up oak leaves from underneath the snow—presumably to find a stray acorn or two.

Stay to the left at the sign for parking lot 13, and then cross the park road again. After crossing over a bridge, the trail slopes down leisurely while accompanying a dry streambed. Crossing the road again, the landscape regains its rolling quality. Here, the trail skirts a wooded hillside above a picturesque ravine sprinkled with fallen trees. Soon, on the left, you'll pass a trail that leads—if you care to take it—to a plot of spruce trees. Continuing straight ahead brings you back to the Big Rock Visitor Station.

For a quick introduction to the types of environments within this section of the arboretum, follow the short paved path bordering the backside of the visitor station and peruse the informational signs along the way.

Find the beginning of the Big Rock section of the hike next to the shelter. Fifty yards ahead, turn right at two closely spaced trail junctions. After the second junction, the trail proceeds alongside a small stream on the right that has carved a shallow ravine. Growing in these low spots amid the deadfall are trees tolerant of moist soil, such as red oaks, basswood, and green ash. As the trail swings left and slowly starts to rise, you'll see trees that require dryer ground, such as white oak, maple, and ironwood. Off to the right, the landscape drops down toward power lines and a marshy area. While the trail curves, dips, and rises through fairly dense woodland, keep an eye out for a few enormous white oaks (growing to 100 feet, the white oak—Illinois state tree—has wide-spreading branches, leaves with rounded lobes, and ashen-gray bark that is plated and scaly). After passing a junction on the right, the trail gradually descends toward a rock the size of a small car.

Weighing in at 12 to 14 tons, the Big Rock hitched a ride on a glacier many thousands of years ago from either northern Michigan or Canada. Geologists point to particular surface scratches on the rock and its position on the ground as possible evidence that farmers moved it out of the adjoining field about 100 years ago. Up until the 1980s, the clearing west of the rock operated as a hayfield.

Passing a trail junction on the left, proceed straight ahead into the former hayfield. Now a restored prairie, this big open space is bordered by oaks and a few stands of birches. After a quarter-mile hike through the prairie, the trail crosses a two-wheel track, and then enters a savanna that is often alive with avian activity: look for woodpeckers, flickers, juncos, and cedar waxwings in the winter, and a host of migrating species such as warblers, vireos, and scarlet tanagers in the spring and fall. Local birdwatchers say that the arboretum's variety of plants and berries makes it one of the better birding spots in the area. After crossing a small bridge, the trail gradually turns left, and then starts to rise into dense woods. Stay right at the next two trail junctions on your way back to the Big Rock Visitor Station.

OAK RIDGE PRAIRIE LOOP

UTM Trailhead Coordinates for Oak Ridge Prairie Loop

UTM Zone (NAD27)   16T

Easting   467107

Northing   4595985

IN BRIEF

Oak Ridge Prairie County Park allows visitors to sample a variety of appealing environments within a fairly small area. During the hike, the landscape swiftly moves from lakeshore to woodland to prairie to marshland.

DESCRIPTION

Tucked in between the northwest Indiana communities of Griffith and Merillville, this 700-acre county park offers a pleasing mix of woodland, marshland, and prairie. On the east side of the park, you'll ramble along the shoreline of a popular fishing lake, through an oak and quaking aspen forest, and then along the edge of a large marsh. After hiking through a savanna dotted with stately oaks, and then mounting a sledding hill in the recreation area in the middle of the park, you'll explore the park's west side, which offers more savanna, as well as an attractive tall-grass prairie, wet prairie, and an isolated lake with an observation deck.

Start the hike at the fishing pier by taking the sidewalk to the right as it leads over the boardwalk and along the shore of the lake. Follow the wide mowed path along the shrubby shoreline, turning right at the trail that appears near the bench and the portable restroom. At 0.2 miles into the hike, take the first junction left, and then take a quick right at the next junction (the path

DIRECTIONS

Take I-90/I-94 south until reaching the Chicago Skyway (I-90), Exit 59A. Follow the Skyway for 10.5 miles to Exit 3. Follow IL 912 (Cline Avenue) east. Proceed along IL 912 for 11.2 miles until you reach IL 6 (Ridge Road). Turn left (east) on IL 6 and drive for 1 mile to North Colfax Street, where you'll turn right (south). The entrance to the park is 2.2 miles ahead on the left.

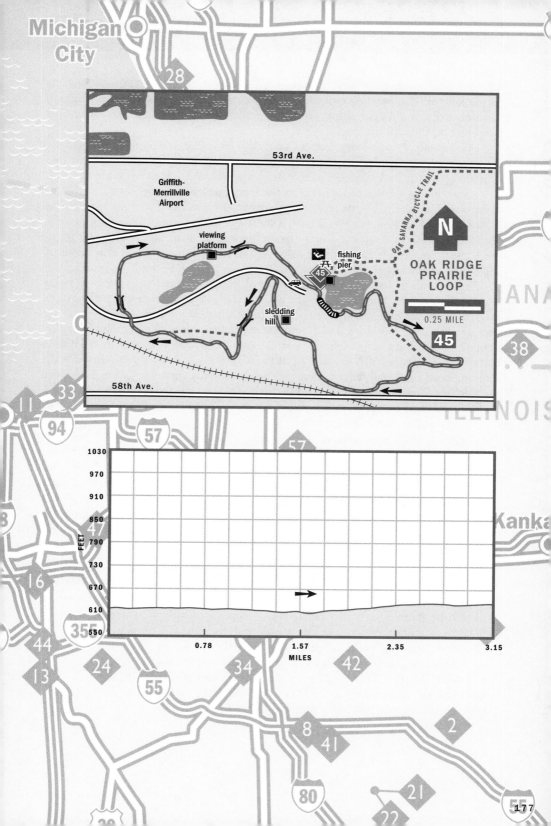

Michigan City

53rd Ave.

Griffith-
Merrillville
Airport

viewing
platform

fishing
pier

OAK SAVANNA BICYCLE TRAIL

N

OAK RIDGE
PRAIRIE
LOOP

0.25 MILE

45

sledding
hill

58th Ave.

ILLINOIS

Kanka

FEET

1030
970
910
850
790
730
670
610
550

0.78   1.57   2.35   3.15

MILES

177

left leads to Oak Savanna Bicycle Trail—see "Nearby Activities" section, below). As you follow this flat, winding trail through stands of oak, sumac, quaking aspen, and sassafras trees, you'll hear acorns crunching underfoot, and you may hear whitetails bounding off through the thickets.

Just ahead, a shrub-laden marsh sprawls out for a quarter mile to the left. On my early morning visit to the marsh, a muskrat cruised through the drainage ditch that runs alongside the trail, while cedar waxwings swirled overhead feeding on berry trees.

After hiking for 0.2 miles between the marsh on the left and shrubs and large cottonwoods on the right, the trail takes a sharp right turn. As the landscape changes from scrubland to savanna, you'll pass a short side trail on the left leading to West 58th Avenue. In the savanna, look for sand cherry, goldenrod, and blazing star growing beneath impressive 80-foot burr oaks. As the oaks multiply, you'll also see ferns and the occasional raspberry bush. At the gravel road, continue straight ahead up the sledding hill; on its backside you'll see a set of train tracks and a savanna sprinkled with quaking aspen. Heading down the other end of the hill, follow the park road to the left, cross the bridge and take an immediate left turn onto the mowed trail that runs alongside the hedgerow and an old drainage ditch. After crossing a bridge spanning a wooded ditch, stay left as the trail twists and turns through stands of shrubs, berry bushes, quaking aspens, oaks, and cottonwoods, as well as a number of still-standing dead trees. Tall sedge grasses, willows, and ferns sprout from wet areas near the side of the trail. When you reach the tallgrass prairie, the trail swings back toward the park road and passes the other end of the trail you passed earlier.

Crossing the park road near several bluebird houses, the trail passes over a bridge and then accompanies a drainage ditch on the left and a cattail marsh on the right. You'll pass sumac, chokecherry, and waving shafts of goldenrod before the trail curves to the right alongside a wet prairie. On this stretch, you'll likely see and hear small planes taking off and landing on the single 4,900-foot runway at the Griffith-Merrillville Airport on the other side of the fence. Soon you'll come to an observation deck with benches and interpretive signs that overlooks the wetlands and pond on the right. After walking through a bit more prairie, and passing through a cluster of small oak trees, cross the bridge that leads to the playground, picnic area, and the parking lot.

▶ NEARBY ACTIVITIES

In Oak Ridge Prairie County Park you can catch the west end of the Oak Savanna Trail as it heads east for 6.25 miles to the community of Hobart. The recently completed paved trail follows an old rail bed alongside savannas, remnant prairies, wetlands, lakes, and residential neighborhoods. Catch another local rail-trail—the Erie Lackawanna Bike Trail—0.7 miles south of the entrance to Oak Ridge Prairie Park on South Colfax Street. This 11.25-mile trail runs through several small towns and neighborhoods, as well as grasslands and wetlands. The mapboard at the trail's Colfax Street parking area will help you plot your journey.

PALOS/SAG VALLEY FOREST PRESERVE: CAP SAUERS AND SWALLOW CLIFF LOOP

▶ IN BRIEF

As part of the larger Palos/Sag Valley Preserves, Cap Sauers Holdings and Swallow Cliff offer great hiking close to Chicago. The terrain is varied and sometimes dramatic, with bluffs and ravines, pristine oak savannas, scenic stream crossings, and one of the state's best examples of an esker.

▶ DESCRIPTION

In a county of more than 5 million people, the wild and isolated ambience of Cap Sauers Holdings seems like an impossibility. Named after the first superintendent of the Cook County Forest Preserve District, Cap Sauers is the largest roadless tract in the county and the largest nature preserve in Illinois. One of the most striking parts of this hike is the section toward the end that runs along the top of a sinuous ridge known as an esker. Another section features an 80- to 100-foot-high bluff known as Swallow Cliff, formed by torrents of meltwater as the most recent glacier retreated about 12,000 years ago. As the last glacier shrank, Lake Michigan swelled. The growing lake eventually released some of its meltwater by carving a couple of channels in the Palos area. One of these outlets sculpted the bluffs and the basin of the nearby Des Plaines River, and the other created Swallow Cliff and the Calumet Sag Channel, which flows just a quarter mile north of the cliff.

Swallow Cliff rises up immediately south of the Teasons Woods parking lot where the hike starts. Heading east—away from 104th Avenue—

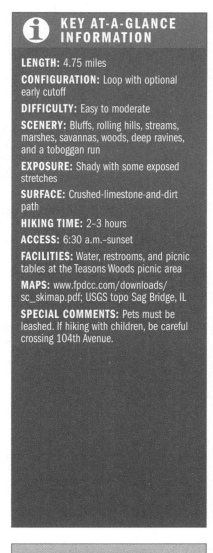

ℹ KEY AT-A-GLANCE INFORMATION

LENGTH: 4.75 miles

CONFIGURATION: Loop with optional early cutoff

DIFFICULTY: Easy to moderate

SCENERY: Bluffs, rolling hills, streams, marshes, savannas, woods, deep ravines, and a toboggan run

EXPOSURE: Shady with some exposed stretches

SURFACE: Crushed-limestone-and-dirt path

HIKING TIME: 2–3 hours

ACCESS: 6:30 a.m.–sunset

FACILITIES: Water, restrooms, and picnic tables at the Teasons Woods picnic area

MAPS: www.fpdcc.com/downloads/sc_skimap.pdf; USGS topo Sag Bridge, IL

SPECIAL COMMENTS: Pets must be leashed. If hiking with children, be careful crossing 104th Avenue.

▶ DIRECTIONS

Take I-55 south until reaching Exit 274. Follow IL 83 (Kingery Highway) left (south). At 4 miles, continue to follow IL 83 as it turns left and becomes 111th Street. After 3 more miles, turn right on 104th Avenue and park in the lot for Teasons Woods immediately on the left.

UTM Trailhead Coordinates for Palos/Sag Valley Forest Preserve: Cap Sauers and Swallow Cliff Loop

UTM Zone (NAD27)   16T

Easting   427247

Northing   4614853

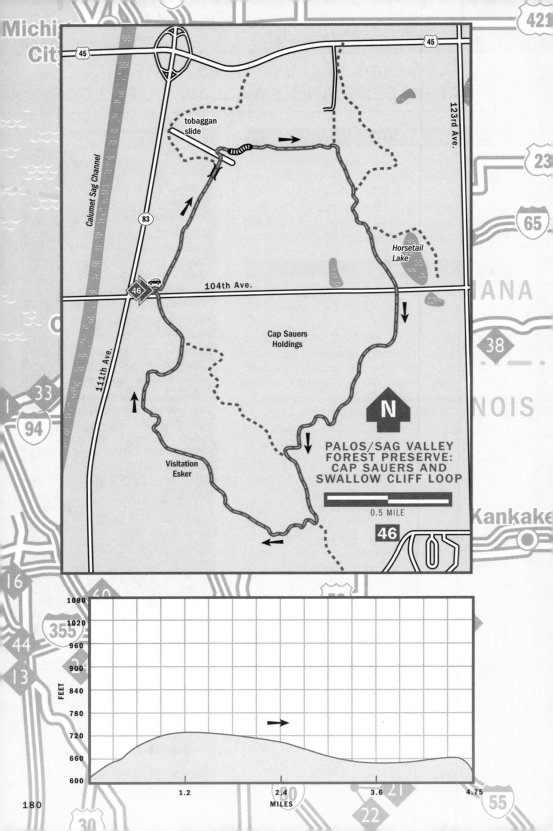

Michigan City

Calumet Sag Channel

tobaggan slide

83

46

104th Ave.

111th Ave.

123rd Ave.

Horsetail Lake

Cap Sauers Holdings

Visitation Esker

N

PALOS/SAG VALLEY FOREST PRESERVE: CAP SAUERS AND SWALLOW CLIFF LOOP

0.5 MILE

46

Kankake

INDIANA

NOIS

FEET

1080
1020
960
900
840
780
720
660
600

1.2   2.4   3.6   4.75

MILES

A serene grassy marsh in Cap Sauers Holdings.

on the crushed-limestone trail at the base of Swallow Cliff, hikers will see at once orange trail markers on the right for trails going up the slope. Those in the mood for exploring can find dramatic ravines and bluffs within this several-mile network of unmarked trails. Be warned, though, some sections are not quite so beautiful. Despite the signs banning bicycles on these trails, damage from off-road biking is clearly a problem. Since this cluster of trails can be confusing, bring a map and compass or carry a GPS unit.

While hiking along the base of Swallow Cliff, look for the points where steep ravines intersect the bluff. At 0.6 miles, cross a small bridge with chain-link fencing on the sides, and follow the first marked trail on the right after the bridge. This trail leads to the end of a steep toboggan run. Cutting across the end of the toboggan tracks, follow the lengthy stone staircase to the right. Continuing on the trail as it heads south, orange markers again provide multiple access points for the tangle of trails on the right. After passing a marsh on the left at 0.8 miles, turn right when coming to a T intersection. As the terrain flattens, an attractive oak canopy develops overhead. At 1.2 miles into the hike, the first of two trails links up from the left; continue straight ahead at both of these intersections. After the second intersection, Horsetail Lake will be visible through the trees on the left.

On summer weekends, the first half of this hike from Swallow Cliff south to Horsetail Lake is active with runners, equestrians, bikers, and hikers. If solitude is what you're after, visit this section during off-peak hours. Within the 1,520 acres of Cap Sauers, however, solitude is usually in abundant supply.

Crossing 104th Avenue into Cap Sauers Holdings, the terrain is flat and shrubby, offering little evidence of the farming that once took place in this section of the preserve. Two miles into the hike, the trail drops down alongside a marsh and then continues through stunning oak savannas, sometimes thick with deadfall. At 2.7 miles, the trail joins up with the first wide gravel trail after crossing 104th Avenue. Turning left allows for a total hike of 4.75 miles. If a shorter hike is on the agenda, take the cutoff to the right for a complete distance of 3.8 miles. Following this cutoff trail brings you through a semi-open area, over a shallow stream, and alongside a few ravines. As traffic noise from 104th Avenue comes within earshot, the trail loses elevation and winds through wild rose bushes before reaching a grove of stately walnut and oak trees. At 104th Avenue, the Teasons Woods parking lot is straight ahead.

Taking the longer route to the left brings you deeper into the preserve, and apparently closer to where much of the wildlife resides. On this section of the hike, tunnel-like animal trails into the shrubbery are a frequent sight. Look for mud at the entrances to these trails to determine what creatures recently passed by. Coyotes, rabbits, and raccoons are common in Cap Sauers. So are deer; in fact, at dusk they become as common as squirrels in a city park.

After hiking 0.4 miles beyond the intersection with the cutoff trail, take the first trail on the right indicated with a marker. This is the trail leading to the esker. (To add a few more miles to your hike, instead of turning onto the esker trail, continue straight ahead on the crushed-limestone trail for 0.7 miles until reaching a fork. At the fork, the trail to the right continues for 0.9 miles, ending at IL 83. The trail to the left continues for 1.25 miles, ending at Will-Cook Road.) Right away, the esker trail passes over a hilltop and then through a labyrinth of dense shrubbery. At 3.5 miles into the hike, turn right at a trail intersection at the edge of a savanna. Shortly after passing through a small muddy ravine and alongside a marsh on the left, the trail starts to snake along the top of what is known as Visitation Esker. Sloping down 40 to 50 feet on each side of the trail, the esker looks like a perfectly shaped winding mound. Indeed, some geologists maintain that this landform—created by a subglacial stream—is one of the most well defined examples of an esker in the state. On the sides of the esker, look for the occasional remnants of controlled burnings: charred stumps and blackened tree trunks lying on the ground. These burnings clear out the invasive plant species and the understory, and, in turn, allow for open vistas of the rolling terrain sprinkled with oaks.

Passing a serene grassy marsh at 3.7 miles, a steep ravine develops on the left. At 4 miles, the esker disappears and the trail intersects with another trail at the top of a bluff. Take the trail to the right, which leads to the open space at the bottom of the bluff. (Stay on the dirt path; avoid the grassy, less trodden trails that sometimes appear.) For the next quarter mile, hikers will encounter a few short, steep sections with loose gravel.

The final leg of this trail passes through wet and lush lowlands, sometimes dense with shrubs. It also leads closer to IL 83, bringing some traffic noise into range. At 4.2 miles into the hike, the trail crosses a small stream, climbs a hill, and then drops you off on the main trail at 4.5 miles. Turn left for a quarter-mile downhill hike back to the parking lot.

PALOS/SAG VALLEY FOREST PRESERVE: LITTLE RED SCHOOLHOUSE HIKE

IN BRIEF

With 2.5 miles of laid-back hiking and plenty of engaging exhibits, Little Red Schoolhouse Nature Center is particularly appealing for kids and beginning hikers. The trails run next to Long John Slough, through oak forests and savannas, and the occasional prairie.

DESCRIPTION

When the first incarnation of the Little Red Schoolhouse opened its doors more than a century ago, it was a place where children from local farms learned the three Rs. Over time, as the Palos Forest Preserve expanded, the school building was moved and eventually shut down. The schoolhouse and the grounds now serve as a place where adults and a new generation of kids can delve into the natural world—and receive a quick lesson on the history of rural education.

Inside the former one-room schoolhouse are taxidermy specimens of a coyote, a loon, an opossum, an assortment of birds, and a five-legged bullfrog named Mr. Lucky. More plentiful are the live animals, such as an American kestrel (a small falcon), a boisterous crow, and a variety of local frogs and snakes. A beehive covered in Plexiglas allows visitors a close view of bees in action. Mixed in with the nature exhibits are details about the old school. On display are photos and a diorama depicting life at the school when it was located just to the west along what is now the Black Oak Trail.

DIRECTIONS

Heading south from Chicago, take I-55 to Exit 279A. Follow La Grange Road (US 12, US 20) south for 3.5 miles. Turn right (west) on 95th Street. Follow 95th Street for 1.25 miles, turning left (south) on 104th Avenue (Flavin Road). Little Red Schoolhouse Nature Center is on the right, a half mile south of 95th Street.

KEY AT-A-GLANCE INFORMATION

LENGTH: 2.5 miles

CONFIGURATION: 2 loops

DIFFICULTY: Easy

SCENERY: A scenic lake, oak woods and savannas, rolling terrain

EXPOSURE: Mostly shaded

SURFACE: Dirt with some gravel

HIKING TIME: 1.5–2 hours

ACCESS: March–October, 8 a.m.–5 p.m., weekends, 8 a.m.–5:30 p.m.; November–February, 8 a.m.–4:30 p.m. Schoolhouse exhibit building opens at 9 a.m., closes one-half hour earlier than the grounds and is closed Fridays. Entire center closed major holidays.

FACILITIES: Water, restrooms, benches

MAPS: Available in exhibit building; USGS topo Sag Bridge, IL

SPECIAL COMMENTS: No pets allowed on trails. The nature center offers educational programs year-round for kids and adults. Ask in the exhibit building for a listing of programs.

This hike includes the Farm Pond Trail, the Black Oak Trail, and the White Oak Trail. While the park map indicates that these trails are a total length of 3 miles, my GPS device measured a total distance of 2.5 miles.

UTM Trailhead Coordinates for Palos/Sag Valley Forest Preserve: Little Red Schoolhouse Hike

UTM Zone (NAD27) 16T

Easting 427091

Northing 4617601

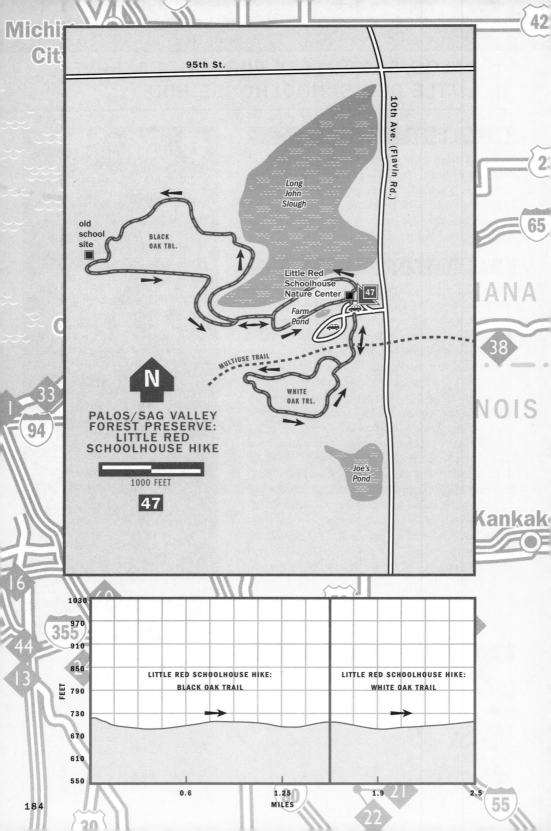

Michi... City

95th St.

10th Ave. (Flavin Rd.)

old school site

BLACK OAK TRL.

Long John Slough

Little Red Schoolhouse Nature Center

47

Farm Pond

MULTIUSE TRAIL

N

WHITE OAK TRL.

PALOS/SAG VALLEY
FOREST PRESERVE:
LITTLE RED
SCHOOLHOUSE HIKE

1000 FEET

47

Joe's Pond

Kankak...

LITTLE RED SCHOOLHOUSE HIKE:
BLACK OAK TRAIL

LITTLE RED SCHOOLHOUSE HIKE:
WHITE OAK TRAIL

1030
970
910
850
790
730
670
610
550

FEET

0.6   1.25   1.9   2.5
MILES

Start the hike on the Farm Pond Trail behind the nature center. From the nature center the trail hugs the shore of Long John Slough, a 35-acre shallow lake fringed by cattails and oaks. During autumn and spring, the slough is a popular stopover for migrating water birds. Between June and September, considerable sections of the slough are blanketed with lily pads and thousands of white water lilies in bloom.

At 0.2 miles, turn right at the fork to begin Black Oak Trail as it runs through a small restored prairie with grasses, sedges, and flowers. Passing beyond a gated fence, turn right again at a second fork. Listen for bullfrogs along the marshy edge of the slough.

As the trail turns away from the slough at a half mile, the woods become dense and quiet. The terrain flattens. Deadfall, charred stumps, and other indications of controlled burnings become plentiful. Appearing regularly are trailside benches and folksy hand-painted signs showing the animals and plants found in the preserve. Watch for black oaks, the trail's namesake, which possess jagged—opposed to rounded—lobes on their leaves.

At 0.9 miles is a sign for the former site of the schoolhouse. First built here in 1870, the school burned to the ground in the mid-1880s and was quickly rebuilt. At about this time, 68 children were enrolled at the school, but only a third showed up for class, particularly in the spring and fall when they were most needed on their farms. Life in the area began to change in 1915, when the forest preserve started acquiring many of the local farms. School enrollment dwindled. As families moved, the location of the schoolhouse was no longer convenient for many students. Shifting populations combined with flooding problems on the site prompted school officials to move the building in 1932. A local man using one mule and log rollers earned $75 for moving the wood structure three-quarters of a mile east to 104th Avenue. The forest preserve continued to expand, and the school was eventually closed; the last class graduated in 1948. In 1955, the school was moved to its present location and reopened as a nature center.

After passing the former school site, the trail follows straight along Old 99th Street. Beyond a marsh on the right at 1.2 miles is a short trail leading into a prairie. Nearby is an enclosure that park staff use to monitor the feeding habits of deer in the area. Finish the loop at 1.4 miles, then head back through the gate, turning right to regain the Farm Pond Trail. At 1.6 miles, the trail ends at a display of old farm equipment. Be sure to check out the small enclosed garden on the left; there is a nice variety of native plants, as well as a literal rendering of the phrase, "bed of flowers." Beyond the garden are three enormous cages containing a great horned owl, a barred owl, and a red-tailed hawk. Before moving on, swing toward the rear of the schoolhouse, where young hikers will enjoy watching the turtles in the small pool.

Even on busy weekends when the Black Oak Trail and the nature center are hosting a steady stream of visitors, you're still likely to find a quiet atmosphere on the White Oak Trail. Start the hike directly across the parking lot from the Little Red Schoolhouse. Just beyond a bench on the left overlooking a small pond, the trail crosses a multiuse path that runs through many sections of the 14,000-acre Palos/Sag Valley Forest Preserve. When reaching a fork at 0.2 miles, stay to the right as the path leads through lightly rolling terrain. Watch for woodpeckers, flickers, and Eastern

Water lillies bloom on Long John Slough for much of the summer.

bluebirds within the canopy of oak leaves overhead. Joe's Pond, one of the many small bodies of water in the area left behind by glaciers, can be seen through the trees on the right at 0.6 miles. As the trail turns back toward the schoolhouse, there's a small ravine to the right. Lush with plants, this ravine is a favorite spot for deer during the summer. Complete the loop at 0.8 miles and head back to the parking lot.

▶ NEARBY ACTIVITIES

One mile south on 104th Avenue is the trailhead for the Cap Sauers and Swallow Cliff hike, found on page 179.

PILCHER PARK LOOP

▶ IN BRIEF

Pilcher Park offers an appealing mix of graceful ravines, lush bottomland forest, and small winding streams. Toward the end of the hike, you'll see a couple of area landmarks from the 1920s: a still used public water well and the recently renovated Bird Haven Greenhouse.

▶ DESCRIPTION

Harlow Higginbotham, an important figure in Chicago during the late nineteenth century, once owned Pilcher Park. Higginbotham was the president of Chicago's extremely successful Columbian Exposition in 1893, a world's fair commemorating the 400th anniversary of Columbus' arrival in the Americas. After the exposition, Higginbotham used many of the trees that were part of the exhibits to establish a private arboretum on this property. Specimens such as southern magnolia, sweet gum, cypress, tulip tree, pecan, black birch, and various hickories were added to a park that already contained about 75 native species of trees.

In 1920, Higginbotham sold the arboretum to Robert Pilcher, a businessman, self-taught naturalist, and "sturdy pioneer," according to the inscription on his statue near the park's nature center. Eventually, Pilcher donated his 327 acres of virgin woodland to the City of Joliet, with the stipulation that the land be left wild. Higginbotham's

▶ DIRECTIONS

From Chicago take I-90/I-94 south. Continue on I-94 until reaching I-57. Take I-57 south for 13.5 miles to I-80 west. After 13.7 miles on I-80, take Exit 137 and follow US 30 (West Lincoln Highway) for 0.6 miles left (west). Turn right (north) on South Gouger Road and follow it for 0.3 miles until you see the first of two entrances for the park on the left. Take either entrance and follow the signs pointing toward the nature center.

ⓘ KEY AT-A-GLANCE INFORMATION

LENGTH: 3.3 miles

CONFIGURATION: Loop

DIFFICULTY: Easy

SCENERY: Bottomland forest, ravines, streams, river, a historic well, and an impressive public greenhouse

EXPOSURE: Mostly shaded

SURFACE: Dirt with sections of new pavement and deteriorating asphalt

HIKING TIME: 1.5 hours

ACCESS: The park is open from dawn to dusk. The nature center is open 9 a.m.–4:30 p.m. on weekdays; 10 a.m.–4:30 p.m. on weekends.

FACILITIES: Nature center, restrooms, picnic tables and shelters

MAPS: Ask for a trail map at the nature center; USGS topo Joliet, IL

SPECIAL COMMENTS: Contact the nature center at (815) 741-7277. To find out about special flower shows at the Bird Haven Greenhouse, call (815) 741-7278.

UTM Trailhead Coordinates for Pilcher Park Loop

UTM Zone (NAD27)   16T

Easting   414711

Northing   4598196

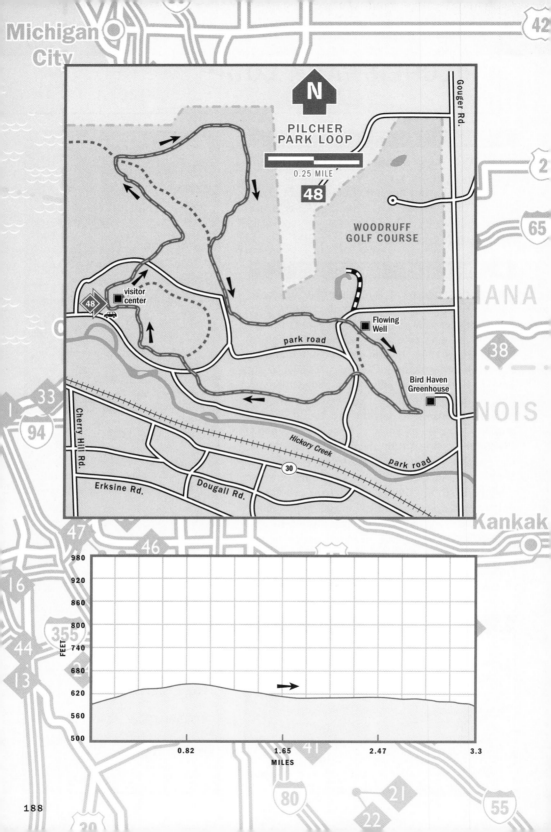

PILCHER PARK LOOP

0.25 MILE

48

WOODRUFF GOLF COURSE

Gouger Rd.

visitor center

48

Flowing Well

Bird Haven Greenhouse

park road

Cherry Hill Rd.

Hickory Creek

park road

30

Erksine Rd.

Dougall Rd.

Michigan City

Kankak

FEET

980
920
860
800
740
680
620
560
500

0.82   1.65   2.47   3.3

MILES

name is preserved across the street from Pilcher Park in another park called Higginbotham Woods (see "Nearby Activities" section).

Thanks to the efforts of Higginbotham and Pilcher, visitors can still explore the park's 420 acres of ravines, streams, and forested bottomland. The ravines roll through the northern section of the park, and the bottomland forest—where you'll see trees such as the bur oak, American elm, and slippery elm—occupies the southern section along Hickory Creek. Come springtime, the landscape in many sections of the park is carpeted with wildflowers.

The first stop at Pilcher Park ought to be the attractive log-cabin–style nature center that hosts a large colorful totem pole in front, built in 1912. Inside, kids will enjoy the turtle pond; several aquariums containing catfish, sturgeon, crappie, and perch; live snakes; and a live Eastern owl. Also inside is a large window where you can watch the park's birds (and squirrels) feeding at a cluster of bird feeders.

To begin the hike, follow the sign for the North Pilcher Trail on the left side of the parking lot as you're facing the nature center. After the trail dips down to meet the edge of a small pond, follow the sign to the right, and then bear left over the footbridge. Just ahead, the trail passes over several drainage culverts before crossing a gravel path and then the park road. On the other side of the park road, the landscape starts to rise.

Reaching the hilltop, the terrain levels out, and the trail curves left and runs above a pleasant wooded ravine containing an intermittent stream. Keep straight ahead at the sign pointing left for the North Pilcher Trail. At 0.6 miles into the hike, where several asphalt trails come together, follow the sign for the Upper Loop Trail on the right. Right away, the Upper Loop Trail enters a flat and dense woodland with a few intermittent streams. After passing an open area where a number of small- and medium-sized trees have been cut, the path starts to lose elevation. Just after crossing a stream, you'll see the beginnings of an expansive wooded ravine on the left. Farther ahead is a nicely situated bench where you can pause and take it all in.

From the bench, the trail descends gradually through a mature oak forest, and then curves right and passes a trail junction. When you reach the gate at the park road, keep straight ahead on the park road until you see the "Hiking Trail, No Horses" sign on the left, just before the paved trail that crosses a steel bridge. After crossing the wooden footbridge, you've suddenly entered a flat bottomland forest. Up ahead, beyond the paved service road, the Woodruff Golf Course appears on the left. Taking a right at the fork leads you over a footbridge, across the park road, and into a picnic area with tables, a shelter, an open grassy area, and the Flowing Well, where you'll likely see a few people filling up their water bottles. Drilled in 1927 to a depth of 207 feet, the park district maintains that the mineral content and the 51-degree temperature of the water have remained constant throughout the life of the well. If you don't mind the slight taste of iron and other minerals common in well water, take a drink.

From the well, follow the concrete path left of the restrooms for 0.3 miles to the Bird Haven Greenhouse, which hosts indoor plants and flowers, outdoor formal gardens, seasonal flower shows, and a children's garden. The greenhouse—designed by the same architectural firm that designed the Central Park Greenhouse in New York

Springtime wildflowers blanket a hilltop in the north section of the park.

City—was built in 1929 and underwent a major renovation in 2003. Displayed in front of the greenhouse is the original clock face from the Will County Courthouse, built in 1887 in Joliet.

Proceeding with the hike, find the dirt path at the back of the greenhouse just to the left of the paved path. A quarter mile away from the greenhouse, after passing a small pond and a marshy area thick with shrubs on the left, the trail crosses a park road and a footbridge, and then heads back into the bottomland forest. This section of the trail is one of the places in the park where you may see wildflowers such as jack-in-the-pulpit, spring beauty, May apple, and red trillium. Crossing the park road again, keep straight ahead, soon reaching a footbridge over a small rocky stream. After crossing another footbridge, the trail runs next to the park road and Hickory Creek. At the next trail junction, bear left, and the nature center should be visible through the trees. Cross one final footbridge and then turn left on the interpretive trail that runs toward the backside of the nature center.

▶ NEARBY ACTIVITIES

Higginbotham Woods, also owned by the Joliet Park District, is across Gouger Road from Pilcher Park. You can walk an old gravel road that traverses the park from east to west. This is accessible from Francis Road, which heads west from Gouger Road just south of the Bird Haven Greenhouse. Near the parking area is a large boulder with an inscription describing a French fort that was allegedly built on this land in 1730 and a trading post built in 1829. Recent archeological studies show, however, that the supposed indications of an early French fort are actually irregularly shaped earthworks created by Native Americans of the Hopewell period, which ranges from 200 B.C. to 400 A.D.

PRATT'S WAYNE LOOP

IN BRIEF

As the largest forest preserve in DuPage County, Pratt's Wayne Woods has no shortage of marshes, ponds, and prairies to explore. The west section of the preserve hosts sprawling open spaces interrupted now and then with picturesque wetlands and groves of elm and cottonwood.

DESCRIPTION

Located in the far northwestern corner of DuPage County, this 3,432-acre county forest preserve was pieced together with help by an assortment of landowners. Some landowners grew corn and grain here, some mined gravel, while others used the setting for a hunting and fishing club. After the preserve got its start in 1965 with the donation of 170 acres by the state of Illinois, a couple of the parcels were sold to the county by George Pratt, a local township supervisor and county forest preserve commissioner. The preserve gets part of its name from Pratt and part of it from the nearby community of Wayne.

The hike begins by circling the tree-fringed ponds on the northwest side of Pickerel Lake. Find the trailhead by heading to the right along the shore of Pickerel Lake and looking for the crushed-gravel path at the far edge of the last parking lot. Once on the trail, you'll pass the east end of Catfish Pond on the right, and then pass a paved wheelchair-accessible trail on the left that

DIRECTIONS

Follow I-90/I-94 northwest from Chicago. After the expressways split, continue on I-90 for 24.5 miles. Exit on IL 59 (New Sutton Road) and drive south for 6.6 miles. Turn right (west) on Stearns Road and go for 1.6 miles. Turn left (south) on Powis Road and continue for 1 mile to the main entrance for Pratt's Wayne Woods Forest Preserve on the right. Park in the first lot on the left.

KEY AT-A-GLANCE INFORMATION

LENGTH: 6 miles

CONFIGURATION: Loop

DIFFICULTY: Easy to moderate

SCENERY: Ponds, lakes, prairies, savannas, marshes, and woodland

EXPOSURE: Mostly exposed

SURFACE: Crushed gravel, mowed grass

HIKING TIME: 2.5–3 hours

ACCESS: 1 hour after sunrise to 1 hour after sunset

FACILITIES: Restrooms, water, picnic tables and shelter, fishing piers

MAPS: Maps are available in the parking lot; USGS topos Geneva, IL and West Chicago, IL

SPECIAL COMMENTS: Although Army Trail Road is not terribly busy, use caution while hiking a short segment along the road. Also, proceed with great care through the equestrian jumping area if horses are present.

UTM Trailhead Coordinates for Pratt's Wayne Loop

UTM Zone (NAD27) 16T

Easting 396947

Northing 4646629

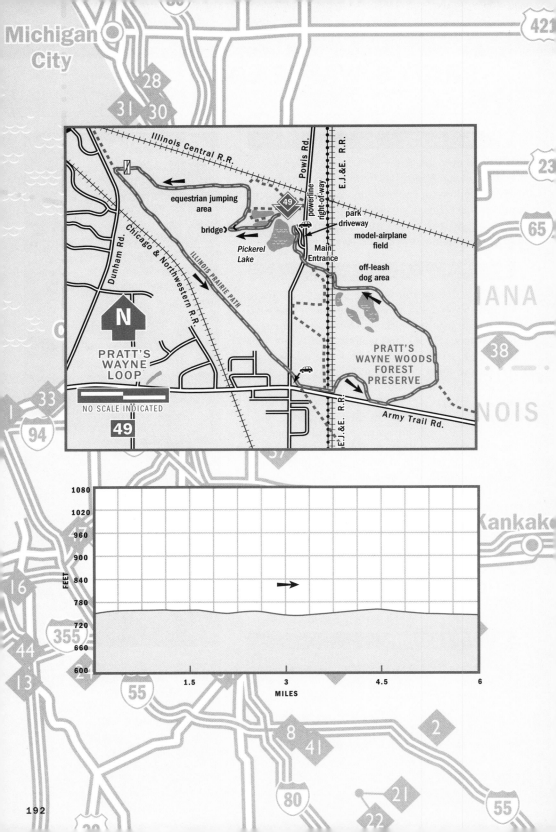

Michigan City

Illinois Central R.R.

Powis Rd.

E.J.&E. R.R.

equestrian jumping area

powerline right-of-way

park driveway

49

bridge

model-airplane field

Pickerel Lake

Main Entrance

off-leash dog area

Dunham Rd.

Chicago & Northwestern R.R.

ILLINOIS PRAIRIE PATH

N

PRATT'S WAYNE LOOP

PRATT'S WAYNE WOODS FOREST PRESERVE

NO SCALE INDICATED

49

E.J.&E. R.R.

Army Trail Rd.

1080
1020
960
900
840
780
720
660
600

FEET

1.5   3   4.5   6

MILES

leads to one of the two fishing piers on Pickerel Lake. After the trail to the pier, follow the next trail left, which brings you to the shoreline of Beaver Slough. Many of the banks of Beaver Slough are reinforced with stacks of limestone that sometimes serve as steps leading to the water's edge. All three of these ponds, as well as Pickerel Lake, were gravel pits about 50 years ago.

Keep straight ahead at the connector trail on the right that divides Beaver Slough and Horsetail Pond. At 0.3 miles, the trail takes a sharp right onto the metal bridge spanning the west end of Horsetail Pond, and then passes a pleasant picnic area and a connector trail dividing Horsetail and Catfish ponds on the right. Just beyond the connector trail, turn left on the two-track (be sure to take the trail to the right of the sign for Pratt's Wayne Woods; don't take the fainter trail to the left of the sign).

Leaving behind the woods, the trail enters a wide-open savanna bordered by groves of oak. Follow the next junction left, and you'll begin to see dozens of obstacles for horse jumping—everything from small logs to wooden fences to giant tree trunks stacked 5-feet high. The 100-year-old Wayne-DuPage Hunt Club organizes equestrian events here during the warmer months.

After hiking for 0.7 miles through the horse-jumping area, the trail veers right through the trees and then turns left before passing through a gate (you may have to duck under a cable stretched across the gate). At one-and-a-half miles into the hike, turn left onto a lovely slice of rail-trail known as the Illinois Prairie Path. This section of Prairie Path—called the Elgin Spur—runs for about 15 miles between the towns of Wheaton and Elgin. Once you're on the path, keep to the right side. You'll notice right away that this 5-foot-wide crushed-gravel path is well-liked by local hikers, runners, and cyclists.

For the first 0.3 miles on Prairie Path, the route shoots straight as an arrow behind a few houses, alongside dense woods, and next to a sizable cattail marsh. Soon the cattails on the left give way to open water, much of it covered in algae. On the far side of the open water, look for large water birds perched on fallen logs. The wooden railings mark the spot where Brewster creek passes under the path. After the creek, open water comes and goes on the left, and eventually shrubs rise up on each side of the trail.

To the left over the wooden railings at the Norton Creek crossing is a wide treeless swath of marshland and wet prairie. Farther along, the thick woods and a dense, leafy canopy turn the trail into a shadowy tunnel. You'll encounter an elementary school on the right and then cross Powis Road before arriving at Army Trail Road at 3.4 miles into the hike, where you'll find a portable restroom, a water pump, a bench, and a mapboard showing the entire 55-mile route of the Prairie Path. The hike continues less than 100 yards to the left along Army Trail Road. While walking along the side of Army Trail Road, skip the mowed path on the right that appears before the train tracks; instead, take the second mowed path on the right, just after the train tracks.

Following the mowed path as it enters the grassland and then swings around the backside of the farmhouse on the right, you'll encounter wet prairies, stands of shrubs, and the occasional savannas. After returning to Army Trail Road for a short sweep, the trail heads back into the grassland, takes a dip, and then rises to meet a trail on the right heading to Munger Road. Turning left at the fork takes you through a grove of smaller trees and next to a wetland on the left. Keeping left at another spur trail, you'll cut through a grove of elm, cottonwood, and cherry trees on your way to a high spot with the best view so far of this sprawling open space. Except for the big cluster of homes off to the east, you can see for nearly a mile in every direction.

As you approach the 23-acre off-leash dog area, you'll pass a cattail-fringed pond with open water on the left. For the next 0.3 miles, the trail follows the dog fence straight ahead and then to the right. At 5.5 miles into the hike, use caution as you cross over the train tracks. On the other side of the tracks, you'll see the horse-trailer parking lot as you approach the park road. Take a left on the park road, then cross Powis Road into the forest preserve's main entrance. Stay to the left, heading toward Pickerel Lake. Follow the shore of the lake for 0.15 miles back to the parking lot.

▶ NEARBY ACTIVITIES

Just north of Pratt's Wayne Woods is the recently opened Tri-County State Park, offering 3.8 miles of multiuse trails through 500 acres of prairie and wetlands. Once agricultural land and now bordered by various developments, the prairies at Tri-County are in the process of being restored. The Big Bluestem Trail takes you to the point where Cook, DuPage, and Kane counties come together. From the Pratt's Wayne Woods main entrance, follow Powis Road for 0.9 miles north (left). Head west (left) on Stearns Road and follow it for 0.7 miles to the park entrance. For information, call the visitor center at (847) 429-4670.

For those interested in exploring more of the Illinois Prairie Path either on foot or on a bicycle, you can connect to the Fox River Trail about 5 miles north of Army Trail Road in Elgin. To the south, the Great Western Trail is about 4 miles away, and downtown Wheaton is about 9 miles. These sections of the Prairie Path are maintained by the DuPage County Division of Transportation, which can be contacted at (708) 682-7318. The map sold by the Chicago Bicycle Federation (www.biketraffic.org) is indispensable for getting around on all the rail-trails and bikeways in Chicagoland.

RYERSON WOODS HIKE

IN BRIEF

The trails in Ryerson Woods wind through some of the most stunning forestland in the Chicago region. Along the shore of the Des Plaines River and its backwater, expect to see waterfowl, wildflowers, and old rustic cabins left behind by the families that once owned the property.

DESCRIPTION

What was a once a weekend getaway for a local industrialist and his friends is now a hikers' heaven, with trails leading through one of the finest woodlands in Northern Illinois. Much of what is now the south section of Ryerson Woods was purchased in the 1920s by Edward L. Ryerson and his friends. Ryerson, who became president of Ryerson Steel Company upon the death of his father in 1928, built a rustic cabin on his riverside plot. In years to come, his friends also built cabins on the land. In 1938, Ryerson bought 250 acres of farmland in what is now the northern section of the conservation area, and then a few years later built a summer home that now serves as the visitor center. Motivated by a desire to maintain this forest sanctuary, in the 1960s Ryerson and his friends decided to donate and sell their land to the Lake County Forest Preserve District.

Given Ryerson Woods' startling beauty and its proximity to Chicago, one would expect it to be swarming with hikers and nature watchers. Fortunately, this is not the case. Perhaps it's the

KEY AT-A-GLANCE INFORMATION

LENGTH: 4.5 miles

CONFIGURATION: Loop within a loop

DIFFICULTY: Easy

SCENERY: Lush forest along Des Plaines River

EXPOSURE: Shady, with brief exposed stretches

SURFACE: Dirt with numerous boardwalks and bridges

HIKING TIME: 3–4 hours for both loops

ACCESS: 6:30 a.m.–sunset

FACILITIES: Water, restrooms, visitor center

MAPS: Trail maps available at the visitor center; USGS topo Wheeling, IL

SPECIAL COMMENTS: The visitor center is open 9 a.m.–5 p.m. daily, except major holidays. Ryerson Woods is open 6:30 a.m.–sunset. No pets or picnicking allowed. Visit www.ryersonwoods.org to learn about Ryerson's plants and animals, and programs offered throughout the year.

DIRECTIONS

From Chicago, head north on I-90/I-94. Follow I-94 as it separates from I-90. Continue on I-94 to Deerfield Road. Turn left (west) on Deerfield Road and proceed for a half mile. At Riverwoods Road, turn right (north). Two miles ahead, turn left at the sign for the Edward L. Ryerson Conservation Area. Follow signs to the visitor center.

UTM Trailhead Coordinates for Ryerson Woods Hike

UTM Zone (NAD27)   16T

Easting   424391

Northing   4670259

N

RYERSON
WOODS HIKE

0.25 MILE

50

Westwood Ln.

overlook

Start 3-mile
section

50

visitor
center

Start 1.5-mile
section

50

Riverwoods Rd.

Des Plaines River

Ryerson
Cabin

dam

Smith
Cabin

Michigan City

Kankak

421

23

65

38

33

94

16

355

44

13

55

21

22

930
870
810
750
690
630
570
510
450

FEET

1.5-mile section

3-mile section

1.12

2.25

3.37

4.5

MILES

The Smith Cabin was left behind by one of the former owners of Ryerson Woods.

restrictions on pets, bicycles, and picnicking that keep the crowds away. Despite the lack of traditional park amenities, Ryerson is still a great place to bring the family. At the farm exhibit in the north section of the preserve, kids will enjoy the pigs, goats, chickens, cows, beehives, and turkeys. Also, the layout of trails allows for easy shortening or lengthening of a hike.

Mapboards are posted at trailheads and at a handful of trail intersections. Picking up a map from the visitor center will ensure that you always know where you are. The first part of this hike, which starts near the visitor center, takes you on a 1.5-mile loop through the northern section of the preserve. The second part of the hike, which starts near the farm, takes you on a 3-mile loop more or less along the perimeter of the preserve. Catch the beginning of the hike's first part just left of the driveway that leads into the visitor center parking lot. Right away on the trail, on the right, you'll notice a high fence, which allows Ryerson Woods staff to monitor the amount of browsing done by deer.

At about 0.2 miles, near a couple of boardwalks spanning intermittent streams, you'll get a taste of what makes the Ryerson Woods landscape so beautiful: tall oaks, hickories, elms, dense canopies, minimal understory, and a lush, leafy ground cover. Coming out of the woods, the trail takes a sharp right turn as it begins to run alongside a park road that borders the farm property. Keep going on this mowed path, passing the intersection with the perimeter loop trail, and then crossing the park entrance road. In the clearing across the road, keep an eye out for bluebirds and indigo buntings, and—if it's dusk—for the bats leaving the bat house. The trail continues to the left, running between the two cabins, which are used for programs and exhibits when school groups visit.

At the next junction, turn right and cross a boardwalk. After you walk through a grove of large shagbark hickories and cross a bridge next to a couple of sizable oaks, the Des Plaines River will appear on the right. In a short distance, you'll find a bench at a modest overlook of the river. After the overlook, take the next trail to the right, which takes you back to the park entrance road. The hike continues on the other side of a parking lot and the farm building in front of you. Before getting back to the trail, you may want to stroll around the farm to see the livestock. Although Edward Ryerson kept dairy cattle and Yorkshire pigs, his main interest was Arabian horses, which were kept in these structures designed by Edwin Hill Clark, the architect who designed the famous Brookfield Zoo in Brookfield, Illinois.

Back on the trail, you'll cross a bridge and enter the forest. In this area and in others, don't be alarmed when seeing garbage bags on the trail waiting to be picked up. Most likely the bags contain an invasive, quickly spreading plant called mustard garlic, which has been pulled up by volunteers. Turn left at the T-intersection and continue along this wide gravelly path until coming to a trail branching left. Follow this short trail through an open area and back to the parking lot.

Pick up the 3-mile perimeter hike at the parking lot by the farm. Starting in the corner of the parking lot closest to the woods, this trail traverses the edges of the open space for a quarter mile, and then rambles alongside the backwaters of the Des Plaines River. During spring and summer, watch for trilliums as well as irises, which are called blue flags and yellow flags. At about 0.4 miles into the hike, as the trail approaches the main thread of the river, consider slowing your pace: it's a favorite place for great blue herons. In the low spots, receding water has left logs strewn about.

Stay to the right at the intersection, and at 0.9 miles you'll reach Ryerson Cabin and a small dam in the river. From the back-right corner of the cabin, continue with the trail as it runs along the bank of the river and over a boardwalk that protects the softer, erosion-prone areas of the riverbank. Ahead is the intersection with another trail and the Smith Cabin, as well as a bench and a mapboard. Beyond the Smith Cabin, cross a bridge over a twisting stream, and head back into the forest. If rain has recently fallen, hikers in Ryerson Woods should expect to get mud on their shoes, particularly on this section of the trail, as it weaves among small marshes and intermittent ponds. After crossing the stream again, you'll pass through groves of elms, patches of May apples, and towering oaks.

At 2.3 miles you'll see a mapboard and a bench at a trail intersection. Continue straight ahead through more dense woodland and marshy areas with boardwalks. The path turns left just before reaching a metal gate, and soon runs alongside the park entrance road. A short way up, pass a trail intersection on the left, and come out on the road that borders the farm area. Return to the parking lot by following the road on the right to the other side of the farm.

▶ NEARBY ACTIVITIES

Just across the river from Ryerson Conservation Area is the southern terminus of the Des Plaines River Trail, an excellent crushed limestone biking trail that runs along the Des Plaines and through a number of forest preserves. In the future, the county plans to bring the River Trail through Ryerson. Until then, a good place to start is 2 miles north of Ryerson at Half Day Forest Preserve. From here, the trail heads north for 30 miles, nearly to the Wisconsin border. For information, visit www.lcfpd.org/preserves.

SHABBONA LAKE STATE PARK LOOP

▶ IN BRIEF

For a man-made artifact, Shabbona Lake is strikingly beautiful and varied. As you make your way around the lake, you'll encounter grasslands, hills, streams, marshes, dense woodlands, ponds—and the lake itself is in view for nearly the entire hike.

▶ DESCRIPTION

It's hard to believe that nearly all of Shabbona Lake State Park in DeKalb County was rolling farmland just 30 years ago. Since then, small forests were expanded, grasslands were established, and a 319-acre lake was created in the center of the park. If it weren't for the earthen dam and spillway on the south end of the lake and the occasional dead tree jutting out of the water, one would readily assume that the lake has been cradled in this landscape since northern Illinois emerged from the deep freeze.

The park is named for Chief Shabbona, a Potawatomi Indian Chief from the area who was known for befriending white settlers at the time of the Black Hawk War. Waged by Chief Black Hawk of the Sac tribe, the Black Hawk War was intended to keep white settlers from taking land held by Native Americans in the area. Shabbona helped to convince other Indian leaders that a war

▶ DIRECTIONS

From Chicago, take I-290 west to I-88. Follow I-88 west to the Sugar Grove exit, which is 2.5 miles west of the Aurora tollbooth. From the Sugar Grove exit, take US 30 (IL 56) west for 25 miles. At Indian Road, 4.4 miles west of Waterman, turn left (south). Go south for a half mile and turn right (west) on Preserve Road. The entrance to the park is 0.4 miles ahead on the left. Stay to the right on the Shabbona Park main road for 2.2 miles until you reach the Shabbona Grove Picnic Area.

ℹ KEY AT-A-GLANCE INFORMATION

LENGTH: 4.9 miles

CONFIGURATION: Loop

DIFFICULTY: Moderate

SCENERY: Lake, prairies, woods, marshes, streams, hills, and a man-made earthen dam

EXPOSURE: Mostly exposed

SURFACE: Mowed grass, dirt

HIKING TIME: 3 hours

ACCESS: November–January, 8 a.m.–5 p.m.; February–March, 8 a.m.–6 p.m.; April, 8 a.m.–8 p.m.; May–October, 6 a.m.–10 p.m. The Tomahawk Trail section of this hike (on the east side of the lake) is closed from October 1 to the end of archery deer season. Call the park at (815) 824-2106 for exact dates.

FACILITIES: Restrooms, water, picnic tables and shelters, playgrounds, and fishing access are available. Campground, camp store, boat rental, and restaurant are open during the warmer months.

MAPS: Park maps are available in the park office parking lot on the south side of the park on Shabbona Grove Road; USGS topos Shabbona Grove, IL and Waterman, IL

SPECIAL COMMENTS: Due to strained finances for the past couple of years, the park has been unable to maintain the Tomahawk Trail on the east side of the lake. Despite the restricted-access sign, this trail is still open for hikers. During the warmer months, the park brings in a steady stream of anglers, campers, and picnickers. The rest of year, the park is surprisingly quiet.

UTM Trailhead Coordinates for Shabbona Lake State Park Loop

UTM Zone (NAD27) 16T

Easting 345023

Northing 4621974

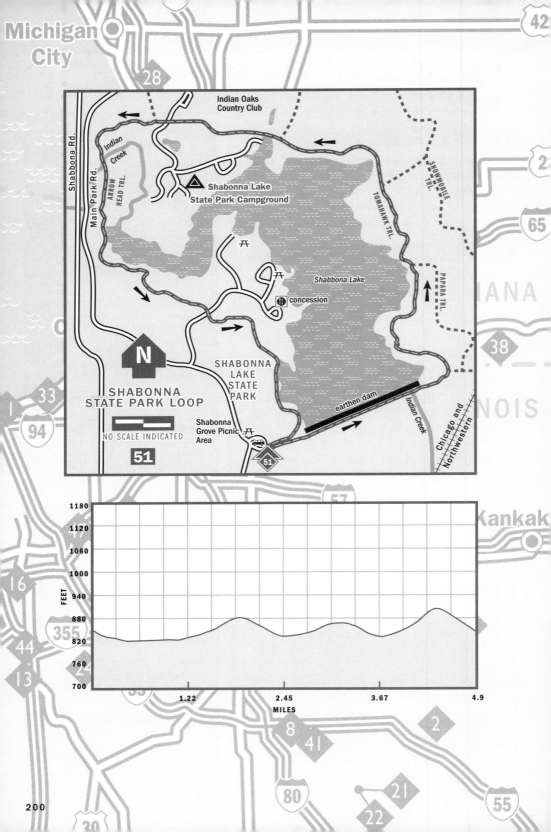

Michigan City

Indian Oaks
Country Club

Shabonna Rd.

Main Park Rd.

Indian
Creek

ARROW HEAD TRL.

Shabonna Lake
State Park Campground

SNOWMOBILE TRL.

TOMAHAWK TRL.

PAPARA TRL.

Shabonna Lake

concession

SHABONNA
LAKE
STATE
PARK

earthen dam

Indian Creek

Chicago and
Northwestern

N

SHABONNA
STATE PARK LOOP

NO SCALE INDICATED

Shabonna
Grove Picnic
Area

51

FEET

| 1180 |
| 1120 |
| 1060 |
| 1000 |
| 940 |
| 880 |
| 820 |
| 760 |
| 700 |

1.22   2.45   3.67   4.9

MILES

Ice-encrusted grasses on the shore of Shabbona Lake.

against the U.S. government would be a futile undertaking. Following Black Hawk's surrender in 1832, the tribes remaining in the area, including the Potawatomi, were relocated to Iowa. Chief Shabbona is buried about 35 miles southeast of the park in the town of Morris, but his wife and several children are buried near the park.

For a counterclockwise hike around the lake, follow the sign pointing to the dam and the Tomahawk Trail from the east side of the Shabbona Grove Picnic Area. Just beyond the sign, stay left as you merge with the snowmobile trail. At the next junction, near the grove of pine and sumac, stay to the right as the trail mounts the half-mile-long earthen dam that was constructed in 1975 in order to create the lake. The dam offers a great spot for watching geese, ducks, and other water fowl that congregate here during much of the year. At the end of the dam, the trail passes over what looks like a big washbasin, which collects water and directs it down a 60-foot concrete spillway that slopes gradually into Indian Creek on the right. The creek meets up with the Fox River about 20 miles south.

After crossing the spillway, the trail rises and runs through an open area before coming to a junction with the Tomahawk Trail, where you'll turn left. As you pass into the hardwood forest, you'll see a little ravine on the left, which was cut by an intermittent stream that runs through a culvert under the trail. Just ahead, the trail passes a bench in a clearing at the edge of the lake. Several dead trees sticking out of the water offer evidence that this lake is younger than it looks.

Don't be alarmed when you see a red sign announcing that the continuation of this trail is closed. While funding shortages prevent the park staff from maintaining this trail, the park still invites hikers to use this trail with the warning that they should be prepared to step over fallen branches and the occasional fallen tree. Other than a few minor obstacles, the trail is wide, well marked, and very easy to follow.

Beyond the sign, the trail passes over another drainage ditch, and begins winding through a gently rolling landscape. Throughout the hike on this side of the lake, the trail alternates between hugging the shoreline and going inland for short stretches. After cutting through an area thick with shrubs, the trail moves closer to the lake, and soon meets the Papara Trail. Stay on the Tomahawk Trail by turning left (watch your step—this area can be especially muddy in the spring).

As the trail comes out into the grassland, it swings to the right, climbs a small hill, and then passes a trail branching to the right. From the top of the hill, the trail takes a steep 40-foot drop before it runs between a pond on the right and a finger of the lake on the left. For the next quarter mile, as you head toward the campground, the path runs parallel to the sometimes marshy shoreline.

Getting closer to the campground, keep straight ahead when the Tomahawk Trail merges with the snowmobile trail. Passing a marshy inlet of the lake on the left, you'll see the Indian Oaks Country Club golf course on the right. At the campground, restrooms are on the left; a camp store and a playground are on the right.

Keep straight ahead on the trail as it rises to a clearing and crosses the campground access road. After crossing the road, follow the sign for the Arrowhead Trail to the left. Turning right on the Arrowhead Trail, suddenly you'll enter a dense woodland. (These sudden transitions from grassland to dense woodland will happen regularly for the remainder of the hike.)

As the trail curves left, it begins a half-mile stretch running parallel to the main park road. Near where the trail crosses Indian Creek on a wooden footbridge, keep an eye out for signs of beavers: cone-shaped tree stumps with wood chips at the base. After continuing for a bit alongside Indian Creek, the trail rises to higher ground, and then meets a short connector trail on the right that leads to the park road.

Soon the trail passes a wetland down below on the left, which is where Indian Creek enters Shabbona Lake. This marshy area is a great spot to look for waterfowl; some 30 species are said to drop in annually at the park during their migrations. While walking the edge of this wetland, you can get closer to the water by using a few access points along the way (signs are posted indicating that access to this area is not allowed between October 1 and the marsh's first freeze-over).

Not long after crossing a park road again at 4.1 miles into the hike, you'll see the park's concession stand and restaurant. The trail turns right before reaching the parking lot, and soon runs near restrooms on the left. As you approach the lakeshore, a connector trail heads left toward the buildings you just passed. For the remainder of the hike, the trail mostly runs alongside the lake through the open grassland. Stay to the right at the final junction near the grove of sumac and pine. From here, the parking lot is just ahead.

▶ NEARBY ACTIVITIES

A few eateries can be found on US 30 in Waterman, which is 4.4 miles east of the turnoff for the park.

Four-and-a-half miles east of Waterman, keep an eye out for parachutes drifting downward in the vicinity of the Hinckley Airport. Chicagoland Skydiving (look for the big sign on US 30) is one of a few places in the Chicago area for pursuing this pastime. Be sure to call ahead for information and reservations at (815) 286-9200. The website is www.chicagolandskydiving.com.

SILVER SPRINGS STATE PARK LOOP

IN BRIEF

Silver Springs offers a wealth of scenic pleasures. While hiking over ridges, through woodlands, along Loon Lake and the Fox River, you'll encounter a variety of trees, birds, and wildflowers.

DESCRIPTION

About 30 miles upstream from where the Fox River flows into the Illinois River, the Fox runs through a beautiful state park named for its sparkling water that seeps from the ground all year. Like many parks in the area, Silver Springs State Park was largely farmland before being bought by the state in 1969. Now it's one of only a few refuges for hikers in Kendall County. While Silver Springs is a popular spot for walkers, it's also well liked by local hunters and anglers. Keep in mind that some of the lesser trails (listed in "Nearby Activities" section) are closed for part of the season to accommodate hunters. The hike that follows, which is open all year, is not the longest or the most isolated hike in the park, but it's the most beautiful and varied.

Start the hike in the northeast corner of the parking lot, opposite the restrooms. From the sign indicating that the Silver Springs are 0.2 miles ahead, follow the wide mowed path until reaching a junction, where you'll turn left. At the bottom of

KEY AT-A-GLANCE INFORMATION

LENGTH: 2.6 miles

CONFIGURATION: Loop

DIFFICULTY: Easy to moderate

SCENERY: Woods, ridges, lakes, wide river, and a natural spring

EXPOSURE: Mostly covered

SURFACE: Dirt

HIKING TIME: 1–1.5 hours

ACCESS: Sunrise to sunset

FACILITIES: Restrooms, water, concession stand/bait shop, paddleboat rentals, and playground

MAPS: Park map available at concession stand; USGS topo Plano, IL

SPECIAL COMMENTS: Bring a fishing pole if you'd like to cast a line into the 2 man-made lakes near the parking lot. Boating is allowed on these lakes; boat motors are not.

There is a free wildflower checklist you can pick up at the concession stand or park office—a great help to those interested in identifying the park's 130 flower types.

DIRECTIONS

From Chicago, follow I-55 south until reaching Exit 261, where you'll take IL 126 southwest for 15.8 miles. Turn right (north) on IL 47 and proceed for 1.6 miles. Turn left (west) onto US 34 and follow it for 5.2 miles until you reach County Road 15 (Fox River Road). Turn left (south) on CR 15 and proceed for 1.2 miles until turning left (east) on CR 1 (Fox Road). Follow CR 1 for 0.9 miles past the park's main entrance, and turn left at the sign for the east entrance.

UTM Trailhead Coordinates for Silver Springs State Park Loop

UTM Zone (NAD27)   16T

Easting   373339

Northing   4609724

SILVER SPRINGS STATE PARK HIKE

N

0.25 MILE

52

Fox Rd.

421

231

65

Michigan City

Fox River

Fox Ridge parking area

park office

SILVER SPRINGS STATE PARK

concession

Beaver Lake

Loon Lake

River Rd.

33

94

Fox River Rd.

park road

Fox River Rd.

Kankakee

38

INDIANA

ILLINOIS

6

44

13

355

FEET

930
870
810
750
690
630
570
510
450

0.65   1.3   1.95   2.6
MILES

Once it seeps from the ground, the springwater from Silver Springs flows toward the Fox River.

a short incline, a platform overlooks a gravelly spot where water seeps from the ground all year. As the water trickles out, it gathers in a small pool before flowing through patches of watercress and alongside a lush stream bank on its way to the Fox River. Continuing ahead on the trail toward the river, look for orange jewelweed flowers near the stream.

Before turning left at the trail that runs parallel to the river, check out the rocky shoreline ahead. Depending on the water level, a small island or two may be visible within this wide, slow-moving waterway. As you follow the trail to the left alongside the riverbank, look high up in the trees at the water's edge for ospreys, a rare sight in Illinois. Brown on the top of its body and white underneath, this is a large hawk that dines on fish it grabs from the water. The two different times I saw ospreys on this stretch of river, they were high up in a tree, apparently waiting for a meal to surface.

As the trail follows the river, you'll pass several short connector trails on the left. The first one leads back to the parking lot where you started, while the subsequent trails lead to Beaver Lake and beyond to Loon Lake, beside the parking lot. At both of these lakes, benches are on hand, offering pleasant spots to have a seat, eat a lunch, and watch the water birds. After following the river for a half mile, you'll pass through a brown metal gate, and then cross the park road. Regain the trail just to the right of the restrooms. Moving away from the river, the trail winds through a mostly maple bottomland forest, and skirts the edge of a small pond. Follow the arrow markers as you pass a few connector trails leading to nearby picnicking spots. This is an area where you may like to have the park's wildflower checklist, which includes 130 flowers listed by color, habitat, frequency, and season in which they bloom. Pick up the checklist for free at the concession stand or at the park office.

After passing a playground on the right, the trail crosses the park road again at 1.1 miles into the hike. On the other side of the road, the trail brushes against a pond and then quickly starts to gain elevation on the way up Fox Ridge. Once you've climbed for about 40 yards, keep walking straight ahead when the trail reaches a grassy open space next to a parking area with picnic tables and another playground. While following Fox Ridge for the next 0.7 miles, you'll notice that there are a couple of trails running parallel to and occasionally intersecting with one another. To follow the lower trail, stay to the left; for the higher one, stay right. There are plenty of confidence markers along the way for guidance on either, and you can look to Loon Lake on the left to reassure yourself of your location.

While following the ridge under a thick oak canopy, watch your step as the trail runs next to the small ravines. Once the trail descends the ridge, cross the park road at 1.8 miles into the hike. After passing the parking lot where you started the hike on the left, keep straight ahead for about 100 yards to pick up the rest of the trail in the back-right corner of the Fox Ridge parking area.

Back on the trail, you'll first cross a small bridge, and then follow an arrow to the right at the trail junction. As you move up on the side of a ridge, the trail passes a wetland in the low spots on the right. Continue to follow the arrows at a few more trail junctions that will appear in the next half mile. Higher up on the ridge, you'll see several houses and an open field on the right. At 2.25 miles into the hike, follow the arrows through a hairpin turn to the left. Soon the trail reaches an open area, with power lines visible on the right. After crossing the open area, turn left at the sign for Silver Springs and head back to the parking lot.

▶ NEARBY ACTIVITIES

For more hiking at Silver Springs, consider the 1-mile-long Duck Creek Trail, the 2-mile-long Beaver Dam Trail, the 1-mile-long Grasslands of the Fox Trail, and the 6-mile-long Prairie View Equestrian Trail. The Duck Creek and Beaver Dam trails are wooded and hilly. The Grasslands and Prairie View trails are, as you might guess, flat and grassy. The Duck Creek, Beaver Dam, and Prairie View trails are closed for part of winter for hunting season. Call the park office at (630) 553-6297 for exact dates.

If you're interested in renting canoes or kayaks to take on the Fox River, Freeman Sports is in Yorkville, 5 miles from Silver Springs, at the corner of IL 47 and Hydraulic Avenue. The phone number is (630) 553-0515.

SKOKIE LAGOONS AND RIVER HIKE

▶ IN BRIEF

Surrounded by urban development, the islands and the scenic waterways of the Skokie Lagoons provide a wooded refuge just 15 miles north of the Loop. After skirting the southern edge of the lagoons, this route delivers you to the quiet, tree-laden banks of the Skokie River.

▶ DESCRIPTION

The Skokie Lagoons have undergone many changes since they existed as marshland that the local Potawatomi Indians called Chewab Skokie, meaning "big wet prairie." Like other wetlands in the area, the marsh was drained by farmers who arrived in the late 1800s. Their efforts to create farmland fell flat, however; during wet years, the land still flooded, and during dry years, the peat marsh would catch fire, and smoke would drift into the surrounding communities for extended periods.

When Cook County acquired the marshlands in 1933, the Civilian Conservation Corps (CCC) started a project of digging a series of connected lakes for flood control and recreation.

▶ DIRECTIONS

By car, take I-90/I-94 northwest. Stay on I-94 for 10 miles after it breaks off from I-90. Exit at Willow Road (Exit 33B). Park in the Erickson Woods parking lot, 0.2 miles ahead on the left.

By bicycle, follow the North Elston Avenue bicycle lane until North Elston Avenue merges with North Milwaukee Avenue. Catch a connector trail leading to the North Branch Trail from the Caldwell Woods Forest Preserve parking lot at the corner of North Milwaukee Avenue and West Devon Avenue. Turn left at the North Branch Trail, and follow it to Willow Road. Alternatively, bring your bike on the Blue Line to the Jefferson Park stop. Follow North Milwaukee Avenue to Caldwell Woods.

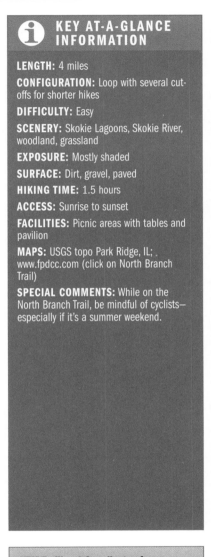

ⓘ KEY AT-A-GLANCE INFORMATION

LENGTH: 4 miles

CONFIGURATION: Loop with several cut-offs for shorter hikes

DIFFICULTY: Easy

SCENERY: Skokie Lagoons, Skokie River, woodland, grassland

EXPOSURE: Mostly shaded

SURFACE: Dirt, gravel, paved

HIKING TIME: 1.5 hours

ACCESS: Sunrise to sunset

FACILITIES: Picnic areas with tables and pavilion

MAPS: USGS topo Park Ridge, IL; . www.fpdcc.com (click on North Branch Trail)

SPECIAL COMMENTS: While on the North Branch Trail, be mindful of cyclists—especially if it's a summer weekend.

UTM Trailhead Coordinates for Skokie Lagoons and River Hike

UTM Zone (NAD27) 16T

Easting 437475

Northing 4661092

Michigan City

Skokie Lagoons

Winnetka
Golf Club

Union Pacific R.R.

NORTH BRANCH TRL.

Old Willow Rd.

94

Forestway Dr.

Erickson
Woods

53

dam

Willow Rd.

Happ Rd.

Lagoon Dr.

Harding
Rd.

Hibbard Rd.

dam

Winnetka Rd.

Winnetka Rd.

N

West
Center
Academy

Chicago River North Branch Middle Fork

SKOKIE
LAGOONS AND
RIVER HIKE

Meadowview Rd.

Longmeadow Rd.

tunnel

0.25 MILE

Skokie River

Kankake

53

94

Loyola
Academy

Illinois Rd.

FEET

930
870
810
750
690
630
570
510
450

1   2   3   4
MILES

Using mostly wheelbarrows, picks, and shovels, workers excavated 4 million cubic yards of earth in what became the largest CCC project in the nation. When work finished in 1942, 7 miles of waterway connected seven lagoons. Fed and drained by the East Fork of the North Branch of the Chicago River (often called the Skokie River), three low dams and a main dam at Willow Road were added to control the water level in the lagoons.

At the Erickson Woods parking lot, look for the plaque commemorating the former site of the Skokie Lagoons CCC camp. From the plaque, take the dirt road on the left that runs between the picnic area and the ditch, which contains treated wastewater (since the water in the ditch remains warm year-around, it often draws birds during the winter). After entering a dense wooded area, the trail curves left, bringing you closer to the noise of I-94. A short stroll ahead, the trail turns right and then crosses a bridge over the water ditch.

After crossing the bridge, you'll meet up with the North Branch Trail, a 20.1-mile paved path that runs north for 3.6 miles to the Chicago Botanic Gardens (see page 40), and south for 16.5 miles to the corner of North Caldwell Avenue and West Devon Avenue. As you turn right on the trail, feel free to cut through the bottomland forest on the left to get a closer view of the lagoon and its resident water birds (despite the thick suburban development in the area and a major expressway that borders the preserve, the birdwatching is often very good around the lagoons). At 1.4 miles into the hike, you'll pass another bridge on the right and a picnic area on the left with a pavilion, picnic tables, and water pump set in an open grassy area that juts into the lagoon. When the paved path curves right to cross Willow Road, continue straight ahead on the gravel trail that passes over the Willow Road Dam.

Marking the south end of the lagoons and the beginning of the Skokie River, local anglers flock to this bridge and the nearby concrete embankment. The county has worked hard over the years to keep the fish biting in these waters. Since the lagoons were dug in the 1940s, the open water has been slowly returning to marshland. Eventually, the stocked and native fish were unable to survive winters in water that was only 5- or 6-feet deep. To solve this problem, in 1988 the U.S. Environmental Protection Agency deepened many of the lagoons to 12 feet, dredging 1 million cubic yards of sediment. Now the lagoons are some of Cook County's most productive fishing spots for bass, pike, and walleye.

After the bridge, keep straight ahead until you reach North Forest Way, where you'll turn right toward Willow Road. On the other side of Willow Road, look for the wide dirt path heading into the woods (this quieter dirt trail runs parallel to the North Branch Trail for 8 miles, from Tower Road south to Dempster Street). After a couple of turns in the trail, you'll be walking on top of a levee alongside the wooded banks of the 20-foot-wide Skokie River. Once you've passed a little dam on the right with a concrete platform, a side trail drops down from the levee on the left and runs for a quarter mile to Hibbard Road. Continuing ahead, don't take the narrow trail that continues directly on the other side of Winnetka Avenue—this trail dead-ends a half mile ahead at I-94. Instead, cross the Winnetka Avenue bridge and take the wide dirt trail immediately on the left. Again, the trail follows a levee along the pleasant wooded banks of the Skokie River.

As you approach the expressway underpass, cut over to the paved North Branch Trail on the right and then turn right for an 0.8-mile trip back to the parking lot. (Continuing south along the North Branch Trail, the trail ends 11.7 miles later at the corner of North Caldwell Avenue and West Devon Avenue.) Heading back toward Winnetka Road, the trail runs through an open grassy area revealing a few houses on the left. For the remaining stretch to Willow Road, the trail meanders in and out of wooded and grassy areas.

▶ NEARBY ACTIVITIES

Head north from Erickson Woods for 2.6 miles along the North Branch Trail for a pleasant hike around the largest island in the Skokie Lagoons. While not technically an island because it's connected to the shore with a narrow levee, the landscape on this 2.8-mile hike offers a surprisingly remote feel for such an urban area. To reach this trail via the North Branch Trail, stay to the right at the fork at Tower Road. At 1.1 miles north of Tower Road, look for the gravel trail at the bottom of a small dip on the left as the path splits from Forest Way Drive. If driving from Erickson Woods, take Willow Road left to Forest Way Drive. Follow Forest Way Drive to the left for 2.4 miles. Park on the side of the road near the trailhead.

On the gravel path heading out to the island, take a left at the first fork. Stay to the left close to the shore for much of the way around the island as you pass through woodland, stands of shrubs, and open grassy areas. After the dam, take the next major fork to the right. Keep to the right until you meet up with your earlier route. A GPS unit is a good idea on this hike because of the number of unmarked trails. If you're in the mood for more exploring, you can also wander through a jumble of trails on the northern part of the island.

Kayakers and canoeists are attracted to the quiet channels and wooded islands within this series of slow-moving waterways (motorboats are not permitted). A few low dams require portaging. Paddlers can launch at spots along Forest Way Drive and Tower Road. Rentals are available at the Chicagoland Canoe Base: 4019 North Narragansett Avenue, (773) 777-1489, www.chicagolandcanoebase.com.

STARVED ROCK STATE PARK:
EAST HIKE

▶ IN BRIEF

This eastern section of Starved Rock State Park offers canyons galore, each with slightly different shapes, sizes, and colorings. Cool and shady, overgrown with ferns, trees, and flowering plants, the numerous canyons on this hike are a delight to explore. You'll also encounter scenic overlooks 100 feet above the Illinois River.

▶ DESCRIPTION

While the views from atop the bluffs and cliffs are spectacular and well worth a visit, the real show-stoppers at Starved Rock are the numerous sandstone canyons that were carved deep into the bedrock as upland streams drained into the Illinois River. During the wet seasons, waterfalls cascade through some of the canyons. In the winter, dramatic ice sculptures take the place of the waterfalls.

The canyon rock is primarily St. Peter sandstone—formed in a huge inland sea more than 425 million years ago and later brought to the surface. Several factories east of Starved Rock use St. Peter sandstone for making a variety of glass products, including bottles and car windows. While the easily scratched sandstone seems consistently soft, the hardness actually varies, depending on the amount of calcium carbonate cementing the sand grains together. The rock's

❶ KEY AT-A-GLANCE INFORMATION

LENGTH: 6.4 miles

CONFIGURATION: Combo

DIFFICULTY: Moderate

SCENERY: Numerous deep sandstone canyons, several rocky cliffs overlooking Illinois River and surrounding woodland

EXPOSURE: Shaded

SURFACE: Dirt

HIKING TIME: 3–4 hours

ACCESS: 5 a.m.–10 p.m.

FACILITIES: Restrooms are available in nearby parking areas; otherwise all facilities, including the visitor center, are at the other end of the park.

MAPS: Maps are available at the visitor center; USGS topo Starved Rock, IL

SPECIAL COMMENTS: Dogs must be leashed. This section of the park tends to be quieter compared to the trails closer to the visitor center.

▶ DIRECTIONS

From Chicago, take I-55 to I-80. After driving for 35.5 miles on I-80, take Exit 90. Turn left (south) on IL 23 and proceed for 2.5 miles, passing the community of Ottawa. Turn right (west) on IL 71 (Hitt Street) and drive for 5.8 miles. Continue driving past the Lone Point parking area on the right and the Salt Well parking area on the left. Park in the Illinois Canyon parking area, the next parking area on the left.

UTM Trailhead Coordinates for Starved Rock State Park: East Hike

UTM Zone (NAD27) 16T

Easting 337658

Northing 4574642

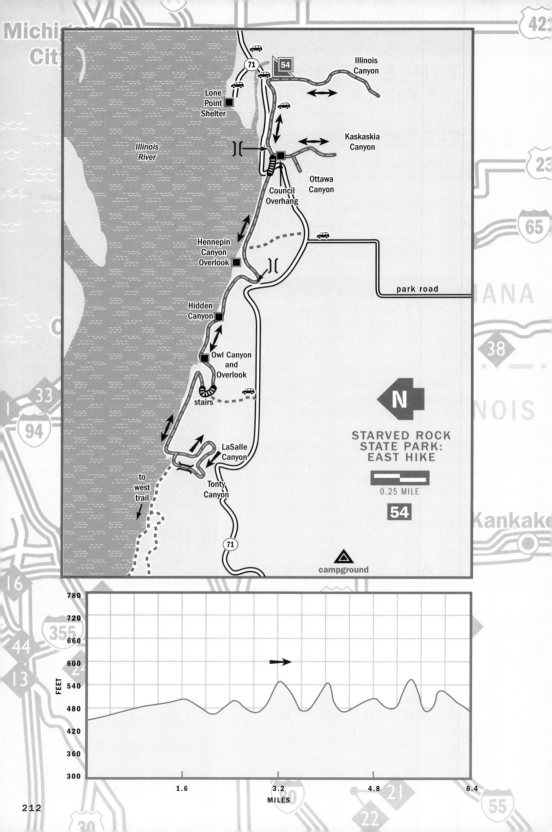

Michigan City

421

71
54

Illinois Canyon

Lone Point Shelter

Illinois River

Kaskaskia Canyon

Council Overhang

Ottawa Canyon

Hennepin Canyon Overlook

park road

Hidden Canyon

Owl Canyon and Overlook

stairs

N

STARVED ROCK STATE PARK: EAST HIKE

0.25 MILE

54

to west trail

LaSalle Canyon

Tonty Canyon

71

campground

Kankake

94

33

38

65

23

16

44

355

13

FEET

780
720
660
600
540
480
420
360
300

1.6
3.2
4.8
6.4

MILES

varying hardness is evident in sections of the canyon walls that are pockmarked or scooped away by erosion.

The hike starts with an exploration of the longest and one of the widest canyons at the park. At the east end of the parking lot, follow the wide dirt trail as it heads underneath a canopy of cottonwoods. After a short way, you'll notice cliffs rising up beyond the trees on both sides of the trail. The farther you hike, the closer the walls come to the trail—in some places the sandstone walls are streaked with yellow on what looks like a bleached white background. Sugar maples and basswood thrive on the wide canyon floor and jewelweed grows thickly on the edges of the shallow creek that accompanies the trail. Watch your step while crossing the creek on a jumble of logs, rocks, and concrete blocks. At the end of the canyon, a large fallen cottonwood offers a pleasant spot to sit and watch a small waterfall emptying into a serene pool. Heading back toward the parking lot, you may consider exploring parts of the canyon off the main trail; getting closer to the sides of the canyon will enable you to see some of the small cave-like openings at the base of the sandstone walls.

Continue the hike at the other end of the parking lot. From here, the trail runs through another parking lot and then crosses a bridge over a stream. After the bridge, stay left and head up a small hill, following the sign for the Council Overhang. The overhang is an impressive white sandstone cavern 40-feet high and 30-feet deep. Following the sign for Kaskaskia Canyon to the left brings you to a narrow trail winding along a streambed that turns into a series of puddles during the summer. The walls of this canyon are sometimes craggy and in places shaded with bluish-green lichen. At the end of the canyon, in springtime, water flows from a moss-covered shelf-like opening that sits above a small shallow pool. Continuing on to Ottawa Canyon, you'll notice that the tall, straight walls create a darker and damper atmosphere. If you're hiking on a hot day, you'll notice the moist air and cooler temperatures upon entering the canyons.

Back at the junction on the other side of the Council Overhang, stay to the left as you navigate a steep, rough section of the path, and then mount a flight of stairs leading up to the park road. On the other side of the park road, another flight of stairs takes you up to a trail that leads along the bluff. At 2.4 miles into the hike, pass a trail on the left that branches to a parking lot, and then follow a side trail that leads to the Hennepin Canyon Overlook. To the right at the overlook, the Illinois River is almost a mile wide; nearly 2 miles to the left is the Starved Rock Lock and Dam. From the overlook, the trail turns inland and moseys along the bluff above the Hennepin Canyon. The park road is right above as you pass over a bridge crossing the stream that drops into the canyon.

After the bridge, the trail runs between a fence and a concrete embankment, and then back out to the bluff's edge. Just beyond the steep cliffs of Hidden Canyon, you're afforded another great view of the Illinois River at the Owl Canyon Overlook. Passing a trail leading to another parking lot, you'll descend a bluff and drop to the river's edge via a long set of stairs. Watch for the thick, knotty roots that emerge from the surface of the trail on this stretch along the riverbank. Just before the arched footbridge, turn left into LaSalle Canyon. As the trail runs along a terrace at the base of the wall, the canyon narrows, and the sandstone surface becomes pitted and lightly grooved. Farther along, the beige stone takes on a gold color and pits become pot-holes. At the end of the canyon, a steady waterfall pours off an overhang and into a small basin before flowing out toward the river.

Heading out of LaSalle via the terrace on the opposite wall, you'll cross a bridge and then turn left before crossing a longer bridge. Coming into the next canyon—Tonty Canyon—feels a bit like you're entering a jungle: the air is damp, while ferns and vines grow on the canyon walls. Jewelweed and sedge grasses grow beside the slow-moving stream on the canyon floor. At the end of the canyon, instead of a waterfall, there's a steady drip coming down from the overhang, with caverns underneath. If you decide to climb around on the low-banked walls, you'll notice that the sandstone is wet with the consistency of sugar, and is easily scratched with a fingernail.

Retrace your steps out of Tonty Canyon, taking a left at the bridge, and then crossing a couple more bridges and several short flights of stairs before arriving back on the riverside trail. Once you reach the river, turn right and cross the arched bridge over the 20-foot-wide creek flowing out of the two canyons. From the bridge, stay to the left for 2.2 miles back to parking lot.

STARVED ROCK STATE PARK:
WEST HIKE

▶ IN BRIEF

After hiking through deep sandstone canyons, you'll encounter a series of overlooks from the wooded bluffs and rocky cliffs high above the Illinois River. This classic northeastern Illinois hike requires considerable stair climbing.

▶ DESCRIPTION

While there are dozens of points of interest throughout Starved Rock State Park, the dominant feature is a narrow bluff that runs 4 miles along the south bank of the Illinois River between Ottawa and LaSalle. Carved deeply in the sandstone of the bluffs are many narrow canyons of varying lengths. In the western section of the park, where this hike takes place, visitors can't help but notice what is perhaps the most popular attraction in the area: the sandstone pedestal from which the park gets its name. Topped off by white pines and cedar, Starved Rock towers 125 feet above the river, offering a commanding view of the nearby islands, the surrounding wooded landscape, and the river, particularly to the east, where it swells to a width of nearly a mile.

Artifacts such as human bones and weapons reveal that different groups of Indians lived on and used the rock for nearly 10,000 years. In 1682, the French took advantage of the easily defended location on the rock and built a fort, as part of their plan to keep the British from gaining control of the Mississippi River Valley (on display in the park's visitor center is a miniature model of this fort built

▶ KEY AT-A-GLANCE INFORMATION

LENGTH: 2.9 miles

CONFIGURATION: Loop, with options for increasing or decreasing the distance

DIFFICULTY: Difficult, primarily because of the number of stairs

SCENERY: Sandstone canyons, wooded bluffs, and rocky cliffs—all at the edge of the mighty Illinois River

EXPOSURE: Nearly all shaded

SURFACE: Dirt, sand, wooden boardwalk and stairs, and short paved sections

HIKING TIME: 2 hours

ACCESS: The trails at Starved Rock are open 5 a.m.–10 p.m.

FACILITIES: Visitor center, snack shop, campground, picnic areas

MAPS: Pick up park maps from the visitor center; USGS topo Starved Rock, IL

SPECIAL COMMENTS: The visitor center offers exhibits, a snack shop, and a small store with books and other items. Between the visitor center and the boat launch to the west is a large picnic area alongside the river. Hotel rooms, cabins, and a cafe are available at a 1930s wood-and-sandstone lodge just south of the visitor center. (See "Nearby Activities" section)

A 133-site campground is located a couple of miles southeast of the visitor center. Not included in this hike are several canyons west of the visitor center. These canyons are comparatively smaller, except for St. Louis Canyon, which is furthest to the west, near a parking area on IL 178.

▶ DIRECTIONS

From Chicago, take I-55 to I-80. After driving for 45 miles on I-80, take Exit 81 south to Utica. Proceed south along IL 178 for 3.2 miles, passing through Utica. The entrance to Starved Rock State Park is on the left, after crossing the bridge. Follow the signs to the visitor center.

UTM Trailhead Coordinates for Starved Rock State Park: West Hike

UTM Zone (NAD27) 16T

Easting 333213

Northing 4575943

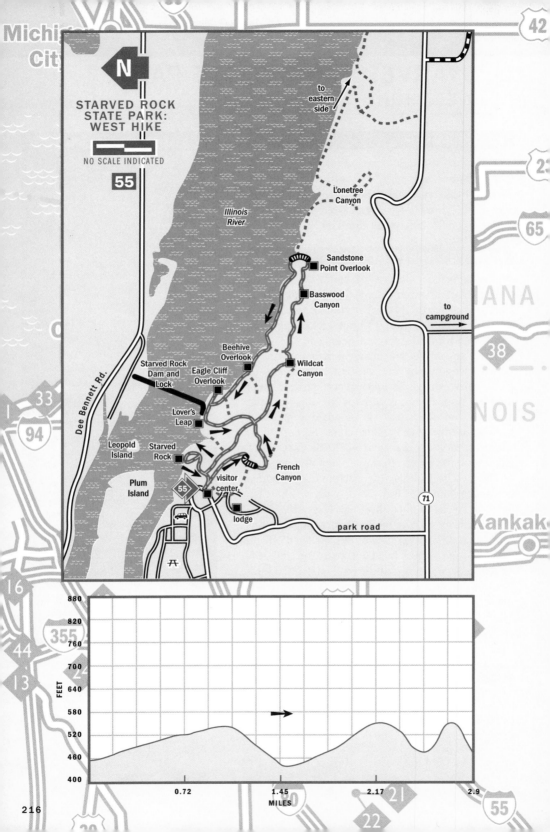

STARVED ROCK
STATE PARK:
WEST HIKE

NO SCALE INDICATED

55

to eastern side

Lonetree Canyon

Illinois River

Sandstone Point Overlook

Basswood Canyon

to campground

Beehive Overlook

Wildcat Canyon

Starved Rock Dam and Lock

Eagle Cliff Overlook

Lover's Leap

Leopold Island

Starved Rock

Plum Island

visitor center

French Canyon

lodge

park road

71

Dee Bennett Rd.

by a group students and teachers in Aurora). The formation got its name from a leg-end about a group of Illinois Indians who fled to the rock for protection while being pursued by Fox and Potawatomi Indians. The Fox and Potawatomi were seeking revenge because one of the Illinois Indians had killed their leader, Chief Pontiac. Unable to escape, the Illinois Indians eventually starved to death.

Given all the history, the unusual rock formations, and the scenic vistas, it shouldn't be a surprise that Starved Rock is often busy. Consider arriving during the week or visiting early in the day if you're looking for tranquility—particularly in this section of the park. At the beginning and the end of this hike, you'll encounter no shortage of trail junctions. Fortunately, the trails are very well marked, and detailed mapboards situated at most major trail junctions show your location within the net-work of trails.

Start the hike on the paved path that runs on the left side of the visitor center, and follow signs for French Canyon and the lodge. Soon the trail runs alongside a ravine which grows into a canyon featuring 50- to 60-foot-high moss-covered walls. Before taking the stairs up toward the lodge, be sure to follow the trail farther into the French Canyon, where it dead-ends in a rounded chamber of layered sandstone. In French Canyon and in other canyons throughout the park, you'll see variety in the surface of the stone: in some places the sandstone is deeply pitted and ridged, while in other places it's smooth and flat. The sandstone takes on different colors, too. Sometimes it's green and moss-covered, or bleached and nearly white, or it may be covered in various shades of blue and green lichens.

After climbing the stairs out of French Canyon, the trail offers a great view from above the rocky walls as it follows the canyon's upper lip. Once you've passed the trail on the right leading to the lodge, take the next left on the East Bluff Trail as it crosses a bridge, which spans the now-intermittent stream that once carved out French Canyon. From the bridge, the trail winds along on the opposite side of French Canyon and then traverses a high bluff. Along the bluff, the elms, oaks, and conifers open up in places to provide striking views of the river and the opposite bank. After reaching a high point and then following a flight of stairs and a boardwalk, stay to the right at the junction, heading toward Wildcat Canyon.

On the way to Wildcat Canyon, you'll encounter the smaller Pontiac Canyon and you'll take in sweeping views of the Illinois River before mounting more stairs and boardwalks. Soon you'll arrive at a lookout platform that offers a stunning view of Wildcat Canyon as it opens to the river. As you follow the boardwalk to the view-ing platform on the opposite side of the canyon, look for the cliff swallows entering and leaving their mud nests built under the rocky overhangs.

From Wildcat Canyon, follow the signs for Sandstone Canyon. Not long after passing Basswood Canyon, the trail arrives at Sandstone Point, the final overlook before the trail descends to the river. After the overlook, the trail skirts the edge of Lonetree Canyon and then leads you down a long series of steps.

At the bottom of the stairs, take the trail to the left along the wooded riverbank (taking the trail to the right leads to trails on the east side of the park, featured on pages 211–214). As the junctions come and go along this busier section of the hike, keep following signs to Starved Rock.

Soon you'll head up a set of stairs to Eagle Cliff, which provides a great view high above the dam. On a cold day in January, during my first visit to this spot, I saw a half dozen bald eagles soaring above the river, waiting for dead fish to turn up in the open water by the dam (attracted to the open water by the dam, bald eagles begin to arrive in November and grow in numbers into January and February). Continuing on, the platform at Lover's Leap provides a great view of the rocky pedestal of Starved Rock.

Getting closer to the visitor center, follow the paved road through the woods and the stairs up to Starved Rock. On the west side of the observation platform, look for Leopold Island No. 1 on the right, and the larger Plum Island on the left. (In recent years, Plum Island was spared from a massive development plan that would have eliminated prime habitat for bald eagles during the winter.) From Starved Rock, the visitor center is just a couple of signposts away.

▶ NEARBY ACTIVITIES

The stone-and-log lodge at Starved Rock State Park was built by the Civilian Conservation Corps in the 1930s. The lodge offers 72 hotel rooms and 22 "cabin rooms." In the new hotel wing of the lodge, there is an indoor swimming pool, saunas, a whirlpool, and an outdoor sunning patio. The lodge's original "great room" is a comfortable space centered around a massive stone fireplace. The lodge's restaurant is open seven days a week and offers a number of house specialties. For lodge prices and reservations, call (800) 868-7625.

TEKAKWITHA–FOX RIVER HIKE

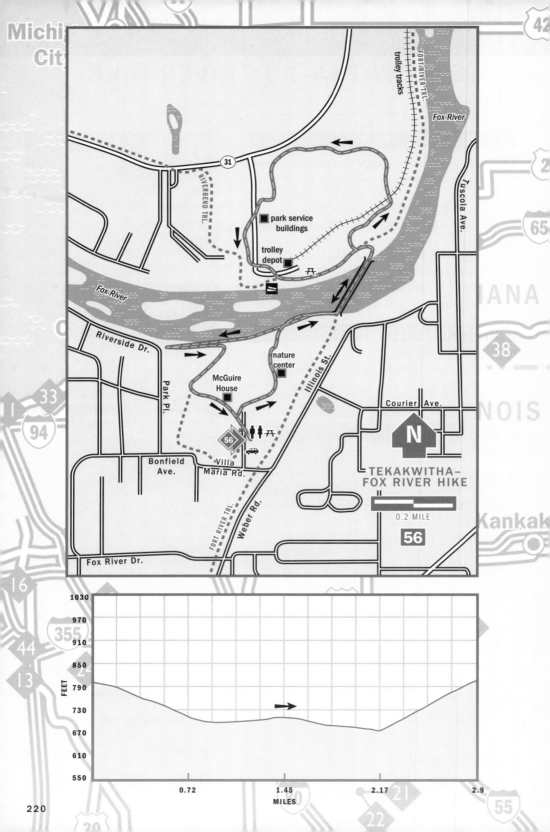

is now the administrative offices for the forest preserve district, was the home of Father Hugh McGuire. Upon his death, he left the house and adjacent land to the Sisters of Mercy, a Catholic women's congregation. In 1990, when Kane County bought Tekakwitha from the Sisters of Mercy, the county agreed to name the preserve in honor of the first Native American to be considered for canonization by the Church. Surviving a childhood bout with smallpox, Kateri Tekakwitha (pronounced Tek-uh-with-uh) lived from 1656 to 1680 in the northeastern United States and Canada. Along with St. Francis of Assisi, she is regarded by the Church as the patron of the environment and ecology.

Starting the hike from the parking lot, a sign instructs visitors to follow the dirt trail for 350 yards through the woods to the nature center. As you approach the nature center, cross a footbridge spanning a picturesque V-shaped ravine. The nature center—formerly a dance hall, when the preserve served as a public recreational area called Five Island Park—hosts activities for kids, a library, a wildlife-viewing room, as well as two recently added exhibits on bison and the Fox River Watershed.

Continuing down the hill toward the river (keeping straight at the fork), the trail winds beside a ravine thick with leafy specimens such as white oaks, sugar maples, and hackberry trees, some of which are identified with signs.

When you reach the wooded riverbank, turn right toward the lengthy foot-bridge, passing an enormous sugar maple hanging over the water. The bridge serves as the route for the Fox River Trail, a 32-mile bicycle and pedestrian path that runs through a number of parks on its route from Aurora north to Algonquin (from the bridge, South Elgin is 1.7 miles north and St. Charles is 4.6 miles south). The 0.15-mile-long iron-and-wood bridge connects with a small wooded island in the middle of the river. This section of the river is named Five Islands for a series of wooded islands along the river to the west. Beyond the islands, outside of your view, the river takes an abrupt hairpin turn on its way south to St. Charles.

On the other side of the bridge, follow the paved path to the left and then take the woodchip trail heading right. Along this trail sit a couple of small monuments commemorating two soldiers from General Winfield Scott's Army who died during the Blackhawk War in 1832 and are buried in the park. This park was called the Blackhawk Forest Preserve until the summer of 2004, when it was renamed Jon J. Duerr Fox River Bike Trail and Boat Launch, after the former executive director of the Kane County Forest Preserve District. Turn right at the second monument for the soldiers, and head down a hill to cross the train tracks.

Now a prairie undergoing restoration, Illinois Central Railroad mined this area for gravel before it sold the property to a gravel-mining operation. According to the county, the forest preserve sits on top of a large aquifer, 250 feet deep, comprised of water and gravel.

After crossing the train tracks, follow the paved park service road that rises up the small hill and turns left. The road runs between an embankment on the right and mounds blanketed with sumac and cottonwood rising on the left. Shortly after passing a junction with a gravel road, the paved road curves left again, and then arrives at several forest preserve service buildings. At the service buildings, cross the main park road and walk along a mowed grass trail that runs parallel to the park road.

Approaching the river, you'll pass the boarding platform for the Fox River Line, where passengers can board a renovated electric intercity railway train for a 2-mile-long trip through the forest preserve and along the Fox River to the Fox River Trolley Museum in South Elgin. The trolley museum has 20 or so electric railway cars on display, including locomotives, a post office car, old passenger coaches from the South Shore Line, and a number of retired Chicago Transit Authority cars. The Fox River train line dates back to 1896, when electric trains ran for 40 miles along the river, from Carpentersville south to Yorkville, and also connected to the streetcar systems of Elgin and Aurora. The line provided passenger service until 1935, and then served as a freight line until 1972.

After passing the boarding platform, head to the left side of the parking lot where the paved trail parallels the river. (The trail on the right side of the parking lot—known as the Riverbend Trail—goes for about 7 miles, mostly along roads, to the Leroy Oaks Forest Preserve, where it connects with the Great Western Trail. At 1.2 miles out, the Riverbend Trail passes a surprising 8-foot natural waterfall gushing over a limestone outcropping.) Continuing along the river to the left, you'll pass some pleasant picnicking spots before getting back on the bridge and returning to the riverbank trail at Tekakwitha.

Back at Tekakwitha, continue along the riverbank trail for a half mile past the trail you took down to the river from the nature center. Before reaching the turn-around point at Park Place, you'll pass a few big piles of logs at the river's edge, a major trail junction on the left, and stands of maple trees, as well as hickory and walnut. You'll also see four of the five wooded islands. Returning from the turn-around point, take the first major junction heading up the bluff. Continue past the junction on the left, which leads back to the nature center; the trees soon thin out and the thick canopy opens. Passing through a savanna studded with quaking aspen and oak, take the path to the left, which crosses a bridge over a small ravine and then leads to the forest preserve manager's residence on the right and the McGuire House on the left. The parking lot is just ahead, on the paved road leading to the right.

THORN CREEK HIKE

▶ IN BRIEF

This lightly used nature preserve is a gem: after exploring the ravines, the pine plantations, the wooded hills, and the streams surrounded by bottomland forest, be sure to check out the former country church that now serves as a nature center.

▶ DESCRIPTION

Considering how much it's been hauled around the neighborhood, the little wooden country church that serves as the Thorn Creek Nature Center is in surprisingly good condition. An Emmanuel Evangelical Lutheran congregation built the church in 1862, several miles northwest of its present location at the corner of Sauk Trail Road and South Cicero Avenue. After 100 years, Emmanuel Lutheran gave the church to Village Bible Church of Park Forest, which moved it just north of the nature center off Monee Road. Ten years later, when the Village Bible Church built a new structure, the congregation passed the old church to the Village of Park Forest. The village spruced it up and put it on a new foundation in its present spot.

Inside, where generations of churchgoers came to hear ministers' sermons, school kids now sit in the pews while park naturalists explain the features of the Thorn Creek Preserve and

ℹ KEY AT-A-GLANCE INFORMATION

LENGTH: 2.5 miles

CONFIGURATION: 2 connected loops

DIFFICULTY: Easy to moderate

SCENERY: Ravines, bottomland and upland forest, pine plantations, creeks, pond

EXPOSURE: Nearly all shaded

SURFACE: Dirt and some gravel

HIKING TIME: 1 hour

ACCESS: Trails are open 8 a.m.–8 p.m.

FACILITIES: Restroom, water, picnic tables

MAPS: Map signs appear at all trail junctions; paper maps are available in the nature preserve and online at www.fpdwc.org; USGS topo Steger, IL

SPECIAL COMMENTS: Nature center hours are noon–4 p.m., Thursday–Sunday. For more information, call the nature center at (708) 747-6320. A bird checklist is available for free at the nature center.

▶ DIRECTIONS

From Chicago, take I-90/I-94 south. Four miles after I-90 splits from I-94, take I-57 south. Follow I-57 for 18.5 miles to Exit 339. Turn right (east) on West Sauk Trail and proceed for 0.9 miles. Turn right (south) on South Cicero Avenue and go for 1.9 miles until you reach University Parkway. Turn left (east) and proceed for 1.65 miles until reaching Monee Road. Turn left (north) again, and the nature preserve is 0.5 miles ahead on the right.

UTM Trailhead Coordinates for Thorn Creek Hike

UTM Zone (NAD27) 16T

Easting 441618

Northing 4589714

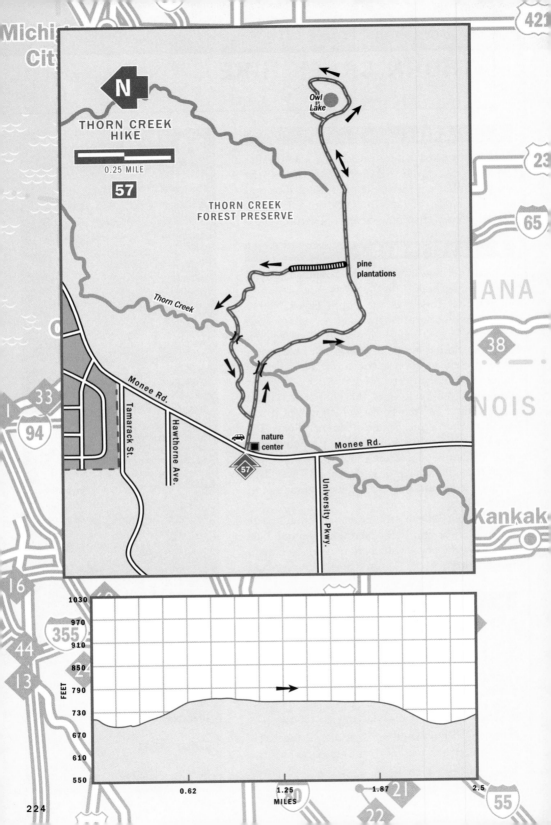

surrounding areas. The large pulpit, elevated 8 feet above the pews, now contains an action-packed taxidermy scene of a red fox chasing a Canada goose through a cattail marsh. Visitors of all ages will enjoy touring the nature center's displays of preserved animal specimens; lichens found in the area; bones, skulls, and arrowheads; photos of animals and plants found in the preserve; and a small nature library in the gallery upstairs. There are also photographs of the farm that occupied the preserve in the early 1900s.

Currently under ownership by the state, the county, and two nearby villages, the nature preserve was formed in the 1960s when private and governmental organizations joined forces to save the property from development. During the summer of 2004, Thorn Creek was in the process of developing more trails on land it recently acquired across Monee Road.

The hike starts in the backyard of the nature center, on a gravelly path that immediately crosses a bridge over an intermittent stream. As the trail starts to descend a slight hill, watch for the logs half buried on the trail surface that serve to direct runoff away from the trail. Stay right at the first junction, and you'll soon enter a bottomland forest of black walnut, swamp white oak, basswood, ash, and slippery elm. After passing a second junction on the left, the trail mounts a bridge over Thorn Creek—which may dry up into a series of isolated pools during the summer. Following a short boardwalk, the trail flattens out and winds through a grove of maples.

Soon a shallow ravine develops on the left, and a much deeper 50-foot ravine plunges down on the right. Dominated by maple, ash, and red oak, this ravine contains a tributary of Thorn Creek. As you proceed, listen for wind whispering through groves of red and jack pines planted by farmers in the 1950s (both red and jack pines' needles are in clusters of two, but the red's needles are up to 6 inches long, while the jack's are only one-and-a-half inches long). According to the bird checklist available at the nature center, these pine plantations provide some of the best birding spots in the 880-acre preserve.

As the path curves left, the landscape flattens and the woods are unwrapped from the dense canopy. In these upland areas, you'll see white and red oak, shagbark hickory, and, after passing the junction with the boardwalk on the left, white pine (needles in clusters of five). On this straight and flat route to Owl Lake you'll see a small cattail pond, pasture roses, and open fields beyond the trees on the right.

After circling Owl Lake (you'll see it's more of a pond than a lake), head back to the junction where the boardwalk starts on the right. While traversing the 0.2-mile boardwalk, you may notice a variety of fern species growing in the wet soil on the sides of the platform. Leaving the boardwalk behind, you'll head back toward Thorn Creek and notice that the landscape begins to drop down on the left. After passing an enormous section of a concrete drain duct, the trail takes a sharp left, drops down the slope, crosses a bridge, and then enters a bottomland forest along a 50-foot section of boardwalk. For the remainder of the hike, look for thick trunks belonging to 150-year-old white and red oaks: the white oaks tend to grow in flat spots, while the reds often grow on the slopes. Stay right at the next two junctions to return to the parking lot.

Crete is a pleasant village with tree-lined streets and tidy front yards planted with flowers. The village hosts a number of antique shops and some charming restaurants, including Annie's Café and Old Fashioned Ice Cream Parlor, south of West Exchange Street on IL 1. Farther south on IL 1, horseracing fans are drawn to the Balmoral Park Race Track. To reach Crete, head south on Monee Road for 0.9 miles, and then turn left on University Parkway and drive for 3.6 miles.

Just a few miles northeast of Thorn Creek in Cook County is the Sauk Trail Forest Preserve, which includes a 4.7-mile paved path for hiking and biking. The hilly path runs through mature woods, next to ravines, and along the shore of Sauk Trail Lake. From the nature center, head north (turn right) on Monee Road and proceed for 1.7 miles. Take a left on South Western Avenue and then quickly turn right on West Sauk Trail. A forest preserve entrance that accesses the paved path is 0.8 miles ahead on the left.

VETERAN ACRES–STERNE'S WOODS HIKE

▶ IN BRIEF

This hike offers a surprisingly varied patchwork of scenery featuring beautiful rolling prairie, hilly oak woodlands, pine plantations, a cattail-fringed pond, and a rare type of wetland called a fen.

▶ DESCRIPTION

Both of these parks—Veteran Acres, a city park, and Sterne's Woods, a county park—are individually charming and each well worth a visit. But taken together, they offer an array of scenic landscapes and many miles of enjoyable rambling through quiet woodlands, rolling prairie, and expansive wetlands. The western side of Veteran Acres along Walkup Road hosts typical city park offerings such as playgrounds, ball fields, and basketball and tennis courts. Oak woodlands occupy the middle section of the park, while the west side is home to Wingate Prairie. Northwest of Veteran Acres, Sterne's Woods contains more woodland, steep hills, and an unusual wetland environment.

Before starting the hike, duck into the nature center to see a collection of live animals, including tiger salamanders, an Eastern box turtle, a tarantula, and a ferret. Mixed in with the fauna is a small gift shop, an array of children's

▶ DIRECTIONS

Take I-90/I-94 northwest and continue on I-90 for 18 miles after I-94 splits off. Exit at North Roselle Road and head to the right (north) for 1 mile to IL 62. Turn left (northwest) on IL 62 (West Algonquin Road) and follow it for 12.8 miles. When you reach IL 31, follow it to the right (north) for 5.7 miles. At IL 176 (East Terra Cotta Avenue), turn left (west) and proceed for 1.5 miles until reaching North Main Street. Turn right (north) on North Main Street and the nature center is just ahead on the left.

KEY AT-A-GLANCE INFORMATION

LENGTH: 3.5 miles

CONFIGURATION: Loop

DIFFICULTY: Easy to moderate

SCENERY: Oak and conifer woodland, open parkland, prairie, pond, marshland, stream, fen

EXPOSURE: Prairie section is exposed, while woodland is shaded

SURFACE: Woodchip, grass, and dirt

HIKING TIME: 2 hours

ACCESS: Both parks are open 8:30 a.m.–dusk

FACILITIES: At Veteran Acres, there is a nature center, as well as ball fields, tennis courts, picnic shelters, restrooms, playgrounds, and ice skating during winter. Sterne's Woods has pit toilets and picnic tables.

MAPS: Maps of Veteran Acres available at nature center; map of Sterne's Woods posted at the mapboard located in the Sterne's Woods parking area. Contact McHenry County at www.mccdistrict.org or (815) 338-6223 for a map of the entire 25.9-mile Prairie Trail. USGS topo McHenry, IL.

SPECIAL COMMENTS: Watch for cyclists on the Prairie Trail—especially on the steep segments.

UTM Trailhead Coordinates for Veteran Acres–Sterne's Woods Hike

UTM Zone (NAD27) 16T

Easting 391403

Northing 4678212

exhibits, and a collection of bird's nests. From the front door of the nature center, look for the woodchip trail on the left heading into the woodland. Taking the second junction on the right brings you into the rolling grassy hills of Wingate Prairie.

Among the many prairie remnants in the Chicago region, this 33.5-acre prairie is unique for its beautiful hilly topography and stands of pine. The prairie was named after Bill Wingate, who worked for nearly 30 years with volunteers restoring this prairie and establishing it—as well as Sterne's Woods Fen—as Illinois nature preserves. Once in the prairie, turn right toward the prairie's southern boundary. Along the way, look for summertime plants such as big bluestem grass, goldenrod, and rattlesnake master (stalks topped with prickly balls containing dense clusters of tiny flowers). At the southern boundary of the prairie, turn left and pass through groves of red pine on your way to the parking lot for the Prairie Trail at the corner of Lorraine Drive and View Street.

The Prairie Trail runs for 25.9 miles from Algonquin to the Wisconsin border through areas that are both urban and rural. This nearly mile-long, hilly segment of the Prairie Trail—one of its best parts—starts off in a grove of red pine before descending a steep hill. As the path swings right to accompany a power line right-of-way, yellow-flowered compass plants line the trail. After passing an industrial building beyond the trees on the right, the ribbon of pavement angles into Sterne's Woods through stands of pine (planted by the previous landowner, Ted Sterne), hickory, and giant black and white oak trees with gnarled limbs reaching out over the trail. While the landscape rises and dips, look for short side trails on the right that drop down next to a pleasant little stream running beside a set of railroad tracks.

After following the Prairie Trail for 0.9 miles, keep an eye peeled for a wide gravel trail that runs parallel to you on the left. Taking the gravel trail to the right, you'll see numerous marked side trails heading up the hill to the left. Stay on the gravel trail until you come to a junction with another wide gravel trail. Turning right on this next gravel trail takes you into a 40-acre wetland, a portion of which is known as a fen. As a result of their unusual soil and water conditions, fens often host an uncommon assortment of plants. This fen is home to two types of orchids: the lady's slipper and the state-endangered grass-pink orchid. Other flowers include fringed gentians, cup plants, liatris, and shrubby cinquefoil.

At the other side of the fen, before the house, turn left into a parking area with picnic tables, pit toilets, and a mapboard. From the back of the mapboard, follow the two-track road as it runs between stands of walnut trees on the right and marshland on the left. Keep straight ahead as you pass a major junction on the left, and then climb a big hill.

If you have the inclination to do some wandering, some of the best hiking in Sterne's Woods is found among the maze of side trails on the left. Within this area, dozens of short trails run through pine plantations and rolling savannas, and to the top of a 70-foot bluff that is the former location of a gravel-mining operation. While a GPS device may be useful here, it's not a necessity due to the size of the area and the easy-to-find, wide gravel trail that surrounds it.

After climbing the big hill, continue straight ahead as you pass another wide gravel trail heading left. This brings you back to the right-of-way, where you can see the Prairie Trail heading up the hill on the left. As you pass through the right-of-way and enter Wingate Prairie straight ahead, skip the first trail on the right heading into the woods, and follow the next right, which cuts through open prairie toward the oak woods. Along the way, you'll notice there are a number of short connector trails that would allow you to zigzag for a mile or two through this attractive swath of grassland. Once you've arrived at the stand of oak trees on the western side of the prairie, keep straight ahead and drop down the hill to the ball fields. At the ball fields, head left toward the right shoreline of the pleasant little pond. Take the bridge that runs next to the willows growing on a couple of islands. As you get closer to the fishing pier, the nature center and the parking lot are straight up the hill.

Note: The nature center is open December 1–April 1, Monday–Friday, 9 a.m.–4 p.m. and Saturday, noon–4 p.m.; April 2–November 30, Monday–Friday, 8:30 a.m.–5 p.m., Saturday, noon–5 p.m.; Memorial Day–Labor Day, Sunday, noon–5 p.m. The nature center offers children's programs as well as guided nature hikes for adults. Call the nature center at (815) 455-1763 or visit www.crystallakeparks.org.

VOLO BOG STATE NATURAL AREA HIKE

▶ IN BRIEF

As one of the most unique wetlands in all of Illinois, Volo Bog hosts an unusual assortment of plants and animals. The outlying areas feature rolling hills, thick woods, and open prairies.

▶ DESCRIPTION

Owned by a dairy farmer until 1958, when it was purchased by the Illinois Nature Conservancy, Volo Bog was transferred to the state in 1970, and in 1973 was registered as a National Natural Landmark. One of the reminders of the park's earlier life is a renovated dairy barn that now serves as a park office and visitor center. Sometime during your visit to Volo Bog, take a moment to drop by the visitor center, where you'll see preserved specimens of various birds and mammals found within the park's 1,200 acres, including a sandhill crane (which is often confused with the blue heron), a beaver, a coyote, and several owls.

To begin, pick up the beginning of the Interpretive Trail at the bottom of the hill next to the visitor center. This half-mile loop—entirely on a boardwalk—allows you a close-up view of the plants and trees typical of a bog. Heading out on the boardwalk, you can see plenty of bright green duckweed floating on the surface of the water. Two-hundred feet out, look for the muskrat lodge on your left, just before entering an area dense with 10- to 12-foot shrubs. The winterberry holly,

▶ KEY AT-A-GLANCE INFORMATION

LENGTH: 5.75 miles

CONFIGURATION: 2 sets of loops joined by a connector trail

DIFFICULTY: Easy to moderate

SCENERY: Hilly with marshes, prairies, forests, and a boardwalk to the center of a bog

EXPOSURE: Roughly an equal amount of exposed and shady areas

SURFACE: Mowed grass, dirt, and boardwalk

HIKING TIME: 2-3 hours

ACCESS: Memorial Day–Labor Day, 8 a.m.–8 p.m.; the rest of the year, 8 a.m.–4 p.m.

FACILITIES: Water, restrooms, picnic tables, parking, and visitor center

MAPS: Trail maps are available outside the front door of the visitor center; USGS topo Wauconda, IL

SPECIAL COMMENTS: No pets, other than leashed pets in the picnic area; the free hour-long bog tour is offered year-round every Saturday and Sunday at 11 a.m. and 2 p.m. The visitor center is open Wednesday–Sunday, 9 a.m.–3 p.m.

▶ DIRECTIONS

From Chicago, head north on I-90/I-94. Follow I-94 as it separates from I-90. Continue on I-94 until you reach Belvidere Road (IL 120). Follow Belvidere Road west for 10 miles until reaching IL 59 (US 12). Turn right (north) on IL 59 and travel for 2.5 miles until reaching West Brandenburg Road. Turn left (west), and 1 mile ahead on the left is the entrance to Volo Bog.

UTM Trailhead Coordinates for Volo Bog State Natural Area Hike

UTM Zone (NAD27)   16T

Easting   402075

Northing   4689313

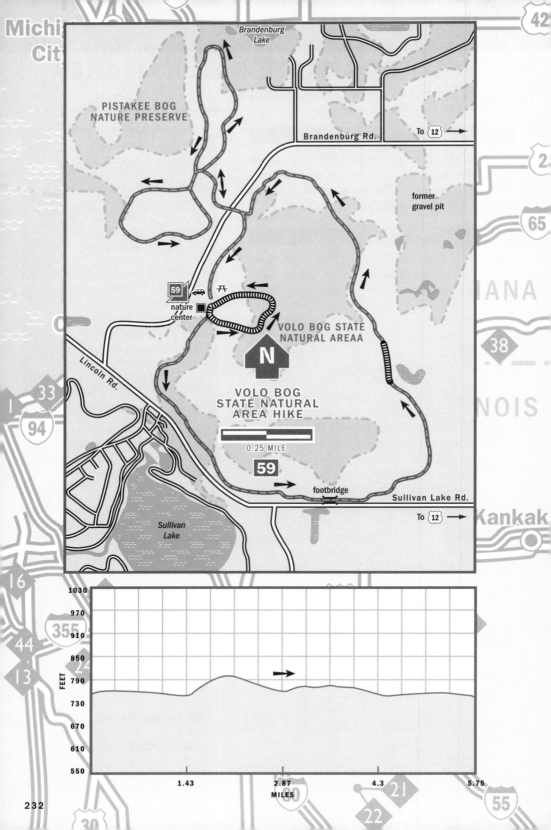

European buckthorn, and poison sumac seem to create a hallway of shrubbery. Be sure to keep your distance from the poison sumac, a tall shrub or small tree with paired leaflets and a single leaflet at the end of the midrib. Whitish-green fruits that hang in loose clusters distinguish the poison sumac from the nonpoisonous variety that produces red fruits. Just touching the bark or leaves can give some people a rash.

This area also contains red dogwood and, during the summer, five different types of ferns, some of which reach heights of six feet. Moving farther into the shrubs, you'll see the moss-covered hummocks, which are floating mounds of decomposing plant material. If a person steps on a mound, the hummocks will sway and shake. This is why Volo Bog is called a "quaking bog."

Next you'll see tamaracks, the pine tree that loses its needles each year. Near the tamaracks, watch for the insect-eating pitcher plant, which looks like a cluster of 4- to 6-inch green-and-red bulbous tubes that are open at one end. At 0.3 miles, you'll reach the open water, the center of the bog. During the spring and summer, this is a spot where you might catch a glimpse of a green heron. Complete the loop by hiking 0.2 miles to the end of the Interpretive Trail, emerging on solid ground very close to where the Tamarack View Trail begins, at the bottom of the hill next to the visitor center.

The 2.75-mile Tamarack View Trail offers a pleasant stroll around the larger basin that includes the bog. The first leg of the hike takes you between the marsh and Sullivan Lake Road. As you enter the wooded area thick with white oaks and box elders, keep an eye out for downy woodpeckers flitting among the trees. Downies are one of a dozen or so birds that may be seen year-round at the bog. In spring, the sparrows, warblers, and other songbirds along this stretch can be overwhelming. In the spring, summer, and fall, expect to see a variety of water birds in the marsh, including kingfishers, mute swans, white egrets, Canada geese, mallard ducks, and great blue herons.

After 0.4 miles, before crossing the bridge over this stream that runs from the marsh toward Sullivan Road, look out into the water among the fallen trees for a beaver lodge.

While following a section of the trail with woods on one side and savanna on the other, you'll come upon stands of walnut trees and willows, and then take a short trip over a boardwalk through a marsh that is thick with shrubs. Beyond the boardwalk, you'll find a nicely situated bench and a few spots that offer views of the marsh. Keep an eye out in this section of the marsh for sandhill cranes. Some birdwatchers maintain that Volo Bog is one of the most dependable locations in Northeastern Illinois for seeing these very large, beautiful birds. Also keep watch for the inhabitants of the bluebird houses that are mounted on posts along the trail. Continue on and you'll pass a few enormous bur oaks, the sentinels of the savanna.

Two miles from the trailhead, you'll leave the prairie-savanna and enter a wooded area. Descend a gentle ravine that leads to an attractive spot with a small pond on one side of the trail and the marsh on the other. Just ahead, look for an observation blind. From here, you can watch for little heads peeking out of the water—both beavers and muskrats have built lodges in this section of the marsh. Farther ahead, take a left turn, and follow the trail along the edge of the water. At the top of a small hill, you'll have the opportunity to hike two more trails and a connector trail, adding another 2.5 miles to your hike. (If you're bound for the parking lot, it's only 0.3 miles from this intersection. After passing a collection of wood benches located within a grove of Scotch pines, the trail drops you off across the parking lot from the visitor center.)

To hike the relatively new Deerpath and Prairie Ridge trails located in the Pistakee Bog Nature Preserve, follow the mowed connector path a quarter mile across Brandenburg Road, then into a savanna and part way up an incline until you see a trail marker. Turning right for the 1.2-mile Deerpath Loop and continuing up the hill, you'll pass through an area thick with young trees, and soon reach a section of the trail that runs alongside stands of older-growth trees. At half a mile from the beginning of the loop, there's a hairpin turn to the left. If the foliage is not too thick, take a look to the right through the trees to see Lake of the Hollow, a quarter mile to the northeast. The trail continues along the edge of the woods another 0.7 miles, and then it descends into a low wooded area thick with box elder, oak, and hickory. If rain has fallen recently, this area likely will be muddy. On your right is an extensive marsh containing two more bogs. After you pass a couple of enormous oaks, one of which has been damaged by lightning, a trail sign indicates that the 0.8-mile Prairie Ridge Loop Trail is to the right.

On the Prairie Ridge Loop Trail, a picturesque hilly prairie immediately opens up in front of you. Taking the trail in a counterclockwise direction takes you alongside the marsh again. At 0.2 miles, you'll turn away from the marsh and start walking alongside a wooded area. In the open space, look for swallows performing their aerial acrobatics. Following the edge of the woods, you'll eventually turn to walk along a small ridge. Reaching the highest section of the ridge gives you an expansive view overlooking a cattail marsh that is active with water birds. Beyond the marsh is the entrance to Volo Bog. Coming down from the ridge, the trail turns left and then drops you off where you left the Deerpath Trail. Follow the signs that read "exit," and in 0.2 miles you'll reach the connector trail that will take you across the road to the Tamarack View Trail and back to the parking lot.

▶ **NEARBY ACTIVITIES**

In the mood for more hiking? If so, you're lucky, since Volo Bog is situated within a cluster of other hiking destinations. Just a few miles to the southwest is Moraine Hills State Park (see page 168). Four other hikes are located about 10 miles away: to the southeast is Lakewood Forest Preserve (see page 146), to the northwest is Glacial Park (see page 80), and directly north are two hikes at Chain O' Lakes State Park (see pages 29 and 33).

WATERFALL GLEN FOREST PRESERVE LOOP

▶ IN BRIEF

This diverse and sometimes rugged landscape includes dense woods of oak and pine, a generous number of ponds and cattail marshes, a prairie, a small waterfall, and an overlook of the Des Plaines River.

▶ DESCRIPTION

Waterfall Glen Forest Preserve surrounds Argonne National Laboratory, one of the U.S. Department of Energy's largest research facilities. Operated by the University of Chicago, over the years Argonne and its previous incarnations have been involved in high-level national research, including the Manhattan Project. The federal government gave the property surrounding Argonne National Laboratory to Du Page County in 1971. While hiking, the only indication that you're circling this world-class laboratory is a fence or two and the occasional access road.

In the parking lot, look for the information board to find trail maps and the beginning of the trail. Once you're on the trail, take the first left for a clockwise hike through the forest preserve. For the first mile, you'll cross three roads—Northgate Road, Cass Avenue, and 91st Street—before reaching the serene 91st Street Marsh. The marsh, which is the size of a small lake, is surrounded by cattails, pine, and oak. There is a bench that offers a nice place to view the marsh, as well as a small pond behind you.

Continuing beyond the 91st Street Marsh, you'll pass under a canopy of oak and maple

ⓘ KEY AT-A-GLANCE INFORMATION

LENGTH: 9.6 miles, which includes a short side trip to a waterfall

CONFIGURATION: Loop

DIFFICULTY: Moderate due to length

SCENERY: Rolling woodlands with ponds, marshes, and stream crossings

EXPOSURE: Shady, with exposed stretches

SURFACE: Hard-packed crushed limestone

HIKING TIME: 4–6 hours for entire loop

ACCESS: 1 hour after sunrise to 1 hour after sunset

FACILITIES: Water, restrooms, a few scattered picnic tables, parking

MAPS: Trail maps are available at the trailhead; USGS topo Sag Bridge, Romeoville, IL

SPECIAL COMMENTS: Pets must be leashed; watch for mountain bikers on weekends

UTM Trailhead Coordinates for Waterfall Glen Forest Preserve Loop

UTM Zone (NAD27) 16T

Easting 420222

Northing 4617429

▶ DIRECTIONS

Take I-55 south to Exit 273A, Cass Avenue. Drive 0.2 miles and turn right (west) on Northgate Road, just beyond the Waterfall Glen Forest Preserve information building. Less than 100 yards up on the right is the parking lot and trailhead.

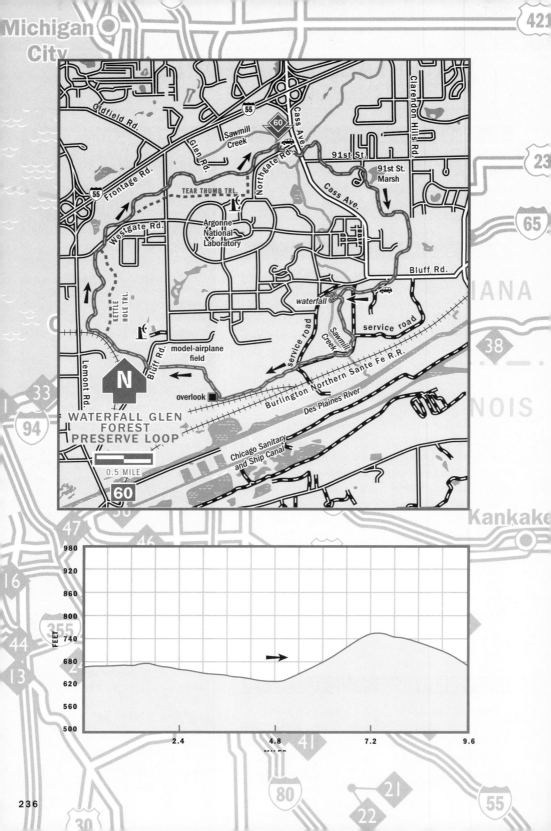

Michigan
City

421

23

65

38

INDIANA

ILLINOIS

Kankakee

Oldfield Rd.

55

Frontage Rd.

55

Glen Rd.

Sawmill
Creek

60

Cass Ave.

91st St.

91st St.
Marsh

Cass Ave.

Clarendon Hills Rd.

TEAR THUMB TRL.

Westgate Rd.

Argonne
National
Laboratory

Northgate Rd.

Bluff Rd.

waterfall

KETTLE HOLE TRL.

Lemont Rd.

Bluff Rd.

model-airplane
field

service road

Sawmill
Creek

service road

Burlington Northern Sante Fe R.R.

N

overlook

Des Plaines River

WATERFALL GLEN
FOREST
PRESERVE LOOP

Chicago Sanitary
and Ship Canal

0.5 MILE

60

94

33

94

47

46

FEET

980
920
860
800
740
680
620
560
500

2.4   4.8   7.2   9.6

MILES

355

44

13

16

30

80

22

21

55

236

The trail at Waterfall Glen runs through a number of pleasant oak groves.

branches and soon you'll reach a plantation of red, jack, and white pine. In the 1950s, Argonne planted these pines to protect the soil from erosion and to serve as a buffer against the surrounding community. Enjoy the aroma while you're here—Northeastern Illinois is not known for its abundance of pine trees.

By now you will have noticed the occasional side trail that branches off from the main trail. Some of these trails are dirt paths and some are mowed lanes. While a few of the mowed lanes show up on the park map, none of the dirt trails are indicated. Despite the lack of markers on most of these side trails, hikers are allowed to venture forth. Many of these trails offer short strolls to nearby destinations such as a pond. Others are longer. On summer weekends around midday, these side trails can provide the solitude that may be hard to find on the main trail. Given that the forest preserve occupies nearly 2,500 acres, be sure to bring a map and compass if you go off the marked trail.

Shortly after crossing Bluff Road, you'll be rewarded with a picturesque waterfall bounded by scenic bluffs and ravines. Before you make your way to the waterfall, which is 3.5 miles into the hike, you'll encounter a parking lot, restrooms, and a water pump. Don't hesitate to top off your water bottle; other than the trailhead, this is the only other spot along the trail with water. After traveling 0.2 miles beyond the parking lot, turn right on the Rocky Glen Trail, which doubles as a gravel service road. There is a mapboard at this intersection showing your location. A hundred feet ahead on the Rocky Glen Trail, turn left to follow a 0.2-mile trail looking down at a ravine and Sawmill Creek. Situated at the bottom of a ravine, the 5-foot waterfall offers a fine spot for a picnic.

Oddly, Waterfall Glen Preserve was not named after this or any other waterfall. Rather, the name honors Seymour "Bud" Waterfall, who served as an early president of the board of the forest preserve district. Also interesting is that the waterfall is not natural, but was built by the Civilian Conservation Corps in the 1930s with limestone from the preserve. During the late nineteenth century, there were three quarries in Waterfall Glen known for producing high-quality limestone. Waterfall Glen provided the limestone for one of the most famous structures in Chicago—the Water Tower, built in 1869 at Chicago and Michigan avenues.

For a shortcut back to the main trail, take the first right up the hill as you head back the way you came. Back on the main trail, you'll get a nice view of the ravine and the 80-foot-high bluffs on the sides of which grow black and white oak, as well as bitternut and shagbark hickories.

A half mile ahead, you'll notice some railroad tracks before passing over Sawmill Creek. This section of the trail leads you through thick shrubbery, as well as oak, pine, and maple. Near the electrical switching station, you'll pass through an area that was used as a plant nursery for Chicago parks. You'll see several concrete-and-stone building foundations from the early 1910s, when the nursery was in operation.

After passing the old foundations, keep an eye out for the overlook at the top of the bluff. This is where the trail takes a right turn, but a service road continues straight up a short hill to a picnic table and an information board. The spot offers a view of the Des Plaines River and the landscape on the other side of the river, which includes the small community of Lemont. Off to the right, outside of your view, is where limestone was quarried. Up ahead 0.3 miles on the main trail, you'll come to a 120-acre short-grass prairie on the right. Among the many plants and animals inhabiting the prairie is a grass called poverty-oat grass, which gives the area its name: Poverty Prairie. On your left is the 500-acre Poverty Savanna, which looks similar to the prairie except for the shrubs and the occasional oak tree.

If you're hiking on a summer weekend, you'll likely witness some takeoffs and landings at the model-aircraft field, just beyond Poverty Prairie. At this spot, you'll also find restrooms and an information board. Crossing South Bluff Road, you'll pass a picnic table and then an idyllic pond likely to be occupied by a few mallard ducks. Just after the pond, you'll see the Kettle Hole Trail on the right.

Continue on the main trail as it meanders alongside Lemont Road, and watch for large, dramatic oaks with curving branches. Along this section, the forest preserve plans to construct an additional parking lot for forest preserve users. After crossing Westgate Road and walking for 0.3 miles, you will see Tear-Thumb Trail as it runs alongside the Argonne Laboratory fence. Continuing on the main trail, you'll begin to catch glimpses of I-55. Following Tear-Thumb Marsh, plantations of pine, and a large wetlands area, you'll cross a footbridge over Sawmill Creek one last time on the way to the parking lot.

▶ NEARBY ACTIVITIES

On the other side of the Des Plaines River is Palos/Sag Valley Forest Preserve, which offers the largest network of trails in the Chicago area. Similar to Waterfall Glen, Palos' terrain is woodsy and sometimes rugged. See pages 179–186 for hikes within Palos/Sag Valley Forest Preserve.

60 Hikes within 60 MILES

CHICAGO

INCLUDING AURORA, ELGIN, AND JOLIET

APPENDIXES
& INDEX

APPENDIX A: OUTDOOR SHOPS

Bass Pro Shop
in Gurnee
6112 West Grand Avenue
(847) 856-1229

Dick's Sporting Goods
in Algonquin
1816 Randall Road
(847) 960-7700

in Geneva
618 Commons Drive
(630) 943-4100

in Glenview
1900 Tower Drive
(847) 730-7400

in Lombard
810 East Butterfield Road
(630) 317-0200

in Niles
5601 Touhy Avenue
(847) 779-8800

in Orland Park
One Orland Park Place
(708) 675-3100

in Schaumburg
601 North Martingale
(847) 995-0200

Erehwon Mountain Outfitter
in Bannockburn
2585 Waukegan Road
(847) 948-7250

in Chicago
1000 West North Avenue
(312) 337-6400

Moosejaw Mountaineering
in Chicago
1445 West Webster Place #9
(773) 529-1111

in Deerfield
740 North Waukegan #102
(847) 914-9999

The North Face
in Chicago
875 North Michigan Avenue
(312) 337-7200

Patagonia
in Chicago
1800 North Clybourn Avenue
(312) 951-0518

REI
in Niles
8225 Golf Road
(847) 470-9090

in Oakbrook Terrace
17 West 160 22nd Street
(630) 574-7700

Uncle Dan's Great Outdoor Store
in Chicago
2440 North Lincoln Avenue
(773) 477-1918

in Evanston
700 West Church
(847) 475-7100

in Highland Park
1847 Second Street
(847) 266-8600

APPENDIX B:
PLACES TO BUY MAPS

▶ LOCATION/CITY

Suburban Map
in Elmhurst
1041 South Route 83
(630) 941-7979

APPENDIX C:
HIKING CLUBS

▶ LOCATION/CITY

Chicago Group of the Sierra Club
200 North Michigan Avenue, Suite 505
Chicago, IL 60601
(312) 251-1680
http://illinois.sierraclub.org/chicago/

Illinois Trekkers Volkssport Club
P. O. Box 25063
Scott AFB, IL 62225-0063
www.illinois-trekkers.org/

Forest Trails Hiking Club
2025 Sherman Avenue, #407
Evanston, IL 60201
www.foresttrailshc.com

Frontrunners/Frontwalkers Chicago
P.O. Box 148313
Chicago, IL 60614-8313
(312) 409-2790
www.frfwchicago.org

Lakeshore Walking Club
3221 Central Street
Evanston, IL 60201
(847) 869-0674

Sole Purpose Walking Club
136 Peach Tree Lane
Westmont, IL 60559
(630) 971-8158

Starved Rock Walking Club
(815) 220-7379
www.starvedrocklodge.com/srwalk.html

INDEX

INDEX

INDEX

INDEX

INDEX